Understanding Sport as a Religious Phenomenon

Understanding Sport as a Religious Phenomenon

An Introduction

Eric Bain-Selbo, Western Kentucky
University, USA and
D. Gregory Sapp, Stetson University, USA

Bloomsbury Academic
An imprint of Bloomsbury Publishing Plc

B L O O M S B U R Y
LONDON · OXFORD · NEW YORK · NEW DELHI · SYDNEY

Bloomsbury Academic
An imprint of Bloomsbury Publishing Plc

50 Bedford Square	1385 Broadway
London	New York
WC1B 3DP	NY 10018
UK	USA

www.bloomsbury.com

BLOOMSBURY and the Diana logo are trademarks of Bloomsbury Publishing Plc

First published 2016

British Library Cataloguing-in-Publication Data
A catalogue record for this book is available from the British Library.

ISBN: HB: 978-1-4725-0610-8
PB: 978-1-4725-1405-9
ePDF: 978-1-4725-0781-5
ePub: 978-1-4725-0698-6

Library of Congress Cataloging-in-Publication Data
Names: Bain-Selbo, Eric, author.
Title: Understanding sport as a religious phenomenon : an introduction / Eric Bain-Selbo, Western Kentucky University, USA and D. Gregory Sapp, Stetson University, USA.
Description: New York : Bloomsbury, 2016. | Includes bibliographical references and index.
Identifiers: LCCN 2016010453 (print) | LCCN 2016018090 (ebook) | ISBN 9781472506108 (hardback) | ISBN 9781472514059 (pbk.) | ISBN 9781472506986 (epub) | ISBN 9781472507815 (epdf)
Subjects: LCSH: Sports–Religious aspects.
Classification: LCC GV706.42 .B34 2016 (print) | LCC GV706.42 (ebook) | DDC 796.01–dc23
LC record available at https://lccn.loc.gov/2016010453

Cover design by Dani Leigh
Cover image © Whit Preston / gettyimages.co.uk

Typeset by Integra Software Services Pvt. Ltd.

Eric dedicates this work to his family—his wife, Laura, and his two children, Zach and Hannah.

Greg dedicates this work to his family—his wife, Lynn, and his children, Kylee, Noah, and India.

Contents

List of Figures

Acknowledgments

The authors want to begin by thanking Lalle Pursglove at Bloomsbury for her commitment to this book and for helping them through the process. Her enthusiasm and expertise has been extremely valuable. We also want to commend the entire Bloomsbury team with whom we have worked, especially Lucy Carroll and Rajakumari Ganessin, whose efforts have been so critical throughout the production process.

In addition, the authors want to acknowledge and thank the following people:

Eric Bain-Selbo

I have to begin by thanking my coauthor and friend, Greg Sapp, for joining me in the journey that is this book. I am proud of the work we have done, and delighted to have done it with him. Many thanks to all those countless colleagues and friends who have talked with me over the years about my work. Special thanks to Matthew Sheffield, one of my former graduate students, who provided significant feedback on some of the chapters and provided research help in the summer of 2014. Thanks to Marc Jolley of Mercer University Press, not only for championing my previous book in the area of religion and sport (*Game Day and God: Football, Faith, and Politics in the American South*, Mercer University Press, 2009), but for being so immediately willing to grant permission for me to use reworked sections of that book in a couple of the chapters in this one. I have received wonderful support from my academic home, Western Kentucky University, and I very much appreciate so many folks at WKU who have helped me over the years. Finally, I want to thank my family (my wife Laura and my two children Zach and Hannah) for accepting my sport fanaticism and, at times, even joining in it with me.

D. Gregory Sapp

I must also thank my coauthor and friend, Eric Bain-Selbo, who so graciously invited me to join him in this project. His wisdom, guidance, and, especially, his patience have been invaluable to me and are greatly appreciated. To my teachers throughout my years—from kindergarten through graduate school and beyond—I owe so much and work to "pay it forward" to my students as my best thanks to them. My colleagues at Stetson have been wonderfully supportive and engaging, helping me think through some of the issues related to religion and sport. I would like to thank Christopher Bell, Mitchell Reddish, Donald Musser, Kandy Queen-Sutherland, Dixon Sutherland, Phillip

Lucas, Ramee Indralingam, and Rajni Shankar-Brown who helped with technical expertise and guidance. Joseph Price remains a primary inspiration in the field of religion and sport and has always been encouraging. I would like to thank my students (too numerous to name) who are fellow learners of life and who challenge me to see the world from multiple perspectives. Finally, and most importantly, I would like to thank my family (my wife Lynn and my children Kylee, Noah, and India) for putting up with my absence the many nights I missed dinner and bedtimes while digging up "just one more source" from the library for this project. They are my favorite team.

1   Introduction

The academic field of religion and sport is fairly new, having originated in the later part of the twentieth century. One of the first important works to address the field was *The Joy of Sports: Endzones, Bases, Baskets, Balls, and the Consecration of the American Spirit* by Michael Novak.[1] He first published this book in 1976 and published revised editions in 1988 and 1994. In 1984, Joseph L. Price first published his piece, "The Super Bowl as Religious Festival," in *The Christian Century*[2] and has since republished it in *From Season to Season: Sports as American Religion*.[3] Novak and Price (who has written or edited other works in the field) are often cited by those of us who work in this emerging field, and rightly so. They have raised issues and questions that need addressing by a larger audience. Since those early days of religion and sport scholarship, there have been many books and articles written that address some aspect of sport and religion. One need only glance at our bibliography at the end of this book to get a glimpse of the work that has been done in the last forty years or so.[4]

Some articles and books look at only one sport, or even at one sporting event, as does Price's article on the Super Bowl. Some focus only on major sports in the United States as does Novak's *The Joy of Sports*. Some scholarship focuses on one aspect of religion in the way Tracy Trothen's article "Better Than Normal?: Constructing Modified Athletes and a Relational Theological Ethic"[5] does. Rather than address one aspect of sport as it relates to religion or one aspect of religion as it relates to sport, we wanted to write a book that we hope serves as an introduction to the field and to provide convincing arguments that sport can be religious whether from the perspective of the athletes or the fans. We illustrate our arguments using sports and religions from around the world so that we really deal with religion and sport in general, not with a particular religion or sport that may or may not represent the whole. We are looking at the human condition in general to see similarities between the practice of religion and the practice of sport.

We want to be clear about what it is we think we are doing here. First, we are not arguing that sport in general or any particular sport is a religion in the same way that Hinduism is a religion. We understand that religions tend to have elements of the "supernatural," for example, and this is not the case with sport (for the most part, a notable exception being the ancient Greek games played in honor of the gods and sometimes with the gods' help). While fans and athletes may argue which sport is better, questions of ultimate truth are not usually raised. For example, some may argue that a card game of poker is not a sport in the same sense that curling is a sport and thus should not receive television coverage by a cable television show devoted exclusively to sport. However, no one is going to argue that curling is truer than poker as one might argue that the teachings of Hinduism are truer than those of Islam. Religious adherents tend to defend the ultimate truth of their tradition because their eternal destiny is thought to be tied up with the truth of that tradition. We have not run across any fans of a particular team who believe that if they are completely devoted to their team showing true dedication and loyalty throughout their lives they will then be transformed at death into a new existence that far surpasses this one in a world, perhaps, where their team never loses.

We are also not concerned with athletes or fans as followers of a particular religion. When we tell our friends, family, even colleagues that we are working in the field of religion and sport we sometimes get a response like, "Oh yeah, Tim Tebow prays a lot and is very religious." Or, "I always wondered if it was okay to ask God for your team to win. Doesn't God love the other team as well?" While the personal religious habits of a particular athlete or fan may be interesting and even inspiring to those who share that athlete's faith, we see no difference between a player making a gesture toward heaven or bowing her head after a good play as if to thank God and a salesperson kneeling at his desk to offer a prayer of thanks after closing a sale. A player who exhibits religious practice on the field or during a postgame interview is no different than someone praying at the office. In both cases, the individuals are merely bringing their religion into the workplace, wherever that may be. An athlete being a practicing Christian does not make her sport religious any more than a US Congressperson being a Christian makes Congress Christian. There are plenty of books by athletes who share their stories of faith during big games or even of their faith getting them through life's trials. This is not one of those books. Nor is it a book dealing with the ethics of one team praying to God for a win against the opponent, though that is an interesting theological and philosophical question.

Finally, we are not arguing that sport is religious because some follow it "religiously." Some would say of devoted fans, "They attend every game religiously." This is no different than someone who watches a television program "religiously" or someone who brushes his teeth after every meal "religiously." Used in this sense, "religious" means being devoted to something in a serious and committed manner and regularly performing the activity. It is a rather shallow understanding of what it means to be religious.

What we are arguing is that the human drives and needs that compel some to be a part of a particular religion are the same drives and needs that compel some to be a part of sport in some way. That is, we believe the activities and beliefs associated with religion per se are similar, if not identical, to the activities and beliefs of athletes and fans of sport. We are saying that sport can be religious for some in the same way that participating in the activities of a mosque, temple, or church can be religious. Sport can function like a religion in that it meets the same needs and desires satisfied or promised by formal religions.

We say "can" because not all who attend games or participate in them as athletes are doing so from a religious perspective. Some might attend a game out of curiosity or because they were compelled by others to go. For these people, the game might just be a social gathering of sorts, maybe even a waste of time. Not all athletes play for love of the game. Some are compelled by other interests, be they financial or romantic. Then again, not all who attend church on a regular basis are doing so for religious reasons, either. Some attend out of a sense of guilt or simply to enjoy fellowship with others and a good potluck lunch. Putting up a building with religious images in and on it does not make the building sacred space. It must be invested with religiousness by the believer who believes it to be sacred. For example, a Hindu temple may be sacred to a practicing Hindu who worships his god there, but to a visiting Christian, it is merely another building with little to no religious significance at all. The Christian may respect the temple as being sacred to a Hindu, but the Christian will not see it as sacred himself. The sacrality of space and time depends on the individual experiencing the time and space.

For our purposes, we will focus only on fans or athletes who are participating for the purposes of the games themselves. We are concerned with those who are committed to sport at some level and will compare them not to the Christian visiting the Hindu temple but to the Hindu who finds meaning in her faith.

There are some who doubt that sport can be seen as religious. For them, traditions like Jainism, Daoism, Judaism, and Christianity are religious. These religions profess belief in the supernatural, going to church, synagogue, or temple, committing to and getting initiated into a group of like-minded believers who claim to believe the same things with regard to God, gods, the afterlife, Heaven, Hell, and on and on. They have sacred buildings, priests, or ministers in sacred robes, and they perform religious rituals to appease their god(s). So for some, sport cannot function like a religion simply because it does not look like what they believe traditional religions look like.

Part of the problem some have with calling sport a religion stems from an ancient practice of denying anything that seems new the status of religion. While sport is, apparently, as ancient as human culture, the sports with which we are most familiar such as basketball, football, and baseball were invented just recently at the end of the nineteenth century. Soccer as we know it today took its shape in the 1860s, for example. If something seems new, it cannot be religious because religion deals with eternal truths, not "truths" that began 150 or so years ago. For most, religion cannot change because that would make God or the gods susceptible to change. In large measure, we can thank the ancient Greeks for the notion that an unchangeable God is best. If God changes, then that means either God was imperfect before and became perfect or that God was perfect and became imperfect.[6] This means that any religion that was new could not possibly be true for the simple fact that it had not been around for very long. A new religion was, in the minds of the establishment, simply made up and, therefore, false. Even those who claimed to have a different (new) perspective on an existing God were deemed suspicious and often persecuted.

Christian apologists of the second century attempted to use reason to convince the Romans that they were not a new religion but were the next step in ancient Judaism which, by the way, preceded Plato. Justin Martyr is, perhaps, the most well known of the early Christian apologists, and he attempted to argue that Jesus was the prophesied messiah that the Jews failed to recognize. Romans tolerated the Jews as long as they paid their taxes and behaved peacefully, but they saw Christians as upstarts and troublemakers promoting a new movement. Justin tried to convince the Romans that Christianity was, in fact, an ancient religion and should, therefore, receive the same tolerance as any other ancient religion. Unfortunately for Justin, his argument failed and he thus earned the title that we now use for his last name.

A more recent example of religious intolerance and persecution can be found in nineteenth-century North America. Joseph Smith (1805–1844) founded what is commonly known as Mormonism in 1830 in the state of New York. Smith claimed to have received a special revelation from God that resulted in the Book of Mormon. In 1843 he claimed to have received another revelation in which the practice of polygamy was sanctioned. He was killed by a mob for his religious beliefs in 1844. When it comes to religion, new is not usually considered good, and this may be part of the reason some balk at the notion of sport functioning as religion.

Perhaps the most common reason some cannot see sport as religion is because sport does not have as its goal a union with the divine or the idea of God. Robert J. Higgs and Michael C. Braswell take this position in their book *An Unholy Alliance: The Sacred and Modern Sports*.[7] They base much of their understanding of religion on *Webster's Dictionary* and quote *Webster's* first definition of religion:

> The service and adoration of God or a god as expressed in forms of worship, in obedience to divine commands, especially, as found in sacred *writings* [ital. added] or as declared by recognized teachers and in the pursuit of a way of life regarded as incumbent upon true believers, as ministers of *religion*.[8]

Because sport does not ostensibly worship God or a god, Higgs and Braswell declare that it cannot be a religion.

They also rely on Rudolf Otto's notion of the "holy" to argue that there is no religious experience in sport.[9] As we will see in more depth in Chapter 2, Otto's idea of the holy is that it is "wholly other" and is experienced as the "numinous," a word he coined to describe what is encountered when one encounters God. Sports, Higgs and Braswell surmise, do not deal with anything like the holy: "What we are saying is that the function of sports as a category of human endeavor is not to connect us to that which is holy or even to remind us of the idea of the holy."[10] For them, for something to qualify as a religion, it has to have a notion of the holy and seek to connect humans with that.

Higgs and Braswell attempt to differentiate between the "sacred" and the "holy." The sacred is a human endeavor while the holy is beyond human control:

> The sacred ... is *set apart* by humans and its significance highlighted by manmade symbols and rites, while the holy is set apart by itself or God and embraces all

of creation. The holy is a reality wholly beyond our power. The sacred is always indicated by place, time, object, or word, while the holy is beyond place and time and language ....[11]

This assertion represents the traditional, theistic view of religion where there is a God no one can see except by special revelation or as mediated by a priestly order to laypersons.

With this understanding of religion, we agree with Higgs and Braswell. As we noted above, sport per se does not promote the idea of God, nor does it encourage fans or athletes to seek God in any way. With this narrow understanding of religion, no one would argue that sports are religions. We, however, do not share Higgs and Braswell's limited understanding of what constitutes religion. The primary fault in their argument from an academic perspective (which is what we are taking here) is that they assume the existence of God as fact and declare that religion can only be defined as seeking unity with that God. Higgs and Braswell use the Christian Bible as though it were an unbiased source of truth.[12] For example, they refer to the Day of Pentecost as found in Acts 2 and (American?) frontier camp meetings for "credible accounts" of people being struck by the holy.[13] This is perfectly fine to do in a Christian context, but not in an academic context where religious documents are not invested with divine authority.

A second fault in their argument is that they use terms like "divine" and "God" without explaining what they actually are. They assume an understanding common to a confessional setting. This practice is quite common among those who have not critically examined the tenets of their faith. There is an assumption that everyone knows what the "divine" is or what the "supernatural" is or what "God" is. Higgs and Braswell claim that sport is not religion because it is not divine. They say in their Preface, "We suggest that while sports are good, they are not inherently divine."[14] Yet they never attempt to define what the divine is. As noted above, they use Otto to say that religion is about seeking the holy, but if the holy is, as quoted above, "beyond place and time and language," then nothing within our grasp is holy.

Higgs and Braswell further demonstrate their overly narrow view of religion when they compare modern sports with ancient religious traditions. They imply that both are brutish. Sport is merely physical competition, not devotional supplication:

> We are not denying parallels between ancient myth and modern sports but raising a question as to why the latter can still be called a religion. Such a religion does not really involve praying at midfield on one's knees, ... but going back to the jungle on all fours as we see to one degree or another in football in every play.[15]

Sport is competitive, an attempt to defeat another person or team. It cannot, therefore, be religious. They regard religion as attempting to help others, not defeat them. While it is certainly true that religions tend to teach love and kindness toward others, religions are also highly competitive as demonstrated by the Crusades, the religious wars in Europe, and the destruction wreaked by terrorists in the name of religion.

According to Higgs and Braswell, if sport is a religion, it is like an ancient religion that is invalid because of its mythology. Sport, therefore, is not true religion anymore than ancient mythological traditions are true religions. They regard their religion as valid and see ancient religious traditions—often the subject of anthropologists and other scholars seeking to understand the human condition—as mere mythology of uneducated people.[16] This is because they have a narrowly conceived view of religion as being about God whose existence and direction of human affairs are taken for granted.

We want to state explicitly that we are in no way denying the existence of God (or of gods). To do so is just as arrogant as claiming to speak for God (or the gods). We are not denying the existence of the divine or the supernatural (whatever those may be) anymore than a fish should deny the existence of air outside the ocean's waters. We are looking at both religion and sport as human endeavors without privileging one over the other. We believe there are elements of the human condition that manifest themselves in different but similar ways, and we are arguing that religion and sport are examples of such a manifestation. Over the remainder of this book, we look at different ways of understanding religion and then analyze elements of different sports, from the perspective of both fans and athletes, and determine that religion and sport do, indeed, share common elements and satisfy the same desires and needs of the human condition.

In Chapter 2, "Sport as a Religious Phenomenon," we use Ninian Smart's "seven dimensions of religion" to gain an overall perspective of what comprises religion in general and then use examples from the world of sport to show that to varying degrees sport shares these same dimensions. For example, Smart says that religion has an ethical dimension where adherents are expected to behave in a certain way. We argue that sport also has an ethical dimension as seen in the fact that athletes are expected to play fairly, by the rules.

Chapter 3 deals with the human endeavor to reach the eternal or infinite, in this case through the theological quest for perfection. Most, if not all, religions prescribe a way of life for the human that is ideal, what we call the "ideal human condition," or "perfection." For many religions, there is an exemplar who demonstrates what it means to be the perfect human being and often serves as the savior of the human race. Also in sport there are various concepts of perfection that athletes and fans seek to achieve. We look at a few ways athletes and teams have achieved perfection in sport.

We look at the psychology of religion and sport in Chapter 4 and see that, according to some notable psychologists, the religious impulse to connect with the infinite may be grounded in our earliest awareness of union with and then separation from the parent. Religion, then, can be seen as an attempt to return to that boundless environment of union with the parent. Indeed, Jesus is quoted in John's Gospel saying that, to enter the kingdom of God, one must be reborn (from above).[17] Similarly in sport, athletes, teams, and their fans recognize their finitude and seek union with the eternal through the winning of championships and/or being inducted into halls of fame.

In Chapter 5, "Come Together: The Sociology of Religion and Sport," we use social theorists like Emile Durkheim and Victor Turner who show that sports are a form of play that brings a community together in much the same way that religions help people experience "collective effervescence" or *communitas*. As is often said, humans are social creatures, and we like to come together to transcend ourselves through the greater reality of a community. Both religion and sport provide that community in similar ways.

We deal with ethics in Chapter 6, "Sport and the Moral Life," and see that the way one behaves is important for the sake of the individual and for the sake of the community. Ethics are about interpersonal relationships and seek to determine the best way to live in relationship with each other. We consider three ways to think about ethics—the deontological (acting on the basis of a sense of duty), the consequential (acting on the basis of what consequences our actions will have), and the virtuous (acting based on an idea we have of what constitutes a virtuous person)—and see parallels between the worlds of religion and sport.

We consider various critical approaches to religion in Chapter 7 in order to understand, first, the ways in which religion can have harmful effects on communities. We then turn to sport to see if it also can have negative effects on communities thus making it susceptible to the critical theories leveled against religion. We find that both religion and sport can have deleterious effects on the community and are, indeed, subject to the same criticisms. However, we also recognize that both can have positive effects that should not be discounted.

Chapter 8, "Religion, Sport, and Secularism," looks at the increasing secularization of societies. The "secular" is that which is not religious. Has sport played a role in the increasing secularization we see in the world? This depends on how one determines what is religious. For those who buy Higgs and Braswell's argument that sport is not religious because it has no concept of or concern with the divine, a strong case can be made that sport has contributed to an increasingly less religious world, at least in Europe and the United States. If, however, we have been convincing in our argument that sport is religious, then we might say that the religiosity of Western cultures, at least, has merely shifted from the church, mosque, and temple to the stadium, pitch, or ballpark.

In the Epilogue, we return to ancient Greece to see the intertwining of religion and sport in the Olympic Games. Just as in ancient Israel there is no separation of religion and political life, so in ancient Greece there was no separation between religion and sport. The two went hand in hand and were often indistinguishable from each other. Today, we see the same human impulses driving both religion and sport in such a way that sport is replacing traditional religion as a means to be in community with others and to achieve the highest possible level of human life. We heed the warning, however, of Dave Zirin who alerts us of the dangerous effects that money and greed can have on our sports. Zirin argues for public ownership and control of sports so that they can achieve their full civic (and, we would add, religious) purposes.

As with anything that is religious, there is no way to demonstrate scientifically the truth of our claim that sport can, and, indeed, does function as a religion for millions of people around the world. On the other hand, we do believe there is more than sufficient evidence to make this claim. Millions of fans see their self-image as inextricably bound with that of their favorite team or athlete to the point that whatever is meaningful in their lives is bound up with the team or athlete. Millions of fans' ultimate concern, to borrow from theologian Paul Tillich, is the success of their team or athlete, and they live and breathe for that success. For some fans, unfortunately, it becomes a matter of life and death as seen when fans attack and kill players for making a costly play on the field or a referee for making what, in the fan's judgment, was a bad call that cost the favorite team a win.

Saint Augustine said that the human soul will be restless until it finds rest in God.[18] Augustine believed that God created every human being with a God-shaped hole in the soul that can only be filled with a relationship with God. As we have seen with Higgs and Braswell, some see religion as the quest to fill that very hole. That millions of fans fill that hole with devotion to a sports team or a particular athlete such that they find their ultimate fulfillment in their team or athlete winning the championship indicates to us that sport can function as a religion, giving meaning and purpose to the individual's life in the very same way that formal, traditional religion can.

Discussion Questions

1. What is the difference between "religion" and "the religious"? Can something or someone be religious without participating in formal religion?

2. What do you think the purpose of religion is? Is that purpose mainly for this life or for an afterlife?

3. What is the purpose of sport? Do you see any similarities at this point between the purpose of religion and the purpose of sport?

Glossary

athlete—one who engages in sport as part of competition against another athlete or as a member of a team in competition with another team.

fan—short for "fanatic;" one who cheers for a particular athlete or team in athletic competition; one who has an emotional investment in the outcome of the athlete's or team's competition.

human condition—all aspects and elements of what it means to be human including (among others) the emotional, social, psychological, spiritual, and material.

numinous—Rudolf Otto's notion of the experience of encountering God as the wholly other, completely unlike any normal human experience.

perfection—in the ancient Greek sense, being complete, not lacking any essential components.

sacred—that which is set apart as special and meaningful, separate from the common and the profane.

Super Bowl—the championship game of the National Football League; one of the most-watched sporting events in the world.

Sport as a Religious Phenomenon

No one claims that her or his particular sport is a religion in the sense that Daoism is a religion, but are there shared elements or functions that would allow us to consider both phenomena "religious?" What does it even mean to be religious? Before we can argue that sport is religious we must first determine what elements or functions constitute religion. In short, what makes religions religious, and are these elements or functions found in sport, as well?

Ninian Smart sees religion as having seven dimensions.[1] The dimensions are: (1) the ritual or practical, (2) the doctrinal or philosophical, (3) the mythic or narrative, (4) the experiential or emotional, (5) the ethical or legal, (6) the organizational or social, and (7) the material or artistic. In this chapter, we will use these seven dimensions as basic categories to understand what makes something religious and to argue that, to some extent or another, sport shares these dimensions with religion and so should be considered "religious." Keep in mind, though, that these are characteristic of religion in general and are not necessarily found the same way in each and every religion. As Smart says, "We may note that diverse traditions put differing weights on the differing dimensions. Religions are by no means equidimensional."[2] For example, Greek Orthodoxy of the Christian religion includes a high level of ritual in its worship whereas the Baptist tradition of Christianity does not. This does not mean that Baptists are less religious; it means only that they have less ritual than do the Greek Orthodox Christians. We point this out to say that sport may not have as much of one dimension or another as other, formally organized religions, but that does not negate its religiosity.

The Ritual or Practical Dimension

We begin with the ritual, or practical, dimension. Smart says that the ritual dimension "is the aspect of religion which involves such activities as worship, meditation, pilgrimage, sacrifice, sacramental rites and healing activities."[3] A ritual is something someone does, and it is intended to have some effect. For example, Mircea Eliade suggests that performing rituals can take one from profane time to sacred time.[4] When one performs a ritual, everyday life—the profane—is set aside and the practitioner moves into sacred time that is removed from life's mundane concerns. The practitioner can then focus on the eternal, the sacred, where ordinary life is no longer a bother. Ritual also creates sacred space. According to Eliade, all rituals take place in sacred space reproducing an act of the gods, an ancestor, or hero:

Any ritual whatever … unfolds not only in a consecrated space (i.e., one different in essence from profane space) but also in a "sacred time," "once upon a time" (*in illo tempore*, *ab origine*), that is, when a ritual was performed for the first time by a god, an ancestor, or hero.[5]

By performing a ritual, the performer imitates the original act of the god and thus infuses his or her action with a power or meaning (sacredness) that it otherwise would not have. At the same time, the ritual helps to unite the performer with the god or eternity. Ritual removes the gap of time from the present to that original time when the world was just created by the god and everything was pristine. In the Judeo-Christian tradition, for example, the rite of marriage recalls the Garden of Eden when God joined Adam and Eve—the first human couple—together.[6]

Rituals are usually performed in the same way each time they are performed, leading to their becoming formulaic. When they become formulaic sometimes the person practicing the ritual comes to see it as manipulative.[7] In other words, one can come to perform a ritual in order to control forces in the world or future events. Smart differentiates between "devic causation" and "mantric causation." With devic causation the person seeks to control spirits or devas that have some control of the natural world. Smart suggests that offering a sacrifice to Neptune—Greek god of the seas—before a voyage would have the purpose of appeasing Neptune so that Neptune would make sure the seas are calm during the voyage. With mantric causation, the ritual intends to manipulate the physical world itself without the intermediary god or deva being involved. Smart says, "Mantric-causation theory is a half-way house towards devic causation, for it supposes not that the events influenced by the mantra are powered by a spirit but that natural objects may jump to our commands as human beings and some animals do."[8] With mantric causation there is a direct connection between the ritual performed and the resulting action of the physical world.

There are many examples of how ritual is a part of sport. A few examples will suffice to show that what we see in religious ritual is clearly found in sport ritual. Smart, himself, notes that ritual is evident in sport:

[M]antric causation too may be evident, as in sportsmen's superstitions. Perhaps the most developed of these are found among batsmen in cricket. They may feel the need to perform certain rites before going out to bat or to wear particular gloves or to carry some magic item in their pocket, or whatever.[9]

Smart believes the rituals may be effective in that they give the player confidence,[10] but this can also be said of religious ritual: it gives the practitioner confidence that his world is ordered and not chaotic.

Baseball Rituals and Football Communion

Baseball, a game that is similar to cricket, is full of ritual, from the group activities of players, coaches, umpires, and fans to individual behavior. As with most sports played in the United States, American baseball games begin with the national anthem. Players from both teams stand at attention, many with their caps over their hearts, while the national anthem is sung or played instrumentally. Fans in the stands will come to their feet and either stand in silence or sing along. Once the anthem is over and the crowd has finished its applause, the home plate umpire will yell, "Play ball!," and the game officially begins. After the first half of the seventh inning is played, the crowd again stands for the singing of "Take Me Out to the Ballgame." Most fans will sing (often raucously) and jam their fingers into the air as they come to the words, "For it's one, two, three strikes you're out at the ol' ballgame." These are rituals done collectively at each ballgame in the same way.

Players and fans also perform rituals before and during the game to ensure a positive outcome. Joseph Price notes that baseball players often have rituals they perform on a regular basis believing that doing so will help their play. These are good examples of mantric causation.

Wade Boggs, long-time third baseman of the Boston Red Sox, performed the same rituals before each game of his career, most notably his eating of chicken before every game. Price adds:

[Boggs] also practiced a five-hour routine that determined actions at certain times and places, including the time that he would leave his home for night games, the length of time that he would sit in front of his locker, and his running of wind sprints at 7:17. In addition, he made sure that as he finished taking grounders in infield practice, he would leave the field by stepping on third, second, and first [bases], in that order, followed by taking two steps in the coach's box and loping in four strides to the dugout.[11]

Boggs is hardly alone. The pervasiveness of ritual in baseball was parodied in the 1989 baseball movie *Major League*.[12] The character Pedro Cerrano practiced voodoo and had a shrine in his locker. Some of the players wanted him to touch his talisman to their bats in order to get more hits in the games. Whether real, as in the case of Boggs, or fictional, as in the case of Cerrano, baseball is a sport that includes many rituals at both the individual and communal level.

Fans of any sport may perform rituals before, during, even after games as part of the act of participating in the sport. Warren St. John recounts his season of traveling with fans on their way to the University of Alabama's football games during the fall of 1998. St. John tells the story of being with two Bama fans who traditionally eat "Bama Bombs" (cherries soaked in pure grain alcohol) before the game for good luck. Describing the passing out and eating of the "bombs" before leaving the recreational vehicle for the game, St. John refers to the ritual as "Communion for fans."[13] Fans of all sports participate in rituals that attempt to manipulate the outcome of the contest, to maintain order in their sports world. Ritual is clearly a dimension of sport as it is of religion.

The Doctrinal or Philosophical Dimension

The second dimension is the doctrinal or philosophical. The word "doctrine" comes from the Latin *doctrina* which means "teaching." A religious doctrine is a teaching that is developed in a religious community (often through practices of the community), taught by an authority (leaders of the community), and is usually based on belief, not on hard evidence. One who believes in a doctrine believes that the teaching is true without having proof of what is taught. Similarly, "philosophy" combines the Greek words *filos* ("love") and *sofia* ("wisdom") to give us "love of wisdom." In a common sense, then, a philosopher is one who loves wisdom. Wisdom is the knowledge of how best to live one's life, knowing which choices to make in a given situation. A philosophy of something is a belief about how that something works best or even what something is. For example, a philosophy of test-taking might hold that it is always best to "cram" right before an examination because that will result in the best scores.[14] A teacher might have a philosophy of testing in which she would have a set of beliefs about what a test is, how best to give one, and how best to use a test to aid in the education of the students. More to our point, a philosophy of life would hold positions about what life is, how best to live it, and what the purpose of life might be (if there is one). With both doctrine and philosophy, belief is central to understanding them. Hard and fast objective knowledge is not usually directly part of either doctrine or belief. One chooses to hold a particular philosophy or believe certain doctrines often with some evidence of sorts, but not conclusive evidence.

Smart points out that, in many religions, one of the primary beliefs adherents hold has to do with the origin of the material universe, or, the cosmos. He says that "creation is taken in many traditions to be crucial because it makes individuals ontologically dependent as well as soteriologically dependent on the Lord."[15] The "Lord" in this case is the Supreme Being of any religious tradition. A creation story explains why the cosmos exists as well as the proper role of humans in it. One of the primary things religion does is order chaos, and in this case, religious cosmogonies explain where humans came from, why we are here, why we are in the state we are in, and how to get to an ideal state of existence, moving from ontological concerns about the nature of being to soteriological concerns about the ultimate fate of human beings. Mircea Eliade says that the "sacred reveals absolute reality and at the same time makes orientation possible; hence it *founds the world* in the sense that it fixes limits and establishes the order of the world."[16] Without a story to tell us where we came from we would have to live with the "chaos" of not knowing. Thus, religions provide these stories (doctrines about the beginning of the cosmos) to give us order in our lives where, otherwise, there is none. Examples from two different religious traditions should suffice to illustrate how teachings about the beginnings of the world provide a sense of order for those traditions.

Many American Indian nations have creation stories that explain the origins of the world and of humans. In one particular Apache version, the Creator joins with Girl-Without-Parents and other gods to create the elements of the earth and the earth itself. While it is not clear how humans were made, a group of 28 humans helped the Creator and the other gods shape the earth. Each of the gods had a specific role in creating the earth, and so each god watches over that particular part of the earth after it is made and people live on it. For example, Lightning-Rumbler is in charge of the clouds and water (presumably, rain), Earth-Daughter is in charge of crops and earth people, and Pollen-Girl is responsible for humans' health.[17] A Crow creation story tells how Old Man Coyote decided to create everything because he was lonely. With the help of two ducks he found mud buried beneath the surface of water and made land out of it. He made humans to keep him company and, because the ducks were bored, he made other animals for them to talk to. Finally, he divided the humans into different tribes with different languages so there could be strife and war between the groups to bring honor to young warriors and to make it possible to steal wives from enemy tribes.[18]

The Jewish creation stories found in the biblical book of Genesis also provide an order for and an explanation of human existence. In the first story—Genesis 1.1–2.4a—a transcendent God speaks the cosmos into being in a particular order structured according to days. The text says, "In the beginning, when God created the heavens and the earth, the earth was a formless void and darkness covered the face of the deep, while a wind from God swept over the face of the waters."[19] God orders the world and then places humans on the earth to take care of it. It is likely that this story was written during the Babylonian Exile (ca. 550 BCE)—a time when the Israelites were in chaos having been decimated and carried off into captivity by the Babylonians. This story was meant to provide them some hope for salvation from the Babylonians with the belief that their God is a God of order and that their current predicament was a part of God's plan.

The second creation story in Genesis is likely much older than the one that appears first in the Bible. It begins at Genesis 2.4b and goes through the end of the third chapter. This story is an etiology that explains why things are the way they are. For example, the existence of animals is attributed to God's having attempted (and failed) many times to provide a suitable companion for the man God had created before any of the other animals.[20] Human death is explained by God's having become concerned that humans will become just like the gods after Adam and Eve eat from the forbidden Tree of Knowledge. Now that they have knowledge, God fears that they will eat from the Tree of Life, thus living forever and becoming just like the gods. So God kicks them out of the Garden of Eden and places an angel with a flaming sword to keep the humans from getting to the Tree of Life.[21]

In both the case of the American Indian and the Jewish creation stories, belief in a certain view of the origin of the cosmos provides those particular communities with a sense of security and order. These beliefs could not have arisen from direct observation but were, rather, developed over time (through dreams? revelation? imagination? secondary experiences?), adopted by the community, and then passed on as community doctrine by teachers of the religious community. By passing down these teachings from generation to generation, the community preserves its sense of order and identity in the world.

So in religion, then, there are beliefs about things that cannot be proven but can only be accepted based on the teachings of authorities, whether those authorities be ancient texts regarded as scripture or learned teachers and priests who hand down the doctrine of that particular community. Those teachings/doctrines provide a sense of order and identity for the community in the world.

Coaching and Team Philosophies

One finds beliefs and philosophies in sport, as well, and those beliefs and philosophies also provide a sense of order and identity for the athlete and/or team. Different coaches have different philosophies as to how they prepare for competition, whether to keep practices loose to keep athletes relaxed or make practices more like a military boot camp with highly regimented schedules and high expectation of effort on the part of the athletes. There are different philosophies for how to approach competition itself. Some believe athleticism is the more important element of competition, while others believe intelligence is the most important. Some believe speed and agility are superior to brute strength, while others believe the reverse.

James Gels, basketball coach and owner of the Web site, "The Coaches Clipboard," writes that every coach should have a philosophy of coaching and that at every interview for a coaching position the applicant will be asked about her or his coaching philosophy.[22] Writing of the different playing styles of basketball a coach might choose, Gels says, "Some coaches are 'go' coaches and like the fast-break, full-court press, gambling, trapping, and like the game to be a track meet....Other coaches are 'whoa' coaches who like a more deliberate, slower-paced game with little risk taking."[23]

Different coaches have different philosophies about how the games should be played, and the coach must convince the players that the approach to the game is the best. Addressing those who would coach, Gels says, "You must get everyone onboard and believe in your system and your style of basketball. Players and assistants must be totally dedicated and believe in what they are doing."[24] If players are going to work together as a team, they must *believe* in the team philosophy in much the same way adherents of formal religion believe in the philosophy or doctrine of that particular organization.

In his book about the National Football League's (NFL) Miami Dolphins and their perfect season, Bob Griese (who played quarterback for the team) says that the Dolphins had a philosophy of playing whether a player was injured or not. He tells the story of defensive end Bill Stanfill who was hospitalized with a lacerated liver. Stanfill received a call from the team doctor while he was in the hospital on the morning of a home game in Miami and was told to leave the hospital and drive to the stadium. He arrived as the team was on the field warming up, and in the locker room the team doctor told him to suit up, that Stanfill was okay to play. Griese continues:

> Stanfill played eighteen pass-rushing downs that afternoon. As he cut the tape off his ankle after the game, he noticed the hospital tag still on it. He asked Virgin [the team doctor] to do the honors by cutting it off. Virgin instead told him to keep it on and return to Mercy [Hospital]....He remained there until later that week,

when he left to pack his bags and board the team flight to Oakland, where he played the entire game.

That was part of the code on the team: anything it takes, anything at all.[25]

The "code" on the team was the philosophy by which the team played. According to Griese, the Dolphins' philosophy of playing through pain was unique to Miami as some of the players found out when they finished their careers with other teams: "After a decade with the Dolphins, [Jim] Langer completed his career with a season near his home in Minnesota. He was stunned by the different mind-set. If a Minnesota player hurt anywhere, Langer discovered, he sat out the game."[26] In Minnesota, the "mind-set" (philosophy) of when to play was different than Miami's. The two teams believed in approaching the sport in different ways, at least as far as playing with pain is concerned.

While the idea of a sport having a doctrine in the same sense of Judaism having doctrines that are written in a sacred text may seem strange, there are, clearly, doctrines and philosophies in sport. These doctrines and philosophies provide an identity for the team and guide the behaviors and beliefs of participants no less than sacred texts and teachings guide the behaviors and beliefs of the ostensibly religious. In the same way that religious doctrines must be believed without concrete evidence, so sport philosophies regarding coaching and playing are also believed even when there may not be good reasons for believing.[27]

The Mythic or Narrative Dimension

In addition to the dimensions of ritual and doctrine, religions have a mythic or narrative dimension. People often mistake the religious use of the word "myth" as being a story that is false. "Myth" is used this way in common language to denote things people believe that are not true. There is even a television show in the United States called *Mythbusters* in which the primary characters test the validity of commonly held beliefs to see if they are true or if they are "myth" (i.e., false). This is not the meaning of the word "myth" in religion. Myths are stories that are told to convey truth about the way life is. They are not intended to be "true" in a historical sense (though sometimes adherents believe that is the case); they are meant to tell us something about ourselves, especially vis-à-vis the divine or the eternal. Smart says myths have a number of functions in a religious context. He notes that

> one function of stories is to serve as the script for ritual action: the story of the Last Supper, the Exodus from Egypt, the Christmas story, the story of Demeter and Persephone, the death of Husayn at Karbala, the myth of Isis and Osiris, and so on.[28]

These stories are relived when the rituals are performed that correspond to them. For example, the Christian ritual of communion takes the communicant back to the crucifixion of Jesus and includes the stories of both the last supper Jesus shared with his disciples as well as the crucifixion itself.[29] When the ritual of communion is performed, the communicant participates in the actual events connected to the ritual.

Smart argues that another "function [of myths] is to explain origins, whether of the cosmos as we now know it, or of certain features of human society, or of death and other problematic features of human life, or of the immediate environment."[30] We have already seen examples of Judeo-Christian and American Indian myths that explain the origin of the world and of humans. These stories explain how our existence came to be the way that it is and, perhaps, how our lives were intended to be by the Creator before some catastrophe made our existence worse. In a similar vein, Smart says that another function of myth is to give humans a picture of "Last Things—stories which depict how things will be at the finish of the world as we know it."[31] So myths can give us a picture of an idyllic past and future as well as explain why this middle period is the way that it is.

In giving us a sense of our origin and our future, myth gives us a sense of who we are by telling stories that characterize our group whether that group be a village, a region, or nation. Smart puts it this way:

> Typically myths can be considered to be relative to a given group or tradition. That is, they are the authoritative stories of such entities. They are recited as part of traditional lore, and in this way have a breathless authority, as I shall figuratively call it. The stories in this category are foundational for the group in question. This is easiest to achieve in small-scale societies, but large-scale traditions are also capable of surrounding a sufficient segment of the population to give their proclaimed narratives unquestioned authority within that segment.[32]

A clear example of such a foundational story is found in the Hebrew Bible in Genesis. There, Jacob—the purported father of twelve sons who become the heads of the Twelve Tribes of Israel—wrestles with a being who turns out to be God. At the end of the wrestling match (which neither competitor wins), God changes Jacob's name to "Israel," which means "strives with God and with humans."[33] As the father of the heads of the Twelve Tribes, Jacob/Israel sets the tone for the nation as it constantly seems to "wrestle" with God and with other nations throughout its history. Myth, then, provides a narrative that sets and represents the character of a group, region, or nation.

Sports Myths and Heroes

The world of sport does not *usually* deal in myth; it deals primarily in competition between competitors. However, there are mythic tales of sports teams and heroes just as there are mythic tales in religion. In Chapter 4 we will see how the ancient Greek and Roman heroes function to give the readers of Homer and Virgil, respectively, a sense of whom they are and from where they came. Those mythic characters engage in athletic competition that demonstrates their physical and mental prowess over fellow competitors. The Greeks and the Romans looked back to their heroes with a sense of pride as they united with the image portrayed in the epic poems recounting their triumphs in athletic competition (as well as in actual battle).

Myths of sports figures are not limited to the ancient past, however. A few examples will demonstrate that sports myths still abound. The first example is that of the supposed "called-shot home run" that Babe Ruth hit in the third game of the 1932 World Series at Wrigley Field against the Chicago Cubs. As the story goes, Ruth had been taunting the Cubs for the entire series so that when he and his wife, Claire, arrived at their hotel for the games at Wrigley, a fan spit on them as they entered. Of the incident Ruth says in his autobiography (written sixteen years after the game),

> I was so hopping mad by the time we got to our suite upstairs that I told Claire I'd fix them somehow.
> "I'll belt one where it hurts them the most," I said, without knowing just what I'd do—or how.
> I guess it was while I was angry that the idea of "calling my shot" came to me. It wasn't exactly a new idea with me. I had hit a few home runs after promising to hit them, and in most of those cases I had been able to pick the very spot.[34]

Ruth goes on to tell of a few instances where he promised to hit a home run for someone. In one case, he says he noticed the team's traveling secretary, Mark Roth, sitting nervously in the stands in an extra-inning game. Ruth claims he asked Roth what was bothering him, to which Roth replied that he was holding a train for the team to get back to New York after the game (which was running very long), and the "railroad was griping." Ruth reports that he told Roth, "I'll take care of it," and hit a home run his next at bat to end the game.[35]

In the third game of the 1932 World Series, Ruth came up to bat in the fifth inning with the score tied. The Cubs players were yelling at him as were the fans in the stands. Ruth claims that before the first pitch was thrown, he pointed to the bleachers in center field indicating that that was where he was going to hit the ball. He then says that, after the pitcher threw two consecutive strikes, he stepped out of the batter's box and again pointed to the center field bleachers. (See Fig. 2.1) According to Ruth, the Chicago pitcher—Charley Root—threw a third fastball that Ruth smashed into the center field bleachers.[36]

Don Meany, a sports reporter covering the Yankees, wrote in 1947 that "[a]fter the game it was unanimously accepted by writers, fans, and players that Ruth had called his shot against Root."[37] Meany admits, though, that as time went on some cast doubt on whether or not Ruth actually called the shot. He even says that Ruth himself became confused about it.[38] Robert Creamer, writing almost three decades after Meany, doubts that Ruth called the shot and presents evidence supporting that position. According to Creamer, only one writer covering the game—sports editor Joe Williams, for whom Meany worked—said that Ruth pointed to the spot where he intended to hit the ball. Creamer quotes Williams as writing, "In the fifth, with the Cubs riding him unmercifully from the bench, Ruth pointed to center and punched a screaming liner to a spot where no ball had been hit before."[39] It seems that Ruth had been raising fingers to indicate the ball and strike count as he taunted the Cubs players in their dugout. Before the decisive pitch was thrown, Ruth appears to have pointed to Root, the pitcher, telling the dugout that it only takes one. He hit the next

Fig. 2.1 Drawing depicting Ruth calling his shot.

pitch out of the park, the ball landing in the center field bleachers. Creamer believes that Williams and Meany both told the story of Ruth pointing to the outfield so many times that people began to believe that he had actually called the shot.[40]

There is more to the story, however. Creamer quotes Ruth talking to John Carmichael about the episode:

> Ruth told John Carmichael, a highly respected Chicago sportswriter, "I didn't exactly point to any spot. All I wanted to do was to give that thing a ride out of the park, anywhere. I used to pop off a lot about hitting homers, but mostly among the Yankees. Combs and Lazzeri and Fletcher used to yell, 'Come on, Babe, hit one.' So I'd come back, 'Okay, you bums. I'll hit one!' Sometimes I did. Sometimes I didn't. Hell, it was fun."[41]

Charley Root, the pitcher, said Ruth did not point: "Ruth did not point at the fence before he swung. If he had made a gesture like that, well, anybody who knows me knows that Ruth would have ended up on his ass."[42] Gabby Hartnett, the Cubs catcher, denies that Ruth ever pointed to the spot where he would hit the ball claiming, "If he had pointed out at the bleachers, I'd be the first to say so."[43] Of course, Hartnett claimed that Ruth hit a fastball thrown by Root, and Root claims it was a low, changeup curveball.[44] Even the people who were involved cannot recall the same events in the same way.

There can be no doubt that Ruth hit a home run in the third game of the 1932 series at Wrigley Field, nor, apparently, that he was making gestures with his fingers during the at-bat. Whether or not he pointed to the outfield before hitting the home run seems to be a matter of interpretation and, probably, one's sympathy for Babe Ruth or the Yankees. Ruth serves as a hero to Yankees fans and to many other fans of the game. His "called-shot home run" is but one story told about Ruth that enlarges his image in the minds of his fans. In all likelihood, Ruth did not call his shot and then deliver it just as he had called it, but the mythic story lives on in the minds of many. It embodies his amazing ability to hit home runs like no one before him and few since, and it creates an image of Ruth and the Yankees that is adopted by contemporary Yankees fans. Ruth and the Yankees not only play the game; they call the shots because they are that good. Contemporary Yankees fans adopt this myth and unite with this image because it allows them to believe that they are the best in baseball. They are at the top of the baseball world.

Another character about whom mythic stories have been told is Notre Dame University football coach Knute Rockne. Rockne was the winningest coach in football history at the time of his death and was wildly popular across the United States. He raised Notre Dame football to an unprecedented level. He was on his way to Los Angeles to sign a film contract to play himself in a movie when his plane crashed, killing all eight on board. One of the myths perpetuated about him was that, when those responding to the scene found Rockne's remains, he was clutching a rosary in his hand.[45] However, Murray Sperber notes that "neither eyewitnesses nor Dr. Nigro [a physician and close friend of Rockne's who was tasked with putting his body in a casket and bringing it back to South Bend, Indiana] ever mentioned this."[46] This legend arose to portray Rockne as a good Catholic to the end.

When Rockne died, the movie studio shifted direction and retitled the film he was to star in, *The Spirit of Notre Dame*, and cast actor J. Farrell MacDonald to play Rockne. Several of Rockne's former football players played themselves in the film. Andrew Hughes quotes Donald Crafton—Notre Dame film, television, and theater chairman—who says the film helped build the legends of Notre Dame and Rockne:

> Notre Dame's reputation as a football powerhouse was still at the mythological stage when the film came out, and it's really developing the myth of Notre Dame as a football powerhouse that has a kind of divine destiny ... I think if one is going to understand how Notre Dame became such a football powerhouse, it's not just Knute Rockne's win-loss record. It's also the construction of the myth around the school as an all-American story with a God-given destiny.[47]

Rockne's win–loss record was 105–12, winning almost nine times as many games as he lost. The film laid the foundation for the idea that Notre Dame's success on the field may be a result of the goodness of its coaches, players, and fans and the favor that God bestows on the team.

Another episode reveals how Rockne came to be sanctified after his death. It was a fairly common practice in the early twentieth century for magazines and newspapers to assign ghostwriters to professional athletes and for those ghostwriters to write pieces in the name of the athlete. Rockne was no exception. John B. Kennedy, an associate editor of *Colliers: The National Weekly*, wrote a series of articles for *Colliers* in Rockne's name that became the basis of Rockne's *Autobiography of Knute*

K. Rockne, published by Bobbs-Merrill. When the book was released in 1931 after Rockne's death, Kennedy wrote to Bobbs-Merrill complaining that he had not been recognized for his work on the *Autobiography*. When it became clear that Kennedy had contributed to the work, Bobbs-Merrill wrote to Mrs. Rockne and former president of Notre Dame, Father John W. Cavanaugh, to say that future editions of the 1931 *Autobiography* would need to make some mention of Kennedy's contributions. Cavanaugh wrote back arguing that they could not recognize Kennedy because the book had already been sold to the public as the work of Rockne. Sperber (upon whose work this recounting is based[48]) concludes:

> For Father John W. Cavanaugh and Bonnie Rockne, acknowledgement of a ghostwriter was totally contrary to the "Saint Knute" version of the coach's life that they wanted to erect, particularly the widow's insistence on portraying her husband as a "scholar" as well as a football coach.[49]

Shortly after his death, the alumni magazine of Notre Dame—the *Notre Dame Alumnus*—published an edition devoted to the death, funeral, and public reaction to Rockne's death. In that edition, editor James Armstrong wrote: "The trip by air during which he was killed was to fill a speaking engagement 'because he did not want to let a friend down,'" though the quotation was not attributed to anyone.[50] There was no mention of the film contract or the $50,000 for which Rockne was to be paid. Sperber suggests that this glossing over the actual reason for Rockne going to Los Angeles was just one example of the rewriting of Rockne's life and that there were many reasons for doing so:

> The transformation of the reasons for the final trip is one small example of the massive rewriting of Knute Rockne's life that begins shortly after his death. The motivations behind the campaign were complex: some revisionists acted out of grief, loss, even guilt; others embraced the sentimental tradition, the glorification of the dead, and the cultural impulse toward myth rather than reality; and many felt a need for a hero and/or a secular saint during a dark Depression.[51]

Whatever the reason(s), many people painted pictures of Rockne that were practically devoid of negativity and elevated him to the status of near-sainthood. In doing so, they created a mythology of the coach's life and raised him up as an example of the good. In much the same way Yankees fans accept the myth of Ruth's called home run, Notre Dame fans (and other Catholics) accept the myths surrounding Rockne and see themselves as elevated as they unite with his image as a great hero.

In some cases, myth may be associated with a team as well as with individuals on the team. The Brazilian national soccer team carries with it an air of mythic greatness begun with the play of a 17-year-old unknown (at the time) player named Pelé. In the 1958 World Cup, Pelé scored a goal in the final game to help Brazil win. With Pelé mostly out with an injury for the next World Cup (held in 1962) Brazil still won, this time with Garrincha playing the star. According to John Carlin, Garrincha played with such "genius" he played more as a performer than a regular athlete and "entrenched the myth—so much a part of Brazilian legend—that in his country people play soccer less

for victory than for fun."[52] That is, Garrincha was so good there was not much competition when he played. He performed, almost according to a prescribed script. Brazil
asserted its greatness in the 1970 World Cup held in Mexico. Carlin says, "Brazil's
apotheosis, and Pelé's, came in the 1970 World Cup in Mexico. The consensus is
absolute among soccer's intelligentsia that this was the greatest team ever to grace
the game." Though there is debate as to whether Pelé or Diego Maradona was the
greatest player, he says, "no one questions the pre-eminence—the peerless combination of flamboyance and effectiveness—of that 1970 Brazil team."[53] Carlin continues:

However, there was a drought of wins following that World Cup:

A lean period followed: it would be 24 years before Brazil won the World Cup
again. But such was the power of the spell cast by that triple-winning Pelé team
that the legend not only remained alive but, as legends do, flourished. It didn't
matter how strong or weak they looked on paper, no team ever got the pulse
racing the way the canary-shirted Brazilians did.[54]

The spell Carlin speaks of is the myth of greatness the team evoked among soccer
fans. Whether it was true or not, fans still expected the mighty Brazilians to win it
all at any given time. In an article previewing the 2014 World Cup held in Brazil,
K. V. Venugopal writes: "The moment people think of soccer, Brazil's name will
linger in their memory. The five-time World champion has created a lasting impact
on the minds of football-hungry fans."[55] The Brazilian team from decades long ago
has created a myth about how good they are, and fans of soccer believe the myth
whether or not the contemporary reality supports it.

The mythic nature of the team has been fed by the players, most notably, Pelé,
but more recently, Ronaldinho. Tostao, who played with Pelé in the 1970 World Cup,
believes there is something about the thinking of the Brazilian players that sets them
apart and above (perhaps as the sacred is set apart) other players from around the
world. He says the Brazilians have a "daring imagination" and that they "have more of
the magic of invention."[56] Other players around the world may equal the talent of the
Brazilian players, but the mindset of the Brazilians makes the difference. Carlin notes
Tostao's position regarding English superstar David Beckham:

The English team captain, David Beckham, Tostao suggests, has the skill to do
what a Brazilian player might, but he doesn't because he is trapped in his English
cultural mind-set. He cannot tap into what Tostao says is "the imaginative unconscious of Brazilian football, transmitted down from one generation to the next."[57]

This "imaginative unconscious of Brazilian football" is mythic in that it is something
that the players believe and has little, if anything, to do with their physical abilities. It
is part of the myth of the Brazilian team.

There is another part of the myth of Brazilian soccer that holds that the players are
so gifted that they do not have to practice much. Ronaldinho and Tostao, however,
would like

to dispel the myth that Brazilian players are so naturally gifted that victory comes
easily to them, no sweat or discipline required. "It's an absolute myth," Tostao says.

"We play a collective game, as disciplined as anybody else's." Ronaldinho says, "We prepare for a game a lot more than people imagine. People think that we run out on the pitch, all the laughter and joy, and then it's goal, goal, goal. No."[58]

This myth that Ronaldinho and Tostao would like to dispel is based on the myth of the greatness of the Brazilian team. It is part of the "story" of the Brazilian national soccer team that has been told at least since the middle of the twentieth century.

Religions have their myths that explain the world and that order it in a particular way. Sport has its myths, as well, that make sense of what both players and spectators experience in sport. Myths tend to idealize and give us something to look up to, or back to in the case of a "golden age," and we have seen them in both religion and sport.

The Experiential or Emotional Dimension

Smart's fourth dimension is the experiential or emotional. Beginning with the experiential, Smart argues that there are two basic kinds of religious experience: the outer and the inner. Smart suggests the outer religious experiences correspond to Rudolf Otto's concepts of the "numinous" and the "mysterium tremendum."[59] Discussing the concept of the "holy," Otto suggests that it is usually used in a sense that means "completely good."[60] However, he wants to sharpen the understanding of the word by suggesting that defining "holy" merely as "completely good" is insufficient. He says, "But this common usage of the term is inaccurate. It is true that all this moral significance is contained in the word 'holy,' but it includes in addition—as even we cannot but feel—a clear overplus of meaning."[61] In focusing on this "overplus" of meaning, Otto develops his own word to capture the meaning of "holy" without the ethical implication of the good. He takes the Latin word *numen*, which can be translated as "the might of a deity," "majesty," or "divinity,"[62] and makes an adjective out of it. Thus, he ends up with "numinous."[63] This word cannot be precisely defined, according to Otto; rather, it must be experienced. Otto suggests that the numinous is much like "creature-consciousness" or "creature feeling." He says, "It is the emotion of a creature, submerged and overwhelmed by its own nothingness in contrast to that which is supreme above all creatures."[64] This creature-feeling is felt only in the presence of the numen—the divine or awesome majesty. So the numinous is "felt as objective and outside the self."[65] The *mysterium tremendum* is that which evokes the numinous experience as it is the wholly other (mysterium or the mysterious)[66] "aweful [sic] majesty" (*tremendum* or "absolute overpoweringness").[67] What Smart means, then, is that those who claim to have religious experiences believe they are experiencing a phenomenon that originates outside the self. One experiences an object separate from the self that evokes the religious feeling. This dualistic experience—the self in relation to the other—is typical of Western religious traditions where the individual seeks the divine.

The other type of religious experience is the contemplative or mystical religious experience. This is typical of Eastern religious traditions like Hinduism and Buddhism, but it is seen also in Sufism (mystical Islam), Kabbalah (Jewish mysticism), and mystical Christian traditions. In this kind of religious experience, the individual meditates or contemplates in order to seek enlightenment from within. According to Huston Smith, Gautama (the Buddha)

> devoted the final phase of his quest to a combination of rigorous thought and mystic concentration along the lines of *raja yoga*. One evening near Gaya in Northeast India, south of the present city of Patna, he sat down under a peepul tree that has come to be known as the Bo Tree (short for *bodhi* or enlightenment). The place was later named the Immovable Spot, for tradition reports that the Buddha, sensing that a breakthrough was near, seated himself that epoch-making evening vowing not to rise until enlightenment was his.[68]

The Buddha set the pattern for what came to be called "Buddhism," so that practicing Buddhists today still seek enlightenment (Nirvana) from within. There is no deity in Buddhism (at least not in the sense found in Hinduism or the Western traditions), so there is no looking for a trace of the divine within the self as there is in theistic mysticism.

In theistic mysticism there is a longing for unity with the divine in such a way that the boundary between the self and the Other is blurred. Evagrius Ponticus (346–399) was a fourth-century Christian ascetic given to writing as well as practicing his Christianity. Evagrius prescribed a regimen for contemplation that began with reading the Psalms, praying, and then meditating on the Bible until reaching a state of serenity (*apatheia*). When seeking union with God, one was not to imagine any shape of God, but instead to clear the mind completely.[69] Evagrius used the word *gnosis* (Greek for "knowledge") to indicate the state of true union with the divine.[70] Augustine, perhaps the most influential thinker in Western Christianity, also described a mystical experience in his *Confessions*. Speaking with his mother on a balcony, Augustine contemplated the heavens and found himself (and his mother!) taking a journey to the eternal. He described it this way:

> As the flame of love burned stronger in us and raised us higher towards the eternal God, our thoughts ranged over the whole compass of material things in their various degrees, up to the heavens themselves, from which the sun and the moon and the stars shine down upon the earth. Higher still we climbed, thinking and speaking all the while in wonder at all that you have made. At length we came to our own souls and passed beyond them to that place of everlasting plenty, where you feed Israel for ever [*sic*] with the food of truth .... And while we spoke of the eternal Wisdom, longing for it and straining for it with all the strength of our hearts, for one fleeting instant we reached out and touched it. Then with a sigh, leaving our spiritual harvest bound to it, we returned to the sound of our own speech, in which each word has a beginning and an ending—far, far different from your Word, our Lord, who abides in himself for ever, yet never grows old and gives new life to all things.[71]

Here we see a classic example of a mystical experience in which one leaves the realm of normal sensibilities and has an experience in which he makes contact with the eternal. The mystic leaves the mundane behind and experiences the holy, the

Other. In many cases, the mystic is unable to speak of his experiences because the experience is unlike anything he has experienced before.

Smart also addresses the emotional side of this dimension, the feeling people have when they have a religious experience, especially in worship. Hearing particular music, singing hymns, smelling scents, and seeing religious images all can evoke emotional responses from the religious. Of singing hymns, Smart says,

> It remains true that hymns create a sense of exaltation, a sublime sense of holiness, sorrow at the death of a Saviour, a feeling of ethical commitment, loyalty to the tradition, and so forth. We need to recognize the power of words and music to fashion these feelings. It is an aspect of ritual which has depth and power. It is something which is a vital part of the phenomenology of religion, even if we find music hard to characterize or come to terms with. Similar effects are brought about by secular equivalents, such as national anthems and military music.[72]

Experiencing the sounds, sights, and smells of a worship service or sacred place can have a powerful effect on the emotions of the devoted. One senses a close presence of the Other, perhaps even unification with the Other. The outer experience and the inner experience are difficult to separate as the religious sense the divine around them.

Smart suggests that the "numinous experience provides a revelation of divinity … and that putative revelation can be applied further to daily experience: we can see the divine handiwork in the world about us."[73] The numinous experience is one of perceiving the divine from without, but that shapes the interpretive disposition of the individual. Once a person believes she has experienced the numinous, she sees the divine in the world all around her, which leads to a desire for more worship which, in turn, feeds the disposition to see the divine in the world.[74] In this manner, then, religious experiences shape the person's disposition to see more evidence of the divine in the world around her, and she feels more connected with the Other. As we will see in Chapter 4, the desire to connect to the eternal is strong, and those who do feel so connected are comforted by the experience.

We should say one more thing about Smart's experiential or emotional dimension of religion before turning to its parallel in sport. There is, Smart says, a tendency of the contemplative person to be drawn to asceticism and for like-minded ascetics to associate together in separated communities.[75] Several of the world's major religions (with the notable exception of Islam) have a monastic subsection of followers who live together in communities separated from the world around them. The word "ascetic" comes from the Greek *askesis* which means "discipline." Ascetics are those who discipline themselves in accordance with the expectations of their particular religious order. Usually, this means that the physical desires of the body—e.g., food, sex, sleep, and material possessions—are controlled by the mind which is often viewed as the spiritual part of the human being. The discipline it takes to deprive the body of these material desires can be quite a challenge, and ascetics often live together in order to encourage each other as well as to be free from the temptations found in the world.

It is a fundamental characteristic of the human condition that we are drawn to be with others who are like us. In any high school cafeteria students will segregate themselves according to groups with which they most closely identify. For example, athletes tend to sit with other athletes, computer "geeks" sit with other computer "geeks," and artistic students tend to sit with other artistic students. There is a certain comfort we feel when we are with others who are like us. Our political positions, our lifestyles, clothing fashions, tastes in music, and so on are not as challenged as they would be if we associated with people who are unlike us. Instead of being challenged by difference, we are comforted by sameness or, at least, similarity. This is clearly true of the religious organizations with which people choose to associate. Christians do not normally attend Daoist temples to worship and Hindus do not usually worship in Jewish synagogues. Even within Christianity, Baptists do not usually worship in Catholic churches and Presbyterians do not usually worship in Seventh-Day Adventist churches. People attend the type of religious organization where they feel supported by people who believe and think in similar ways. As with the ascetics of any religious organization, believers will associate themselves with others who can support them and encourage them to continue faithfully in the tradition and who will afford them the religious experiences and emotions with which they have become familiar.

The Thrill of Victory and the Agony of Defeat

Anyone who has attended a sporting event has experienced the emotional outpouring of fans, coaches, and players. Participants of sporting events usually become emotionally involved in the play and the outcome of the games and express that emotion in obvious ways. When an official makes a call that goes against the home team, most of the crowd gets angry and "boos" or yells at the official (sometimes both). When a player makes an amazing play, fans of her team will be happy and cheer wildly. When one's team or favorite player loses a competition, the fan likely will experience sadness, frustration, and even anger.

In the 2015 NFL Super Bowl, with less than a minute left on the game clock, the New England Patriots were leading the Seattle Seahawks 28–24. The Patriots had just scored the go-ahead touchdown with 2:02 remaining to play. The Seahawks, however, took the ball the length of the field and were threatening to score with less than a minute to go in the game. The Seahawks had the ball at the five-yard line of the Patriots. The Seahawks arguably had the best running back in the NFL during the 2014–2015 season—Marshawn Lynch. With just over a minute left to play, Lynch carried the ball four yards to the one-yard line. With twenty-six seconds left on the clock, almost everyone in the stadium and those watching on television expected Lynch to get the ball and attempt to run it in for a touchdown. Instead, the Seahawks ran a pass play that was intercepted, ending the Seahawks drive and dashing their hopes for a second consecutive Super Bowl title.

As one would imagine, the emotional responses of the teams and the fans of the teams were diametrically opposite each other. Patriots players threw their arms in the air in jubilation. They hugged each other with huge smiles on their faces, some with their mouths and eyes wide open at the sudden change in the game. Expecting the Seahawks to score and take the lead, they instead stopped the Seahawks and won the game. They were thrilled. Their fans were thrilled. Patriots fans went from the feeling of utter despair to extreme joy, shouting obscenities in jubilation, throwing their hands in the air, slapping each other's raised hands, and running around their living rooms.[76] On the other hand, Seahawks fans' emotions went from great expectations of joy—their team was on the one-yard line with one of the best running backs in the league and plenty of time to score—to feelings of sadness, despair, and anger. Seahawks fans screamed obscenities, shouted "No! No!" as if denying the fact they were going to lose, stared at the television in disbelief, and some slunk to the floor unable to hold themselves up.[77] Fans of American football experience various emotions based on the outcome of their favorite team's play and these emotions can range from utter despair to incredible joy in the time it takes to throw a short pass.

We should note that fans are not necessarily responding to the actual play on the field but to what that play *means*. For Seahawks fans, the interception meant that their team would not win the championship and so they (the fans) would not be perceived as champions. For Patriots fans, the interception meant that their team would probably win the game and win the championship and that Patriots fans would be regarded as champions themselves. The emotional response of the individual is tied to his interpretation of external events. In the case of the Super Bowl, the external event was winning (or losing) the game. In the case of religious experience, the external stimulus might be seeing a majestic mountain, hearing a choir sing, or having a minister pronounce divine grace and forgiveness. In both types of cases, the individual perceives something external to the self and interprets the meaning of that event as providing connection with the eternal (winning the championship/experiencing awe at the beauty of the choir) or being cast away from the eternal (losing the championship/being excommunicated from religious fellowship).

Individual Union with the Eternal

What we have described above illustrates, primarily, what Smart calls the outer kind of experience—the fans witness something external to them and respond to it accordingly. The inner experience primarily belongs to the athlete himself, and this inner experience is often a spiritual feeling. Ignacio Götz quotes former surfer, Michael Hynson, who says, "When you become united with a wave … you feel like you are in total harmony with the divine at every level."[78] Götz goes on to describe the spiritual experience of the goalkeeper in soccer:

> His training demands that he learn to focus on the ball with utmost attention. By itself, the soccer ball is a piece of leather sown [sic] to certain specifications, but to the goalkeeper, the ball is as complicated a conundrum as a Zen *kōan*. He has to concentrate on it at all times. If his awareness waivered for a moment, he might miss the most important happening of his life, just as he might miss the most

spectacular save of his career. There is no time to switch off, as it were; his eyes must not blink, for everything is centered on the ball—*life* is focused on the ball, concentrated in it, and he must follow it intently, for this is what it takes to live. If he fastens his attention on the ball to the point of merging with it, then he gains salvation, enlightenment, *satori*, as perfectly on the soccer field as in a Buddhist monastery; for, in fact, there is no difference. What matters is to concentrate to the utmost, not to let the mind wander, to see nothing but the ball, to let his whole being, body and mind, merge with the ball in the flux of reality, to move with the movement of the ball—that is, with the flow of life. The important thing is the exhilaration of belonging, the joy of merging, the utter happiness of losing all form and of blending in the formless streaming that some label existence. This is what it means to be a goalkeeper. For isn't the goal, everybody's goal, to merge, sooner or later, with the spirit of the universe? So, the thing for the goalkeeper to do is to stick to this goal, to keep this merging as his goal, to be a keeper of the goal.[79]

Here we have an example of an internal, subjective experience of the individual. Many athletes express such a feeling of spiritual awareness in exerting themselves in their sports.

All sports require the athletes to be disciplined in that they must train, eat properly, and take care of their bodies. Often, the mind of the athlete has to demand that the body continue to exert itself physically even though the body may be sending signals of pain to the brain pleading for it to rest. As with ascetics of religious traditions, the athlete must control her body's desires (e.g., the desire to rest when being pushed by physical exertion) with the mind thus disciplining the body to submit to the mind's control. This self-discipline is especially necessary in long-distance runners who often train alone as they prepare for competitive runs such as marathons. The hours and hours of running require the athlete to push the body when it does not want to go in order to achieve the desired goal of competing at the highest possible level. This discipline may be rewarded, not only at the time of the competition, but during the training itself.

Many long-distance runners claim to have experienced the so-called runner's high, also considered an inner, spiritual experience. Henning Boecker et al. report that "there is no generally accepted definition as to what runner's high is, but common descriptions include feelings like 'pleasantness,' 'inner harmony,' 'boundless energy,' or even druglike 'orgiastic' sensations."[80] Citing a study done by Dietrich and McDaniel,[81] Robert Sands and Linda Sands show that endurance runners' bodies produce endocannabinoids in the blood that

moderate or reduce pain sensations for both the peripheral and central nervous systems and produce similar psychoactive effects to THC, a constituent of marijuana.... These effects include time distortion, enhanced euphoria, transcendence, reduced anxiety, and intense sensory perception, and for some "touching" the sacred or divine.[82]

For some runners, then, this experience is in some way a spiritual or religious experience. It is one in which they feel a connection to something other and, no doubt, yearn for repeated such encounters as we saw above with ritual.

Jeffrey Summers et al. suggest that there is a connection between the "runner's high" and those who develop an actual addiction to running. When these runners miss a scheduled run they report feelings of guilt, irritability, and even depression.[83] Not all runners have experienced this high, but in their study of middle-aged, non-elite runners running a marathon for the first time, Summer et al. found that 48 percent of those surveyed before the marathon reported having experienced the runner's high. That is a significant percentage of these runners.

Robert Sands and Linda Sands suggest that running helps the person connect with her environment and feel at one with it. They point to American Indian practices of incorporating running in both sport and ritual:

> Looking at running in Native American past and present lifeways, the symbi-otic relationship between ego and nature is played out in cosmology and ritual. Running served many purposes in ancient Native American cultures ... Races and gaming were popular parts of the fabric of Indian ceremony and ritual.[84]

It is possible that by running and feeling at one with the environment, the individual escapes, at least momentarily, the feeling of utter finitude and feels joined to the eternal, the Other. The runner becomes connected with his surroundings. In much the same way that ritual connects the individual with the community and with the Other, running accomplishes the same thing.

The Ethical or Legal Dimension

The fifth of Smart's seven dimensions of religion is the ethical and legal dimension. (Since we treat the ethical aspect of religion in sport in Chapter 6, we will only briefly consider this dimension here.) Smart says that it "is difficult to disentangle ethical from legal require-ments" in the religious realm.[85] He points to Islam's Shari'a law that intends to govern the whole of the Islamic community. In ancient Judaism, the Torah was meant to govern the Jewish people in all aspects of their lives, not just the religious. In fact, one could not separate religious law and secular law in ancient Judaism. Smart points to Confucianism as the best example in antiquity of the ethical and legal being closely aligned:

> Of all the philosophies of the ancient world, Confucianism most clearly exhibits the way in which political life should be governed by moral principles. In effect it is an ideology for the training of political leadership, predicated on a hierarchical society.[86]

The law contains the rules that reflect the ethical values of the community. In many religions, that law tends to be codified in sacred texts that then serve as guidelines for subsequent generations of believers who commit to those traditions.

Another aspect of Smart's ethical and legal dimension is the honor and respect paid to ancestors. Smart says,

> Although in some weak sense every society thinks of the dead as owed some duties (the honouring of wills, for example, and the need to tend graves), it is in societies where the dead are considered really to be living that a special ethos prevails.[87]

In traditional African religious traditions, the dead are honored and thought to be alive as long as they are remembered. However, when all those who have memories of the deceased are dead, the ancestors fade away entirely. Smart points out that in Far Eastern traditions that have long had a history of writing, the memories of the dead can be greatly prolonged by writing them down.[88] Even after everyone who had direct memories of the ancestors is gone, the writing preserves the memories for subsequent generations to honor.

Sinners and Saints

Sport has an obvious ethical and legal dimension to it as well, and this is easily seen in the rules that govern play. In fact, what differentiates one sport from another is, in large part, the rules by which the games are played. To be sure, the equipment used in each sport has something to do with the playing of the game, but not nearly as much as the rules by which the game is played. For example, in non-regulation competition, soccer can be played with a coconut if necessary, and it probably is in parts of the world where the players cannot afford a regulation soccer ball and where coconuts abound. The game of basketball would be much more difficult if played with a football, but the fundamental object of getting the ball through a net (or wooden basket or wired loop) would be the same. Baseball could be played with a volleyball and hockey stick instead of a baseball bat and baseball. However, even with ideal equipment, one cannot change the rules without fundamentally changing the game itself. In golf, the player must advance the ball by striking it with a club. The ball cannot be carried, thrown, or kicked toward the cup. In the shot put, an athlete cannot bring her own shot to the competition that is lighter or of a different shape than a regular shot. The size, shape, and weight of the shot are regulated by rule so that each competitor throws the same-sized shot. This is fair; this is ethical.

When players or coaches do not follow the rules and they are caught, officials tend to penalize them in some way. The National Association for Stock Car Auto Racing (NASCAR) circuit is notorious for teams breaking the rules to gain a competitive advantage in the races. There is a saying that goes, "If you are not caught cheating, you are not trying hard enough." Teams are constantly pushing, and sometimes skirting, the rules to make their cars faster. In the very beginning of the 2007 season, NASCAR suspended four crew chiefs—the primary persons responsible for the preparation of the race cars—because their cars did not pass a pre-race inspection by NASCAR officials. Robbie Reiser, the crew chief for driver Matt Kenseth, and Kenny Francis, crew chief for driver Kasey Kahne, were each suspended for four races and fined $50,000 for their cars not conforming to NASCAR rules. Rodney Childers, crew chief for driver Scott Riggs, and Josh Brown, crew chief for driver Elliott Sadler, were each suspended for two races and fined $25,000.[89] The suspensions and fines were especially noteworthy because they came immediately before the opening of the race season at arguably the biggest race of the year—the Daytona 500 held in Daytona Beach, Florida (USA). NASCAR officials intended to crack down on cheating in the sport and made the unprecedented move of docking the drivers racing points that are earned to determine the season's champion. Drivers Kahne and Kenseth were docked fifty points each while Riggs and Sadler were docked twenty-five points each.[90]

The severe penalties and fines did not stop cheating in NASCAR. In March 2012, Jimmie Johnson's crew chief—Chad Knaus—was suspended for six weeks and fined $100,000 because Johnson's car failed inspection before the Daytona 500. According to Jeff Owens, this was not the first time Knaus faced penalties for violations of NASCAR rules. Owens says that Knaus had been penalized nine times in the previous eleven seasons for violations on Jimmie Johnson's cars. He had been suspended four times and won only once on appeal.[91] Knaus and Johnson won the NASCAR championship five years in a row from 2006 to 2010, but Owens compares that record to Barry Bonds' home run record in Major League Baseball. Many people see Bonds' record as tainted because he has been accused of using performance-enhancing drugs to give him an advantage.[92] According to Owens,

> [s]ome defend Knaus by saying that he's only doing what a good crew chief should do—looking for loopholes in the rulebook and trying to find an edge in a sport that has always applauded and encouraged mechanical ingenuity. But in an era when NASCAR has laid out more specific and more clear-cut rules—some say they're still not specific or clear enough—and cracked down on bending those rules, Knaus has emerged as the sport's most penalized competitor.[93]

What Owens is complaining about is the fact that Knaus should be concerned about his reputation but is not. Owens is appealing to a sense of fairness required for sport to be sport. If a competitor is cheating by breaking the rules set out by the sport, then the competitor is not really playing the sport as it is intended to be played. The cheater gains an advantage over other competitors so that the cheater is not really playing the same game. The game is determined by the rules, and when the rules are broken by one player, that player has removed himself from the game all of the other competitors are playing. The cheater may cross the finish line first, but the cheater has "stolen" the prize by playing what amounts to an easier game than the other competitors while appearing to play the same game. The fans have been cheated because they have not seen a true game where everyone was playing by the rules. There is clearly an ethical sense of fairness inherent in sport and this sense of fairness is most obvious when cheaters are caught breaking the rules. In breaking the rules, cheaters violate the spirit of their sports just as we might imagine "sinners" violate the spirit of their religious traditions.

The other aspect mentioned by Smart regarding the ethical and legal dimension of religion was that ancestors are honored and revered for setting examples of greatness to descendants. The world of sport also honors the greats who have come before by enshrining them in halls of fame. Many sports have a hall of fame where those who have played the game at the highest levels or who have contributed to the game in a significant and lasting way are honored. For example, The Archery Hall of Fame and Museum in Springfield, Missouri,

> seeks to honor those Outstanding [sic] members of the Archery Community through the process of induction into its Hall of Fame. As an integral part of its existence, the Hall seeks to preserve the history and tradition of Archery and Bowhunting for future generations.[94]

Its purpose is to preserve the central aspects of the tradition by lifting up and enshrining those who have been exemplars of the sport and those who have had a lasting impact on it. M. R. James writes of Dave Samuels' 2007 induction into the Hall saying that Samuels "deserved the gratitude of all modern bowhunters now enjoying the fruits of his decades-long pro-hunting and conservation labors .... Dave Samuels has been a true trailblazer and forceful presence in modern bowhunting."[95] Samuels has become someone all bowhunters can look up to as the highest example of what a bowhunter should be. He has made a lasting impact on the sport and so is enshrined for subsequent generations to honor and revere.

In July 2015, Major League Baseball inducted pitcher John Smoltz into its Hall of Fame in Cooperstown, New York (along with pitchers Randy Johnson and Pedro Martinez, and catcher/second baseman Craig Biggio). Speaking at the Hall of Fame, Smoltz said, "This is a pretty incredible place. Some elite people .... To know that I'll be a part of it is something that still hasn't set in yet." He continues:

> When I think of Babe Ruth and Ty Cobb and what's behind me is just incredible … I've always had a decent perspective of the evolutional changes (of baseball), but I never really got a chance to see them up close. To hold a bat, to hold a ball from 1906 or 1905, is pretty incredible.
> The day you get in the Hall of Fame … [p]eople start looking at you differently.[96]

While Smoltz does not elaborate on what he means by the last statement, it is fair to assume he means that people look at him differently because he is in the Hall of Fame—signifying his elevation as a baseball player to a higher status than the normal player. In a sense, he has been recognized as a saint of the game. He is among the elite—like Babe Ruth and Ty Cobb—who have been forever immortalized as members of the Hall of Fame (Ruth's and Cobb's moral character outside of the game notwithstanding). As with the honoring of ancestors and saints in religion, special athletes are honored and remembered.

The Social Dimension

The sixth dimension of religion according to Ninian Smart is the social dimension. As with the dimension of the ethical, we treat this dimension at some length in Chapter 5. Here, we will consider just one aspect of the social dimension of religion, and that is the role of religious leaders in religious organizations. Smart offers a taxonomy of the different kinds of leaders who are a part of various religious traditions. For example, the Hebrew prophet serves as a spokesperson for God.[97]

Often he performs the role of social critic calling the people back to the covenant they made with God. The sage, on the other hand, is a person who is well read and given to studying literature. She is wise and leads by example.[98] The guru is "a spiritual guide or preceptor, very often a single wanderer or celibate teacher, or a Brahmin instructor, and commands absolute obedience."[99] The preacher is similar to the prophet in that she speaks to the congregation on behalf of God.[100] She also interprets the scriptures and urges the congregation to follow the divine teachings. The rabbi is like the sage in that he is learned, but he is different in that the works he studies are more legal and practical than theological.[101] The theologian is the "one who is charged with formulating the doctrines or teachings of a tradition or sub-tradition."[102] Theologians tend to think deeply about the truths of the tradition and they interpret those truths in contemporary culture. All of these leaders are revered for having a special link to the divine or special abilities that make them exemplars of their traditions. They serve to set the standards for what constitutes proper behavior and belief in the religious organization. They also teach the practitioners of their particular religions and help them achieve their goals of becoming the best followers of their religions they can be by mentoring them and setting examples for them.

The Coach

As Smart notes, secular individuals may also serve the same functions as these religious leaders.[103] Most organizations of any size have a structure in which those with more advanced knowledge and training lead those with less understanding of the work of the organization. Athletic teams usually have head coaches who oversee all aspects of play. Often teams have position coaches who focus on one position of a team and equipment managers whose specialty and expertise is in maintaining the proper equipment necessary for players to use. Many teams, both amateur and professional, have team physicians and even psychologists to help with the mental aspect of the game. Having these varying specialties does not necessarily make sport religious. However, just as religions have their "elite" who lead the followers toward spiritual excellence, so sports have their revered leaders who teach and set examples for how to excel in the sport and even in life.

Fisher DeBerry was the head football coach at the United States Air Force Academy from 1984 to 2006. He served as a coach and as a mentor for his players over that time period and was inducted into the Colorado Sports Hall of Fame in 2008. Of his coaching, former Air Force quarterback Shaun Carney says,

> I don't think there is a more worthy candidate for hall of fame induction in the nation and certainly here in Colorado than Coach DeBerry ... He taught us a competitive edge that we brought to the field, and it helped us win games. He taught players to be great citizens, and we'll take those lessons with us for the rest of our lives.[104]

DeBerry functioned in the same way any religious leader would function by helping his players achieve their goals as football players. Whether or not the players knew it, DeBerry also led them to become better persons.

Bela Karolyi is the well-known gymnastics coach who defected from Romania in 1981. By that time, he had already coached one of the world's most famous athletes—gymnast Nadia Comaneci—in the 1976 Olympics, where Comaneci received the first ever perfect score of 10 in an Olympic gymnastics event. After defecting to the United States, Karolyi coached the US women's team that included Mary Lou Retton. Retton won a gold medal in the women's all-around competition in the 1984 Olympics. While some question Karolyi's methods,[105] no one questions his ability to help gymnasts excel at their sport. Karolyi coached nine Olympic champions during his coaching career. Two-time US national champion Kristen Maloney says of Karolyi, "He makes all the girls want to do more....Now we believe in ourselves."[106] Karolyi did what any religious leader would do—he helped his followers maximize their potential by teaching them his methods and philosophies. Just as religions have their leaders to help followers achieve their highest potential, so do sports, at least those sports that have coaches.

The Material Dimension

The final dimension of religion according to Smart is the material dimension, which he treats rather briefly. Using the Greek god Poseidon as an example, Smart points out that there are at least two aspects of the material component of a god. The first is that, as god of the sea, Poseidon actually is the sea; the sea is his body. The sea, Smart says,

> is a person which heaves and billows and tosses ships around yet it is often flat and tranquil. It is a person with varying behaviour, which the worshipper hopes to influence, for instance by sacrifices. It is a person which can therefore be addressed, and which in suitable temples can be realized in statues.[107]

The second aspect of the material component of a god is that humans can make images of the god as Smart notes, for example, in statues. A physical depiction of the god may merely represent the god, or it may be the physical manifestation of the god if the depiction is duly consecrated.[108]

Besides the physical representation of the gods, there are other material aspects of religion. Smart says that there are various aspects of the material dimension including the vestments worn by priests, paintings of sacred places or events, and even the incense that is burned during certain ceremonies and rituals. Perhaps the most obvious material aspect of a religion is the building (e.g., temple, church, mosque) erected by the faithful.[109] Religious buildings serve to house the gods and provide places to perform rituals. They create sacred space where practitioners of the faith can worship.

Mircea Eliade notes that sacred space is set apart from profane space that is "homogeneous and neutral."[110] He says, "Every sacred space implies a hierophany, an irruption of the sacred that results in detaching a territory from the surrounding cosmic milieu and making it qualitatively different."[111] There can be no doubt when walking through the gates of a White Cloud Daoist temple in the middle of massive Beijing or into St. Peter's Basilica at the Vatican amidst the bustling of Rome that one has entered a place that is set apart from the secular world.

Not only is sacred space set apart from the secular; according to Eliade, "it *founds the world* in the sense that it fixes the limits and establishes the order of the world."[112] Organizing space that was once "chaotic" (unknown, undeveloped) imitates the gods as they created the cosmos against chaos:

> An unknown, foreign, and unoccupied territory (which often means, "unoccupied by our people") still shares in the fluid and larval modality of chaos. By occupying it and, above all, by settling in it, man symbolically transforms it into a cosmos through a ritual repetition of the cosmogony. What is to become "our world" must first be "created," and every creation has a paradigmatic model — the creation of the universe by the gods.[113]

This world is created in imitation of the gods as they created the world, but this world still needs a portal to heaven, the eternal. Eliade illustrates this need for communication with heaven using the Achilpa, an Arunta tribe of nomadic hunters and gatherers in Australia. According to their creation story,

> the divine being Numbakula cosmicized their future territory, created their Ancestor, and established their institutions. From the trunk of a gum tree Numbakula fashioned the sacred pole (*kauwa-auwa*) and, after anointing it with blood, climbed it and disappeared into the sky.[114]

The Achilpa have a sacred pole, which they believe is the one Numbakula used, and carry it with them wherever they wander. When they stop at a particular location, they erect the pole which becomes the center of their world. It creates sacred space wherever they go and provides a connection with the sky where Numbakula is.[115] It provides their gateway to the eternal.

Similarly, sacred spaces that are constructed as relatively permanent structures also provide a gateway to the eternal. For example, when one walks into a Catholic cathedral such as St. Paul's Cathedral in St. Paul, Minnesota (USA), it is clear that she is in a different space that is not like the world. The high, domed ceiling strikes in the visitor a sense of awe such that she expects to have an encounter with the divine, or at least such an encounter seems possible. The dome represents the ceiling of the sky, or the heavens, and comes to a central point representing the center of the cosmos, the place where creation began. By returning to the center, the visitor has returned to the world as God intended it to be at the beginning when God first created it.[116]

In some cases, the sacred space is a natural formation such as a sacred river or a stand of trees in the middle of a plain. Often, mountains are revered as sacred. K. C. Hanson notes that the importance of the mountain for religious purposes varies by context:

> Depending on the era, culture, and text, the cosmological emphasis on the mountain might be one or more of the following: the assembly place of the gods, the connection between heaven and earth, the center/navel of the earth (and the locus of creation), the locus of revelation.[117]

Eliade suggests that the sacred mountain serves as the bridge between the earth and the heavens. Like the sacred pole of the Achilpa, the mountain serves as the *axis mundi*, or that around which everything (particularly every meaningful thing) revolves. Eliade says that "around this cosmic axis lies the world (= our world), hence the axis is located 'in the middle,' and the 'navel of the earth'; it is the Center of the World."[118] Just as with the Achilpa, the sacred mountain becomes the center of the world for those who revere it and provides a gateway between earth and the heavens.

Sacred space, then, is one aspect of the material dimension of religion that orders an otherwise chaotic world. Outside of the sacred space, whether natural or constructed by humans, lies the mundane, the ordinary, the profane. One might even say that outside of the ordered, sacred space lies chaos itself.

Stadia and Relics

Sport also has a material dimension to it, including statues of heroes, buildings, clothing, and, of course, stadia. Joseph Price notes that

> baseball has its temples—its stadiums—where the rites are performed, and its shrines—like the Hall of Fame, the commemorative plaques on the centerfield fence in Yankee Stadium, and the bronzed shoes of Johnny Bench at Cincinnati's Great American Ballpark—where the players and games are commemorated.... Baseball, like religions, also has its relics, its tangible artifacts that help to call to mind the journeys to the games and the contact with its heroes. For the fan, the relics are called game balls, players' autographs, and memorabilia—officially licensed souvenirs—that can be purchased at stadium souvenir stands.[119]

These are all material objects that are a part of the game of baseball and a part of the experience of the fans, especially those fans who attend the games in person. The objects that can be purchased in souvenir stands are significantly less sacred than those that have had some contact with the heroes who have played the game. For example, an officially licensed Major League Baseball baseball can be purchased in a stadium souvenir shop, but it does not compare in importance to a ball that has actually been in the game. A ball that has been in the game has been part of the sacrality of the game itself. Fans at most levels of baseball will scramble to get a ball that has been hit in the stands, even if it is only a foul ball (as opposed to a home run ball). This is especially true at the Major League level. A ball that comes out of the hand and off the bat of Major League players has been in contact with the eternal, or the universal, the heroes of the game. Fans can buy jerseys made by the same manufacturer to the same specifications as those worn by the players, but they pale in value compared to a game-worn jersey. A non-game ball or jersey becomes significantly more sacred when a star Major League player has autographed it.

Additionally, a ball or jersey (or bat or pair of cleats) that has been part of something especially significant is even more valuable than an "ordinary" relic of the game. For example, in September 1995, Major League superstar Cal Ripken, Jr., playing for the Baltimore Orioles, broke a record in baseball that some said would never be broken—Lou Gehrig's consecutive games played streak. Gehrig played in 2,130 consecutive games for the New York Yankees before being forced to quit because of Amyotrophic Lateral Sclerosis (ALS)—now known as "Lou Gehrig's Disease." Ripken tied the record on September 5 and broke it on September 6. When the September 6 game became official—after the top of the fifth inning was complete—the Baltimore crowd gave Ripken a standing ovation that stopped the game for twenty-two minutes. Eventually, Ripken took a jog around the entire field slapping outstretched hands and waving to the crowd. The day before, in the game in which he tied Gehrig's record, Ripken hit a home run ball that was caught by Michael Stirn. Stirn sold the ball to an unnamed businessman three months later for $41,736. The businessman attempted to sell the ball to Walmart for $1 million, a figure he deemed reasonable because of the price a buyer paid for the ball Eddie Murray hit for his 500th home run ($500,000).[120] Walmart declined to purchase the ball, but the asking price (and the selling price of Murray's home run ball) is indicative of the value many place on such an important relic of the game. Many such relics find their way to the Hall of Fame and are displayed for visitors to view and revere.

In addition to its "holy" relics, the game of baseball also has sacred space. Certain stadia are revered because of their longevity or because of events that have taken place there. Wrigley Field, the home field of the Chicago Cubs, is widely regarded in its entirety as sacred space by baseball fans of all teams. (See Fig. 2.2)

Sometimes parts of stadia are intentionally set apart as shrines to commemorate players or teams. There is the well-known Monument Park in Yankee Stadium that honors great Yankees players of the past. When the Yankees moved into the

Fig. 2.2 **Exterior of Wrigley Field opening night 2015.**

new Yankee Stadium in 2009, they moved Monument Park to the new stadium. When the Atlanta Braves moved from Fulton County Stadium to Ted Turner Field in 1997, Fulton County Stadium was demolished except for the section of fence over which Hank Aaron hit his 715th career home run surpassing Babe Ruth and becoming Major League Baseball's "Home Run King." That section of fence (along with a commemorative plaque) serves as a shrine to honor Hank Aaron. It is, indeed, sacred space.

Like most sports arenas, the field area is off-limits to fans who must remain in the stands. Any fan who enters the field area without permission violates a taboo and is usually arrested by security personnel and removed from the stadium completely. Baseball's field is unique, however. Price argues that the pitcher's mound represents the cosmic mountain that serves as the center of the baseball cosmos.[121] It is where play begins, which is consistent with the idea that the center of the universe represents the birth of the universe, or the navel. Price sees this navel—omphalos in the Greek—as the "rubber" that sits on top of the cosmic mountain:

> The pitcher's rubber is located at the top of the pitcher's mound, a twelve-inch-high rise that provides the only topical elevation in the field. Rising above the contour of the field, the pitcher's mound corresponds to the cosmic mountains of old and its stature as such is reinforced by the presence of the rubber at its crest.
>
> In the world or cosmos of baseball, the omphalos is located at the top of the cosmic mountain. As the mythical center of the field, the pitcher's mound is the point at which creation of the game begins. The pitcher, who starts play by throwing the ball to the batter, must stand on top of the pitcher's mound and must keep his foot on the rubber until he has released the ball. There is, then, an umbilical connection between the creative activity of the pitcher (as a high priest) and the omphalos itself.[122]

There are many more examples of how the space of a baseball stadium may be seen as sacred including the monuments—statues, commemorative plaques, and larger-than-life pictures of important moments in a team's history—that are erected to honor heroes (saints) and heroic moments of the team. However, this brief treatment should suffice to show that, like religion, sport has a material dimension that helps to order the chaos outside and provide meaningful material culture.

Conclusion

We have seen (at length) the parallels between Ninian Smart's seven dimensions of religion and sport. To be sure, not all sports have every dimension in equal weight. While there is a material element to cross-country running, there is not as much of the material as we have seen in baseball. However, just because one religion does not build massive cathedrals to set apart space as sacred does not mean that those religions are any less religious than those that do build such structures. It seems clear that sport, as an organized activity of humans, shares the same structures or dimensions that organized religions have.

In the following chapters, we build upon the case made here. In the next chapter in particular, we will consider religion and sport from a theological perspective. We will consider what religion seeks to do for the individual and compare that to what sport does for the individual.

Discussion Questions

1. Do you have rituals that you perform on a regular basis? Do these rituals have a purpose? Are people who perform rituals superstitious?

2. Do you have beliefs about things that cannot be proven definitively? Do these beliefs provide a certain order and meaning to your life?

3. Did your parents or guardians ever tell you stories about your ancestors? If so, did those stories help shape how you see yourself as a member of your family? Have you ever had family members disagree about the events of the story because they remember the event(s) differently? If so, how do you determine who is correct?

4. Do you have a favorite sports team that you get emotional about when it wins or loses? Why do you get emotional about a team? If you don't have a favorite team, why do you think others get emotional about their favorite teams?

5. Why do sports have rules? Why do sports have officials (e.g., umpires and referees) to ensure that those rules are followed? Should athletes who are caught cheating be elected to their respective halls of fame? Who determines what is right and wrong?

6. What kind of people do you look to for guidance? Is there someone who provides a pattern for the way you would like your life to be?

7. Why do we build statues of certain people? Do certain places seem more special to you than others, places that you treat with more respect than others? Does a natural structure like a mountain or the ocean evoke certain feelings in you? Are there places you regard as sacred in any sense of the word?

Glossary

ab origine—Latin phrase used by Mircea Eliade to denote that time in the mythic past "in the beginning" when God(s) created the world in its ideal form.

apotheosis—the raising of a normal human being to divine status.

cosmos—the world in its totality, but primarily as experienced by the individual.

cosmogony—a view of the origin of the world, how the world came into being, and what order it has.

etiology—an explanation of how things came to be the way they are, usually told through mythic stories.

in illo tempore—Latin phrase used by Mircea Eliade to denote a time in the distant past ("in that time") when life was ideal as created by the God(s).

kōan—in Zen Buddhism, a question meant to jolt the student from normal structures and patterns of thought, usually apparently absurd to the untrained.

mysticism—the tradition of seeking to have direct contact with the divine or Other.

ontological—having to do with being and existence (from the Greek *ontos* = being).

profane—the ordinary, the common; that which is not sacred.

ritual—any activity that is performed in a very similar way every time it is performed in order to recall a memorable event in the past or, sometimes, to manipulate future events.

sacred—that which is set apart from the ordinary, or profane; of greater qualitative meaning or value.

secular—having to do with the profane world as opposed to that which is sacred.

soteriological—having to do with the salvation of a person in a theological sense.

3 The Quest for Perfection: A Theological Approach

Being "self-aware" means, among other things, having the ability to imagine oneself from outside of oneself. That is, we can imagine ourselves as distinct from the world around us and question our relationship to each other and to the world. We can also imagine ourselves as being different than we really are. That is, we can imagine ourselves being in a state different from the one in which we find ourselves. We can imagine ourselves being taller, shorter, faster, or stronger, for example. We can also imagine ourselves being better than we are in any number of ways, including in decisions we make on a daily basis. Who has not looked back at some point and wished he or she had made a different decision from one that was made? Looking forward, we can imagine that we will improve in our lives to have the best life possible. We can imagine that our lives will get better than they are presently: we will have a better job, earn a higher salary, be in better physical condition, have better relationships, etc. In our imaginations we have an ideal self we wish to be and work toward achieving that goal. What we end up with when we engage in this exercise is a dichotomy between the condition in which we find ourselves currently—the *actual human condition*—and the condition in which we would like to be—the *ideal human condition*.

This difference between the actual and ideal conditions can be applied in any number of temporal situations. For example, most college students' ideal condition as college students is to have graduated and be employed soon thereafter (though this last part may be more the parents' notion of the ideal condition for their child). The actual condition of the college student is to be in college still, working through courses and other requirements for graduation. Or, a person may be taking a road trip lasting several hundred miles so that the ideal condition is to have arrived at the destination while the actual condition is traveling toward the destination.

Having determined the actual state and the ideal state, we can work now on achieving the ideal state. Recognizing where one is in relation to the goal—the ideal state—one can determine how far one is from the ideal condition and perhaps what will be required to achieve the ideal condition. Going back to our examples above, college students should have an idea as to how much they must yet achieve in order to graduate from college. They can compare the requirements for the degree as stated in the bulletin or catalog of the college and then determine how many of those requirements they have met. Determining how many requirements have been met necessarily indicates how many requirements have yet to be fulfilled, thus providing the students with what they still must achieve, or, how far they are from their ideal condition of graduation. In the second example, understanding the distance to the ideal condition can be met easily with a GPS mapping unit that visually presents the gap between the actual condition—where the driver is—and the ideal condition—where the driver wants to be.

In this chapter, we look at the ways in which religious traditions conceive of the ideal human condition and how to move toward it—focusing on Buddhism, Hinduism, Christianity, and Islam. The goal of achieving perfection, or at least union with that which is perfect, also can be found in sport, and we detail this phenomenon in golf, baseball, gymnastics, and American football. In the end, we see a very similar phenomenon happening both in religion and sport.

Religions and the Actual vs Ideal Human Condition

A key element of most religions is that they seek to define in a religious sense both the actual human condition and the ideal human condition in order to determine the gap between the two and what must be done to achieve the ideal. The actual human condition is often described by various religions as a finite one, subject to pain and death, separation from the Creator, being limited in knowledge of reality or, more generally, living in a state of imperfection. Some religions combine some or all of these to describe the actual human condition. The ideal human condition can be defined in any number of ways in a religious sense, including having an eternal life of bliss after death spent in the presence of one's loved ones and of the Creator, spending eternity absorbed into the Creator, being forever free from physical and emotional pain, having complete knowledge of the universe or, more generally, existing in a state of perpetual perfection. Again, some religions combine some or all of these in order to define the ideal human condition.

Helping us to understand the gap between the actual and the ideal is what religion does. It describes the ideal human condition, often referred to as "perfection,"[1] as compared to our actual human condition, thus making it possible to determine what we need to do to obtain our ideal human condition, if that is, indeed, possible. Though we are not able to cover all of the world's major religions, a few examples should illustrate how religion attempts to describe both the actual and ideal human conditions.

Buddhism

Buddhists tend to see the actual human condition as one mired in temporality. In fact, reincarnation (the cycle of birth, death, and rebirth) means that human beings are thrown back into time over and over again—a cycle called *samsara*. In *samsara*, most people are concerned with things that are not eternal—their status in the community, how much money they have, or, for sports fans, whether or not their team will win the championship. The first two of the Four Noble Truths of Buddhism illustrate the actual human condition. The First Noble Truth is that life is suffering. This does not mean we are all in physical pain all of the time (though experiencing physical pain is part of the suffering of life). It means that we find life to be a struggle that is difficult and causes us anxiety, concern, and, sometimes, physical pain. Our existence has moved away from what it should be so that we find ourselves struggling as though we are off-track or disjointed in our lives. The Second Noble Truth states that we experience this disjointedness and unsatisfactoriness, this suffering, because of our desires or cravings. Desires often can have positive consequences, as when we may desire the good for others. Desiring in itself, though, sets us up for suffering because we suffer when our desires are not fulfilled. We may desire to be free of disease (or even to be able to live forever), to be free of physical pain, to receive a raise at our jobs, for our children to succeed, or for our favorite teams to win a championship. Perhaps some of these desires will come true, but not all of them. When they do not come true, we suffer. Even when they come true, we just generate new desires that set us up for new suffering.

The ideal human condition is achieved according to the Third and Fourth Noble Truths. The Third Noble Truth tells us that, if the cause of our suffering is due to our desires, we must overcome those desires to restore our lives to the correct state of existence. The Fourth Noble Truth tells us how to do that: We must first decide to live an intentional life dedicated to overcoming our desires and then follow the Eightfold Path to Enlightenment. The Eightfold Path means having: (1) right views, (2) right intent, (3) right speech, (4) right conduct, (5) right livelihood, (6) right effort, (7) right mindfulness, and (8) right concentration. Once the person has achieved success in each of the elements of the Path, he reaches a point where his mind sees reality as it is, free from temporal, finite distractions. He has then experienced Enlightenment.[2]

Hinduism

Hindus see the actual human condition as one bogged down by desires keeping us from union with Brahman (God). Within each of us is our true, eternal self known as *Atman*, but we are typically unaware of it because of our desires for temporal things. According to Hinduism, people want pleasure and worldly success consisting of wealth, fame, and power. There is nothing wrong with these desires, necessarily, but in order to achieve release (*moksha*) from the temporal (like Buddhism, this is *samsara*) and union with Brahman, we must mature enough to realize that these things will not bring us true happiness. We may begin on the Path of Desire, but we must move to the Path of Renunciation if we are to achieve union with the eternal.

The Path of Renunciation involves, of course, renouncing our desires for temporal goods. Once we realize that temporal goods will not bring us true happiness, we look beyond those things to the things we really want at a much deeper level. The things we really want are being, knowledge, and joy, and we want these things infinitely. What people really want is release (*moksha*) from *samsara* so that we can experience the infinite.

While we ultimately all want the same thing, Hinduism teaches that there are four paths (*yogas*) to union with Brahman depending on one's personality type (though individuals may choose elements from more than one path). For those who are more intellectually inclined, there is *jnana yoga*. This path focuses on learning and under-standing to reach Brahman. For those who are guided more by emotion than by reason, there is *bhakti yoga*. The way to Brahman on this path is to love God for the sake of love alone. The third path to Brahman is *karma yoga*. Followers on this path perform works meant for unselfish purposes, for the sake of others' well-be-ing. The more one acts without regard for the self, the more the self and its binding desires diminish and union with the infinite is achieved. The fourth path to Brahman is through *raja yoga*. In this approach, the individual performs a series of psycho-physical experiments to focus the mind on God without distraction from the temporal world. The body is trained to tune out the world of the physical and focus exclusively on the eternal. Perhaps the most well known physical exercise for this path has the practitioner sitting in the lotus position: legs crossed with each foot touching the opposite thigh, spine erect but relaxed, hands palm up in the lap with thumbs slightly touching each other. Breathing is controlled so as not to be a distraction until the mind is able to block out all external sensory perceptions. When all that is temporal is removed, only the eternal remains.

Hindus also hold to the doctrine of reincarnation. Unlike Buddhists, however, who do not believe in the idea of a soul, Hindus believe that the individual soul goes through a series of birth, living, and death over and over until the soul achieves *moksha*. The final goal, then, is to escape the finite (*samsara*) and unite with the infinite.

Christianity

While much of Christianity focuses on achieving the ideal human condition in an afterlife (i.e., going to heaven), there is a significant ascetic component of Christianity in which practitioners seek to discipline their lives while on earth to achieve the high-est state of existence before death. Adapting the ancient Greek distinction between mind and body in the individual, Christianity tends to see the highest form of human existence as seeking the eternal (God) while not being distracted by the temporal (the world). That is, these Christians seek to nourish the soul that, they believe, is connected to God, and to keep the material body and its desires in check. This is a constant battle because most of Christianity holds that humans are born in a state of separation from God, caught up in the world of sensual pleasures. It is a battle to overcome this attachment to the world and to seek union with God.

In his *Life of Antony*, Bishop Athanasius (ca. 295–373) extols the virtue of a third-century monk—Antony—who left behind great wealth to wage spiritual battle with the forces of evil in the desert.[3] As Athanasius tells the story, Antony is not attempting to escape the material world as much as he intends to live the highest possible Christian life. He goes to the front lines of battle to fight on behalf of others. After living alone for twenty years, some of his friends finally insisted on seeing him and visited his desert home. What they found was a person in ideal shape both physically and spiritually:

> [W]hen they beheld him, they were amazed to see that his body had maintained its former condition, neither fat from lack of exercise, nor emaciated from fasting and combat with demons, but was just as they had known him prior to his withdrawal. The state of his soul was one of purity, for it was not constricted by grief, nor relaxed by pleasure, nor affected by either laughter or dejection. ... He maintained utter equilibrium, like one guided by reason and steadfast in that which accords with nature. ... And when he spoke and urged them to keep in mind the future goods and the affection in which we are held by God, ... he persuaded many to take up the solitary life. And so, from then on, there were monasteries in the mountains and the desert was made a city by monks, who left their own people and registered themselves for the citizenship in the heavens.[4]

The historicity of the account is not as important as the fact that Athanasius, a well-known and powerful bishop in the early Christian Church, presented Antony as an exemplar of the ideal Christian life.

One of the best-selling Christian books of all time is Thomas À Kempis's *The Imitation of Christ*. In this work, Thomas paints Jesus, the exemplar for all humanity, as an ascetic who lived a life of humility, prayer, and devotion to God. Thomas encourages followers of Christ to focus on the spiritual and shun the material:

> Seldom do we find a person so spiritual that he lives stripped of everything. Who can find someone truly poor in spirit and totally detached from all the things of this world? His price is well beyond that of anything on earth! If a person were to give up all his possessions, that would still be nothing. ... Yet no one is richer, no one more powerful, no one more free than the person who can give his whole life to God and freely serve others with deep humility and love.[5]

It is still the case today that many, if not most, Christians see those who live the ascetic life as the highest form of Christian possible. They believe those who renounce the "world" and take holy orders to live the simple life are those who live closest to the way that Jesus himself lived. In Roman Catholicism, the largest branch of Christianity in the world, priests (including bishops, archbishops, cardinals, and the Pope) are expected to remain unmarried and celibate for life giving up the "worldly" union with a human being for the heavenly union with God.

Islam

Muslims—adherents of Islam—trace their origins back to Abraham, seeing themselves as the descendants of Abraham through his first son, Ishmael. (It is through Abraham's second son, Isaac, that Jews see themselves as the offspring of Abraham.[6]) Muslims accept the prophets of the Hebrew tradition as spokespersons for God and even regard Jesus as God's prophet who was born of a virgin and raised from the dead after his crucifixion. While academicians might see the rise of Islam as beginning with Muhammad in the early part of the seventh century, Muslims regard Muhammad as the *final* prophet who received the definitive word from God in the form of the Qur'an. In fact, Muslims refer to Muhammad as "The Seal of the Prophets," meaning that he is the final prophet and that no other legitimate prophets have come (or will come) after him.

Muslims believe that God's creation is good. Humans stand as the highest of God's creation and so are fundamentally good as well. Muslims believe in the dignity of the human being as the pinnacle of God's creation and thus have two basic obligations toward their Creator: (1) being thankful for the blessing of life received from God, and (2) surrendering (the meaning of the word *islam*) one's will to the will of God. If there is a flaw in humans it is that we forget the source of our being and fail to thank God properly throughout life or that we simply fail to surrender our lives to the will of God.

Muslims practice the Five Pillars in order to remain in good standing with God and to be allowed into Heaven at the Last Judgment. The first pillar is the confession of faith: "There is no God but God, and Muhammad is His prophet." At least once in her lifetime, a faithful Muslim must state this belief in public and with conviction. The second pillar is the canonical prayer that is prayed five times a day while kneeling in submission to God in the direction of Mecca. The third pillar is charity. Muslims believe they should give two-and-a-half percent of their worth to help the poor each year. The fourth pillar is the observance of Ramadan. Ramadan is a month-long commemoration of Muhammad's receiving of the Qur'an from God and also of his migration from Mecca to Medina ten years later. Muslims fast from the first light of day until sunset, not allowing any food or drink to pass their lips during this time. The point of the fast is to teach dependence on God, self-discipline, and compassion for the poor (who often may be hungry). The fifth pillar is the pilgrimage to Mecca. Every Muslim who is financially and physically able is expected to travel to Mecca at least once in his lifetime to heighten his devotion to God. If a person has lived faithfully according to the Five Pillars and has avoided prohibited actions such as gambling, murder, eating pork, consuming alcohol, and stealing, he will be granted admission to Heaven at the Last Judgment. Otherwise, Hell awaits as punishment.

In these cases and in others, the goal of religion is to help humans achieve the ideal human state, however that may be understood by the particular religion. In most cases, it is certainly better than what we are experiencing presently. We want to maximize our potential and advance ourselves beyond where we are. We see ourselves as flawed and desire to achieve a state of perfection. Each religion, then, encourages us to discipline ourselves—gives us a sort of training—to help us achieve our goal.

Perfection in Sport

We can see the same impulse to achieve our maximum potential in sport. As with religion, there is talk in sport about "perfection." This attempt to achieve perfection in sport is parallel to the attempt to achieve the ideal human condition in a religious sense. In both cases, one seeks to reach the highest possible goal. There are many examples from the world of sport that indicate this impulse.

Golf

Golf is a relatively simple game—to understand, that is. Each course has a series of holes, usually eighteen. Players attempt to get a small ball in each of the eighteen holes using sticks called "clubs." Each time the player hits the ball toward the cup, the player incurs a "stroke" on her scorecard. The player who takes the fewest strokes to get the ball in the hole over the course wins. Players tee up at varying distances from the different holes with the average number of strokes needed to get the ball in the hole stated as "par for the hole." Some holes are "par 3" holes, some "par 4s," and some "par 5s." The fewest number of strokes possible on any hole is one, as the player must hit the ball off of a tee some distance away from each hole. If a player hits the ball off of the tee on her first swing of the club and the ball goes into the hole, that is called a "hole-in-one." It is the best possible score on any hole in golf. In that sense, one could say that the person hit a "perfect" golf shot.

For those who have never played the game of golf, the hole-in-one may not seem like such a big deal. After all, have not many of us scored the hole-in-one at miniature golf? A hole-in-one in regulation golf, however, is quite difficult to accomplish. Professional players rarely score a hole-in-one and they play on a regular basis, often daily. For the amateurs who achieve a hole-in-one, the Pro Shop at the course on which the score was achieved will usually offer the opportunity to purchase a plaque on which the ball can be mounted with a picture of the hole to commemorate the perfect shot. The hole-in-one is celebrated as an achievement that cannot be bested.

Baseball

In baseball, there is the so-called perfect game. The perfect game in baseball refers to a game in which the pitcher manages to retire every batter he faces without any batter getting to first base for any reason. In a nine-inning game, this means that the pitcher faces twenty-seven batters and gets twenty-seven consecutive outs. These outs could come by the batter hitting a ball that is fielded for an out or by striking out. However it is done, the pitcher gets every batter out that he faces.

This is quite rare in baseball. As of this writing, Major League Baseball (MLB) teams have played over 200,000 games since the National League began play in 1876. More than 200,000 games means that more than 400,000 pitchers have started MLB baseball games since there are two starting pitchers—one for each team—in each game. Of all those games pitched, only twenty-three were perfect games (that is one perfect game for nearly every 18,000 games pitched). Given the current rules of baseball, there is no way to get more outs-per-batter than to pitch a perfect game and get twenty-seven outs in twenty-seven at bats. The pitcher who throws a perfect game has achieved the highest level of accomplishment possible for a pitcher in that no opposing player achieved any level of success against that pitcher (and team) for the entire game.

On May 18, 2004, the Arizona Diamondbacks were visiting the Atlanta Braves at Turner Field in Atlanta, Georgia (USA). Randy Johnson, starting pitcher for the Diamondbacks, became the oldest player in MLB history to throw a perfect game. He was forty years old. After getting Braves batter Eddie Perez to strike out swinging for the final out of the game, Johnson was mobbed by his teammates as he came off the mound. Most of the fans in the stands—overwhelmingly Braves fans—stood and cheered for Johnson as he threw only the seventeenth perfect game in MLB history at the time. Rather stoic afterward, Johnson said he tried not to get caught up in the fact that he was retiring each batter he faced because doing so causes "you to lose your focus." He went on to say, "On days when I pitch, I'm very focused. It's me and the catcher and I know what I want to do. This was special."[7] Indeed. As it is the pitcher's job to prevent batters from reaching base, preventing every batter from doing so is the highest accomplishment a pitcher can achieve.

Gymnastics

There are plenty of athletic events that are scored by judges who determine how well the competitors perform. In rare cases, an athlete has been judged to have completed her performance perfectly and so has received a perfect score. For example, Romanian gymnast Nadia Comaneci was awarded a perfect score on the uneven bars in the 1976 Summer Olympic Games. (See Fig. 3.1) This was the first time in history that any gymnast had been awarded a perfect score in Olympic competition, and Comaneci made headlines around the world for doing so. She went on to record six more perfect scores, and her name still invokes the phrase "Perfect 10" for those who witnessed the 1976 Games. In competition, gymnasts are scored based on their completion of required elements, or moves, in a routine. A gymnast must complete each required element with the necessary strength, form, and grace for that particular competition. Judges score the gymnast based on how well she does and the judges' scores are put together to form a composite score. If a gymnast fails to complete a required element of the routine, a standard deduction in points is assessed. By scoring Comaneci's uneven bar routine a perfect 10, each judge determined that she had completed all of the elements with perfection, without flaw.[8] They determined that she would not have been able to do the routine any better and so awarded her a perfect score.

What Comaneci did in the 1976 Olympics was groundbreaking and still lingers in the minds of many today, especially those who follow competitive gymnastics. Matt Rendell argues that Comaneci's performance reminded "the world what the Olympics were all about ... [and set] the benchmark against which the very greatest in sport will ultimately be judged."[9]

Fig. 3.1 Nadia Comaneci in uneven bar routine.

American Football

While the examples above are all examples of individual accomplishments in sport, there is also the possibility of achieving perfection as a team. As a final example of perfection in the world of sport, consider the National Football League's (NFL) Miami Dolphins' perfect season of 1972. A *perfect season* can occur in any sport in which a series of competitions is held. This type of perfection sees a team or individual win every competition entered, usually culminating with victory in a championship game. These tend to be less rare than other forms of perfection, but in one sports league—the NFL—there has been only one such perfect season in almost 100 years of the NFL, the aforementioned 1972 Miami Dolphins.

The Dolphins won fourteen regular-season games in 1972 and then two playoff games before meeting the Washington Redskins in Super Bowl VII. The Dolphins dominated most aspects of the game and allowed Washington's only score on a fluke play (to be discussed below). During the regular season that year, Miami led the NFL in both offense and defense, statistically speaking. They won nine of their fourteen regular-season games with backup quarterback, Earl Morrall, leading the team because of an injury to starting quarterback, Bob Griese, an indication of the completeness and strength of the team as a whole. Although other NFL teams have come close to matching the 1972 Dolphins, such as the 1985 Bears and the 2007 Patriots, no other team has ever had a perfect season in the NFL. The Dolphins did it by winning each game on their regular-season schedule and then each game in the playoffs—reaching the highest level of possibility for NFL teams.

Don Shula, the head coach of the team, had taken the Baltimore Colts to the Super Bowl as head coach in 1969 and lost to the New York Jets. The year prior to the Dolphins' perfect season, he led Miami to the Super Bowl only to lose in embarrassing fashion to the Dallas Cowboys 24–3. After beating the Redskins, Shula said, "There is no empty feeling this year. This is the ultimate."[10] By "ultimate," Shula of course means "the highest." Nick Buoniconti, who played linebacker for the 1972 Dolphins, was interviewed about their season in 1998. He referred to the scoreboard of the Los Angeles Coliseum (where the Super Bowl was played) and noted that at the end of the game the scoreboard operators put "Best Ever" on the board. Buoniconti said, "That's something no one can ever take away from you."[11] Winning every game of the season including the championship game is as good as it is possible to get in any team sport.

Based on these examples, it seems clear that the achievement of perfection is part of the world of sport. In each example, there is a clear indication that the best that can be achieved has been achieved. The least number of strokes a golfer can use to hit the ball into the hole is one. She cannot hit it in the hole in any fewer strokes. The minimum number of batters a pitcher can face in a nine-inning game is twenty-seven. It is impossible to retire fewer than twenty-seven batters and pitch a complete game. The gymnast can only do each element without mistakes. The Miami Dolphins could only win all seventeen games they played that season ending with a perfect 17–0 record. These are four examples of perfection, the best that could be done in the sport. These performances and accomplishments can only be matched but never surpassed, thus ensuring the competitors' places in eternity as having achieved perfection.

It is telling that these achievements of perfection are still discussed by those who follow these particular sports. Every time a pitcher pitches a perfect game in MLB, commentators note how many perfect games have been thrown and even refer to past perfect games in comparison. Every time an NFL team wins its first ten games or so of the season, talk of the 1972 Dolphins rises in comparison. It is a well-known fact that each year surviving members of the 1972 Dolphins enjoy champagne when the last undefeated team has been defeated that year. These accomplishments of perfection live on in the minds of the players, the fans, and in halls of fame. In each of these sports (and in others) the ideal has been achieved and is rightly remembered and commemorated.

In both religion and sport, most of the time and energy of the participants is spent trying to accomplish the best that one can achieve. We measure ourselves against the elusive standards of perfection and also against other participants. In sport we have head-to-head competitions to determine which individual or team is the best. We can even compete against our best performance on an individual level as in running, rowing, or swimming. In religion we seek to imitate those who are closer to perfection than are we through reading and studying their writings or following the way they conduct their lives. In the case of both sport and religion we strive toward perfection in a temporal, finite setting marking achievements along the way, always working to be better. The goal of perfection remains with us as we seek to improve our imperfect condition. When we achieve perfection, we in a sense touch the infinite. We become immortal. Whether commemorated in a hole-in-one plaque or in sports record books, our achievement transcends our earthly existence. Through the achievement, in fact, we escape time and become eternal—if not in fact, at least in our experience.

Perfection Only an Ideal?

We may ask, though, whether these examples from the world of sport really constitute perfection. Was the hole-in-one shot the result of the perfect swing, or did the golfer have help from an unanticipated gust of wind or a favorable bounce off of a moving tree limb? Did Nadia Comaneci really perform the perfect uneven bar routine at the 1976 Olympic Games, or might the judges have missed something? Because judges are subjective individuals, does their participation in the event necessarily flaw the performance or at least its interpretation? What about the human element in the pitching of a perfect game? Do not umpires miss ball and strike calls (some, it seems on a regular basis), and could not a plate umpire miss a call in *favor* of the pitcher?

Consider the MLB game between the Detroit Tigers and the Cleveland Indians on June 2, 2010. After retiring the first twenty-six batters in a row with only one remaining to complete his perfect game, Tigers pitcher Armando Galarraga covered first base on a ground ball hit between first and second base in what is a fairly routine play in the major leagues. First baseman Miguel Cabrera fielded the ball and tossed it to Galarraga who stepped on the bag for what appeared to be the final out of what would have been the twenty-first perfect game in MLB history. First base umpire, Jim Joyce, called the batter—Jason Donald—safe, thus ending Galarraga's bid for a perfect game. Television replays clearly showed that Donald should have been called out, and a distraught Joyce admitted his mistake after seeing the replay in the umpires' locker room immediately after the game ended.[12] Months later, Joyce reflected: "I can't even explain the feeling, because there are no words. … It's almost worse than my dad's death. That's how bad I felt."[13] Galarraga should have been recognized as having pitched a perfect game but was denied because of human error. If it is possible to make a mistake denying a pitcher a perfect game, it seems possible to err the other way as well. Maybe there have been perfect games that have been the result of similar human error in which an umpire called someone out who was actually safe at first base.

Nadia Comaneci denies that she was perfect in those 1976 Olympics, even when she was awarded a perfect score by the judges. Speaking of the balance beam routine for which she was awarded a perfect 10, she says, "It was not perfect, I had done it better in training. ... I think I was better than everybody, and they had just given the girl before a 9.95, so what could they do? At the time, I was so naïve, I thought maybe the judges just wanted me to feel better."[14] In the eyes of the judges that day, her routine was perfect, but was it really flawless?

Even a perfect season can be filled with flaws. While we may proclaim the Miami Dolphins' undefeated NFL season of 1972 as "the perfect season," mistakes were made along the way. For a classic example of a Dolphins mistake, we turn to the NFL Championship Game (the Super Bowl) itself. Leading 14–0 in the fourth quarter, Miami lined up for a forty-two-yard field goal attempt which, had it been success-ful, would have made the score 17–0. Garo Yepremian's forty-two-yard field goal attempt was blocked by Washington's Bill Brundige, and the ball bounced right back to Yepremian. He then tried to complete a "pass" of sorts to an unknown receiver. Looking more like a failed attempt to set a volleyball, the football tumbled up into the air out of Yepremian's hands and was caught by Washington's Mike Bass. Bass quickly ran the ball back for a touchdown.[15] There can be no doubt in anyone's mind who watched that play that it was a mistake, a flaw, in Miami's season. This is only one example of a mistake in the team's season. We have not even considered the numerous penalties, fumbles, dropped passes, and missed blocks that occurred along the way.

Conclusion

So, we may ask, is there really such a thing as perfection in sport? There is no doubt that many talk as if perfection is something seen occasionally in the world of sport. There are markers that we claim cannot be surpassed including the hole-in-one, the perfect balance beam score, the perfect game in baseball, or the perfect season. These and other markers give us something to shoot for as athletes and fans.

Is there such a thing as perfection of the human condition? Again, this is some-thing that is debatable as many who believe in such a possibility believe it will only be achieved after death and release from this temporal realm. Religions give us something to shoot for, though, goals that keep us working on ourselves to improve ourselves in order to experience existence as best we can. Augustine said that all of life is a recovery from the disease of the original sin; it is a continual and gradual strengthening of the spirit that will find perfection when the faithful are united with God after death. So rather than argue that religion and sport are two different things that are very similar, it seems more the case that they are expressions of the same impulse in the human being to escape temporality and finitude and participate in the perfect, the eternal. For some, the eternal is God; for others it may be the perfect dive, golf shot, or pitched game. In both cases, religion and sport provide human beings with powerful models of excellence and even perfection toward which we can strive.

In the following chapter, we will consider what some psychologists, philosophers, and theologians understand as the psychological basis for the religious impulse in humans. Similarly to what we have seen in this chapter where we have looked at the need for humans to maximize their existence through achievement of the highest possible human condition, in the following chapter we will see how humans desire to become joined with the infinite, gaining a sense of union with the eternal.

Discussion Questions

1. How do you understand the concept of "perfection"? Do you think you have seen it in some form?

2. Is there such a thing as perfection in the world of sport given the human element involved in judging or refereeing sporting events?

3. How does culture affect conceptualizations of the ideal human condition?

4. Which understanding of perfection is more helpful—perfection as completeness or perfection as being without flaw? Is either concept a realistic possibility for humans?

Glossary

asceticism—based on the Greek *askesis*, which means "discipline," the practice of disciplining the body with the mind, usually depriving the body of its physical desires including sex, eating, and sleeping.

actual human condition—the state of imperfect existence in which humans currently find themselves as they work toward perfect human existence.

atman—Hindu concept of the true, eternal self or soul trapped in materiality and bogged down by desires.

Enlightenment—Buddhist concept in which the human awakens to the true nature of reality and is liberated from the suffering caused by desires.

ideal human condition—the state of perfect human existence to which humans strive; defined differently by different people and different religions.

moksha—Hindu concept that describes release from *samsara* and union with Brahman (God).

original sin—a concept developed by the early Christian church that held that Adam and Eve's disobedience of God in the Garden of Eden—eating the forbidden fruit—introduced sin into the human race; given its most prominent exposition by Augustine, Bishop of Hippo (354–430), who said the disease is cured through baptism of the infant leaving the soul in a weakened state that can improve through a life focused on God.

perfection—complete and/or without flaw.

samsara—Hindu and Buddhist concept of the human condition as one in which humans are trapped in materiality and forced to repeat the cycle of reincarnation until they escape.

yoga—in Hinduism, a path to escape from temporality and union with Brahman; there are four possible yogas depending on a person's personality type.

A Psychology of Sport and Religion: Escaping Finitude

The field of psychology deals with how individuals act in and experience the world and how they understand those actions and experiences. Psychologists are concerned with how individuals perceive their place in the world and their interactions with those around them. There are some psychologists who are primarily concerned with the biology of how the brain works such that it is able to form an image of the self as a self that is separate from other selves. Others are more concerned about how the individual's environment and personal experiences work to shape the individual's perception of her world, her self, and the relationship between the two. Some psychologists focus on the developmental process an individual goes through over the course of an entire lifetime, usually dividing a person's life into "stages" in which the individual sees the world in a particular way and behaves similarly to other individuals who are also in that stage of life. Other psychologists focus on abnormal psychology with the intent on understanding how the minds of individuals who are not like most people interpret their surroundings and act on that interpretation, sometimes to the detriment of the community as a whole. In the end, though, psychology is focused on the individual mind and behavior.

In this chapter, we review a number of psychological perspectives (some from psychologists and some from theologians) to understand how religion arises from human psychology and how it serves the human psyche. We then argue that sport—from the ancient Greek and Roman worlds to the present day—functions in a very similar way and that this similar functioning adds to the case that sport can be seen as religious phenomenon.

Psychology and the Origin of the Religious Impulse

Psychology as a distinct discipline arose at the end of the nineteenth century—a time when many academic disciplines were being focused on the study of religion in an attempt to understand the human side of religion. Psychologists also applied the newly developing methodologies of their field to religion as a whole in an attempt to see the human influence in the birth, development, and practice of religion. Some psychologists have even attempted to explain religion as a purely human creation stemming from individual needs and perceptions of the world.

Sigmund Freud (1856–1939) is known as the "Father of Psychoanalysis." Freud believes that the unconscious holds the key to explaining our propensity for religion.

According to Freud, there is probably no better window through which to view the unconscious than the dream. He says, "Dreams are psychical acts of as much significance as any others; their motive force is in every instance a wish seeking fulfillment."[1] Dreams can be divided on this basis into two groups: first, there are the dreams that openly appear as wish-fulfillment; second, there are the dreams in which the wish-fulfillment is disguised and unrecognizable. In the latter case, dream censorship is at work.[2] That is, our subconscious mind hides the fact that what we are dreaming is a wish we have, thus releasing us from bearing responsibility for the dream (and the wish). This would explain why some dreams do not appear as wish-fulfillment dreams, but Freud holds that, upon closer inspection, all dreams will reveal themselves as some form of wish-fulfillment.

Freud goes on to show how religion originates within the individual. He states:

Dreams, which fulfill their wishes along the short path of regression, have merely preserved for us in that respect a sample of the psychical apparatus's primary method of working, a method which was abandoned as being inefficient. What once dominated waking life, while the mind was still young and incompetent, seems now to have been banished into the night—just as the primitive weapons, the bows and arrows, that had been abandoned by adult men, turn up once more in the nursery. *Dreaming is a piece of infantile mental life that has been superseded*.[3]

In other words, the carefree joyful life of the child has been suppressed as the adult grows older, and this life is accessible only through the regressive apparatus of the dream. The wishes of the child are present in the subconscious of the adult, made known through the interpretation of the dream.

One of those wishes is to be protected and cared for by the father, and this is where Freud finds the origin of some fundamental religious ideas. Though buried in the subconscious, the childlike desire for security is present in the adult and is manifested in the creation of religion:

The derivation of religious needs from the infant's helplessness and the longing for the father aroused by it seems to me incontrovertible, especially since the feeling is not simply prolonged from childhood days, but is permanently sustained by fear of the power of Fate. I cannot think of any need in childhood as strong as the need for a father's protection.[4]

This insecurity, Freud believes, remains with us throughout our lives and is manifested in the creation of religion as an attempt to find security in God.

Freud suggests that there may even be something in our pre-childhood subconscious memory that may hold the clues to further understanding of the propensity for religious impulse in the human being. Speaking of the religious impulse originating in the child's need for security in the father, he says, "There may be something else behind this, but for the present it is wrapped in obscurity."[5] Michael Balint believes he can locate the origin of religion as occurring earlier than childhood, before the child recognizes the need for security in the parent.

In his book, *The Basic Fault*, Balint suggests that there is a subconscious region of the psyche that goes back beyond the Oedipus complex. (For Freud, the Oedipus conflict arises in the male child who becomes jealous of the relationship his father has with his mother and wants to eliminate the father from the triangular relationship.) For Balint, this region of the psyche is an area consisting of a two-person relationship as opposed to the Oedipus complex that consists of a three-person triangular relationship.[6] There are four chief characteristics of this level. First, all of the events that happen in it belong to an exclusively two-person relationship; there is no third person present. Second, this two-person relationship is of a particular nature, entirely different from the well-known human relationships of the Oedipal level. Third, the nature of the dynamic force operating at this level is not that of a conflict. Finally, adult language is often useless or misleading in describing events at this level because words do not always have an agreed-upon conventional meaning.[7]

An important aspect of this two-person relationship is that of primary love, and Balint says that this may be the earliest level of cognition.[8] The ultimate aim of this primary love is the ideal state of well-being.[9] This primary love is a rejection of primary narcissism, both Freud's primary narcissism in children and subsequent theories of primary narcissism of the fetus. Clinical evidence has not supported the existence of primary narcissism.[10] As an alternative, Balint offers his theory of primary love, a theory of primary relationship to the environment.[11] Balint says that in this state, the fetus and the environment exist in a harmonious blend.[12] The two are practically indistinguishable. There are no sharp boundaries between the fetus and the environment within the mother. The fetus is totally dependent on this environment. Prior to birth, the two exist in a state of complete "mix-up." In fact, Balint says, "they interpenetrate each other."[13] There is no narcissism here because there are no boundaries between the fetus and the environment. That is, there is no conscious awareness of the self to focus on as opposed to that which is not the self.

At birth, the baby experiences great trauma, coming close to death. It is at this point that the baby and the environment begin to separate. Objects with clearly defined boundaries are present and relationships with those objects are necessarily formed. Narcissism may arise at this point, but it is secondary narcissism at most, according to Balint.[14] It is at this point that what he calls "the basic fault" may be formed as the infant is removed from the boundless connection between her and her mother to separation from everything. The fault, then, is a subconscious awareness of separation and boundaries.

Balint is careful not to set a date or age at which this basic fault occurs, which leaves such a determination to speculation (but within an early framework). The basic fault occurs before the Oedipal conflict, which is a triangular relationship. This triangular relationship can occur in the young child of possibly three or four years of age. That leaves only a couple of postnatal years in which this basic fault occurs, certainly during infancy. Religion, then, arises as we seek to reestablish this boundless connection and repair the basic fault of separation we experience.

In a similar vein, and basing his work on Freud, Heinz Kohut believes that religion is the result of a narcissistic desire for self-preservation. It is one thing to accept that objects are finite, and temporary, but it is even more difficult for humans to accept the fact that we are impermanent and finite.[15] It is certainly possible to come to this acceptance. There are those, he says, who are able to overcome the feeling of hopelessness at the realization of one's finitude, and they do it by seeing themselves as part of the whole of existence, of eternity: "I have little doubt that those who are able to achieve this ultimate attitude toward life do so on the strength of a new, expanded, transformed narcissism: a cosmic narcissism which has transformed the bounds of the individual."[16] The individual sees herself as part of the entire cosmos which will remain after the individual no longer exists as an individual. The individual will have a continuous existence as part of the continuing cosmos.

Similarly to Michael Balint's argument in *The Basic Fault*, Kohut argues that the "original psychological universe" is the mother as the fetus grows into conscious-ness. The developing mind identifies with the mother, and it is this identity to which we seek to unite in a timelessness that transcends our finite existence.[17] There is a desire of the self to unite with the eternal and so maintain a continuity of the self that will overcome one's finitude.

Freud, Balint, and Kohut propose very similar origins of the religious impulse in humans. Freud suggests that religion (in part) arises from the child's need for security in the father. Though childhood may be in the distant past for adults, Freud argues that adults maintain their childhood needs buried in the memories of the brain that often surface in dreams. Throughout our lives, Freud believes, we have a longing for security through a parental figure. Balint suggests that humans experience a trau-matic break from a boundless unification we experience with the mother while in the womb and so seek to regain that boundlessness through union with the eternal. He believes that this break—the "basic fault"—occurs sometime after birth but before the child is aware of the triangular Oedipal complex. The break certainly lies behind conscious memories. Kohut also suggests that a recognition of our finitude causes us to seek to join ourselves with the eternal in order to overcome the awareness of our impermanence and eventual end. In all of these psychologists, then, there is the suggestion that religion serves to help humans overcome the recognition of our finitude by providing an eternal with which we can unite by following the teachings of the religion. Doing so gives us the security that we need in the face of impending nonexistence.

Philosophy, Theology, the Finite, and the Infinite

Philosophers and theologians also have addressed the psychological perception of finitude in their work. Friedrich Schleiermacher (1768–1834) is well known for his contention that particular forms of religion are outward expressions of the feeling of absolute dependence. In *The Christian Faith* he writes that to be self-conscious is to feel absolutely dependent and, at the same time, in a relationship with that on which we are dependent—God:

> As regards the identification of absolute dependence with "relation to God" in our proposition: this is to be understood in the sense that the *Whence* of our receptive and active existence, as implied in this self-consciousness, is to be designated by the word "God," and that this is for us the really original significa-cation of that word. ... Now this is just what is principally meant by the formula which says that to feel oneself absolutely dependent and to be conscious of being in relation with God are one and the same thing; and the reason is that absolute dependence is the fundamental relation which must include all others in itself. This last expression includes God-consciousness in the self-consciousness in such a way that, quite in accordance with the above analysis, the two cannot be separated from each other.[18]

Schleiermacher believes that this feeling of absolute dependence necessarily invokes in humans a sense of the infinite God on whom we are dependent. Particular individuals then express this sense of contingency in religious form in a given place in a given culture at a given time, thus making all particular forms of religion context-specific.[19] For example, in the Jewish tradition both creation stories found in the first two chapters of Genesis indicate that God purposely created humans and without God's action humans would not exist. They did not will themselves into creation but were dependent on God for their existence. Particular religious practices and beliefs are an outgrowth of this universal feeling of absolute dependence. We recognize our limitedness and seek to unite with the eternal.

Ludwig Feuerbach (1804–1872) claims that what we think of as "God" is actually a projection of the absolutized goodness of human nature. For Feuerbach, writing a little later than Schleiermacher in the early 1840s, humans have a sense of their limitedness in the face of apparent unlimited goodness:

> It is true that the human being, as an individual, can and must ... feel and recog-nise himself to be limited; but he can become conscious of his limits, his finiteness, only because the perfection, the infinitude of his species, is perceived by him, whether as an object of feeling, of conscience, or of the thinking consciousness.[20]

The concept of finitude necessarily invokes the concept of infinity, but we see this infinity as separate from ourselves. Feuerbach says that we subconsciously remove the good from human nature and project that goodness onto an infinite God. All of the good qualities of humans are removed in order to create an object outside ourselves leaving us as weak, finite beings in need of salvation:

> Religion is the disuniting of man from himself; he sets God before him as the antithesis of himself. God is not what man is—man is not what God is. God is the infinite, man the finite being; God is perfect, man imperfect; God eternal, man temporal; God almighty, man weak. God holy, man sinful. God and man are extremes: God is the absolutely positive, the sum of all realities; man the abso-lutely negative, comprehending all negations.[21]

So humans are left with a gap between them and God with a need to get back what God now has (infinitude) by uniting with that God, taking that God back into the human:

> To enrich God, man must become poor; that God may be all, man must be nothing. But he desires to be nothing in himself, because what he takes from himself is not lost to him, since it is preserved in God. Man has his being in God; why then should he have it in himself? Where is the necessity of positing the same thing twice, or having it twice? What man withdraws from himself, what he renounces in himself, he only enjoys in an incomparably higher and fuller measure in God.[22]

Once again, the finite limitation of humans is overcome by uniting with the infinity of God.

Paul Tillich (1886–1965) and Reinhold Niebuhr (1892–1971), two Christian philosopher-theologians writing in the twentieth century, also write about the human condition as characterized by the finite/infinite problem. Tillich suggests that the threat of non-being shadows our existence, causing anxiety. Anxiety, Tillich says in *The Courage to Be*, "is the existential awareness of nonbeing."[23] He says that anxiety "is finitude, experienced as one's own finitude. This is the natural state of man as man, and in some way of all living beings. It is the anxiety of nonbeing, the awareness of one's finitude as finitude."[24] Tillich draws on the Latin root of the word "exist," which is *existere*, meaning "to stand out of." To *exist* means to stand out of nonexistence. That we exist means at the same time that we do not *not* exist. Existence and nonexistence together constitute an inseparable pair in Tillich's thinking, and the presence of the possibility of nonexistence, or non-being, is with us always as a shadow causing anxiety and fear. While Tillich's juxtaposition of being with non-being is not quite the same as the juxtaposition of finitude with infinity, he is aware that our sense of being finite allows the threat of non-being to shadow us. In order to overcome the threat of non-being, we must find courage to overcome it and so live without fear. We find the courage to be in the God above the God of theism[25] where "the anxiety of doubt and meaninglessness [is] taken into the courage to be."[26] Again, by joining with the eternal, the threat of finitude and non-being is overcome.

In his *Moral Man and Immoral Society*, Reinhold Niebuhr points to this contrast between our finitude and the infinite quite directly:

> Self-consciousness means the recognition of finiteness within infinity. The mind recognizes the *ego* as an insignificant point amidst the immensities of the world. In all vital self-consciousness there is a note of protest against this finiteness. It may express itself in religion by the desire to be absorbed in infinitude. On the secular level it expresses itself in man's effort to universalize himself and give his life a significance beyond himself.[27]

Humans have an awareness of themselves as limited to a particular place and time, as having a finite existence that has a beginning with an impending end at some point in the future. According to Niebuhr, this sense of limitedness leads us to want to escape our finitude, to rise above it to the level of the universal or eternal. As we have seen, some argue that the desire to escape our finitude is what gives rise to religion as we seek to unite with the eternal, the infinite—God. We also see examples of the desire to escape finitude in the world of sport, where athletes and fans seek to rise above their finitude, their limitations, and attain eternal recognition.

Sport as a Source of Eternal Recognition

When sports fans "participate" in sport, they do so primarily from a mental perspective. While it is true that some fans will, occasionally, jump onto the field of play as if they were participants in the game, those fans are usually apprehended rather quickly by security forces and arrested. Most fans will simply watch and/or listen to the game and interpret the events in various ways. That is, fans watch the game, hear the sounds, and make sense of the events as they understand the game. Fans who know the game well will perceive it in slightly different ways than will the casual fan who is not familiar with the intricacies of the game related to rules, strategy, and personnel. Fans may cheer for their favorite players or teams, but that is usually the extent of their physical involvement in the game. The bulk of their participation is mental.

The word "fan" is an abbreviation of the word "fanatic," a word usually associated with someone who is highly devoted to something, often religion. A sports fan attaches himself to a player or team and then cheers for that team to win. The fan who actually attends the live competition often dresses in team colors and sometimes in authentic team regalia in an attempt to unite with the team. It seems fairly obvious that the fan sees himself as a part of the team so that when the fan's team wins the fan experiences joy, even euphoria, at the triumph, and disappointment, even anger and despair, at a loss. There is clearly a psychological unification with the team in the fan's mind so that the fan rejoices in victory and agonizes in defeat.

As part of psychologically uniting with and physically cheering for the team, fans choose popular athletes to represent the best of the team. Team jerseys bearing the numbers and sometimes the names of the individual heroes are bought by fans who want to be united with a particular athlete and team. It is usually the case that fans want to unite with the most well known stars on the team as they receive most of the national or even international acclaim for their success. Fans tend to want to unite with players who spend a lot of time in the spotlight as they are seen as the best of the best, the top players of the team. These athletes serve as heroes for the fans who cheer not only for team success, but for the individual player's success as well. If the team wins a national or world championship, that team is considered to be the best at the game for that particular season and will forever (eternally) be known as the champions of that season. By uniting with a particular player on a championship team that is "universally" known, the fan escapes her finitude thus becoming eternal herself and/or achieving unification with the eternal.

Mythic Heroes

The athletic champion and our desire to unite with that champion thus escaping our finitude did not appear with the advent of modern-day athletic competitions. We read in Homer and Virgil accounts of champions engaged in competition held at various occasions. In these accounts of the games, the "heroes" engage in competition and are cheered on by those not participating in the games. It is sometimes clear that those cheering choose a champion to support.

In Homer's *Iliad*, the Achaians engage in funeral games after the funeral ceremony of Patroklos. The first competition is a chariot race with several competitors. Antilochos, one of the competitors, is described as having been taught horsemanship by Zeus and Poseidon.[28] While the Greeks may have used these kinds of expressions commonly, that is, that one or more of the gods instructed someone or gave someone special powers without implying that people actually saw Zeus and Poseidon instructing Antilochos, they were probably using the expressions in the same way that people today will say that a certain person has been blessed by God with certain talents. As an ancient Greek might have said that Zeus was with him in victory that day, so a winning coach or player might say, "God smiled on us today." At any rate, it is clear that Antilochos is special as he learned his talent not from humans, but from the gods.

Antilochos is not the only gifted driver, though. Each of the five men who are in the race is special. They are called "strong Diomedes,"[29] "strong Eumelos,"[30] "fair-haired Menelaos the sky-descended"[31] and "spear-famed,"[32] and Meriones, "strong henchman of Idomeneus."[33] Antilochos is himself referred to as "the glorious son of Nestor,"[34] and even the judge of the event is "Phoinix the godlike."[35]

The race is run, of course, with the gods having something to do with the outcome. There is even some "trash talking" among the fans in the stands who argue about who is actually in the lead as the race progresses.[36] Diomedes, who was considered the best of them all at the beginning, wins the race. After the prizes are awarded, though, Achilleus awards a special prize to Nestor, perhaps because Nestor's son, Antilochos, showed humility when challenged by Menelaos for cheating. At any rate, Nestor recounts his many victories to Achilleus, saying that he now no longer has the strength to compete with the younger men. He finishes his recollection by saying: "This was I, once. Now it is for the young men to encounter in such actions, and for me to give way to the persuasion of gloomy old age. But once I shone among the young heroes."[37] So not only in the descriptions of the racers by Homer, but on the lips of one of his characters we see the competitors as heroes, men above the ordinary.

There are other competitions in the *Iliad* in which we see a select group of the men portrayed in larger-than-life imagery. In the boxing match, Achilleus calls for two men to box, the "two best" among all the men.[38] Epeios, "a man huge and powerful, well skilled in boxing," stepped up and challenged all others for the prize.[39] The only one to accept the challenge was Euryalos, "a godlike man."[40] In the wrestling match, Aias and Odysseus, two giants of men, wrestle to a draw.[41] In the fourth contest, a footrace, Aias, Odysseus, and Antilochos are the racers.[42] In spite of the goddess

Athene's intervention for Odysseus, causing Aias to slip on ox dung, Aias finishes first and claims the prize—an ox.[43] In the next competition—close combat—we again see two previous competitors, Aias and Diomedes.[44] In the sixth competition—throwing a weight—Polypoites, Leonteus, Aias, and Epeios contend.[45] Only Polypoites and Leonteus are new. In the archery contest, Teukros competes with Meriones.[46] Only Teukros is new. In the final contest—spear-throwing—Agamemnon challenges Meriones.[47] Agamemnon is new to the competition, but he is obviously one of the main characters of the poem.

Clearly, the champions of the group are competing in the matches, and many of these competitors compete in more than one competition. In these funeral games noted in Book 23, there are twenty-two slots for competitors, but these are filled by only thirteen different men. Certainly there were many men at the site, yet only the few best are competing for the prizes. These are the champions, the heroes, of the group.

In the *Odyssey*, games are played by the Phaiakians, a group of people Odysseus finds himself with on his journey home. In similar fashion as we saw in the *Iliad*, the competitors of the Phaiakian games are mentioned as the best of the group in physical prowess.[48] The Phaiakians have their games and then one of them, Euryalos, challenges Odysseus telling him that he looks soft, that he does not resemble an athlete.[49] Of course, Odysseus has to prove otherwise and takes a larger discus than that thrown by the Phaiakian competitors and throws it farther than the Phaiakians did in their competition.[50] In this manner, Odysseus shows that he is far superior to normal humans.

In Virgil's *Aeneid*—written for a Roman audience toward the end of the first century BCE—Aeneas holds games to mark the one-year anniversary of his father's death. There is a boat race, a footrace, boxing, and archery. The boat race is the first of the competitions and is unusual in that it is a team competition.[51] Most of the events are individual competitions, but here we have teams of rowers. As it turns out, the boats are captained by individuals who are said to be the winners or losers, maintaining the idea that it is an individual competition in much the same way the chariot racing of the *Iliad* largely disregards the horses that are doing the real work. Toward the end of the race, two are vying for the lead, Cloanthus and Mnestheus. While Cloanthus takes the lead, the entire crowd cheers for Mnestheus.[52] While we are not given any indication as to why the crowd cheers for Mnestheus, we still see the crowd aligning itself with one of the competitors and cheering him (or them) on, much as we see crowds cheering today.

In the footrace, competitors are also described in glowing language. Euryalus was "exceptional for beauty and bloom of youth"[53] while Diorës was of the royal line of Priam.[54] Virgil displays the greatness of the competitors most clearly in the boxing match in the *Aeneid*. After Aeneas describes the prizes he asks if anyone will step up to engage in boxing. We read the description of Darës next:

Without an instant's pause, in his huge power,
Darës got up among the murmurous crowd—

The one man who had held his ground with Paris,
The man, too, who knocked out the champion, Butës,
Beside the burial mound where Hector lies:
Butës, a giant boxer, bragged of coming
From the Bebrycian tribe of Amycus,
But Darës stretched him half dead on the sand.
So powerful, the man reared up his head
For combat, showed his shoulders' breadth, his reach
With left and right, threw punches at the air.
Who would fight him? Among all those men
Not one dared put the leather on his hands.[55]

Entellus is urged to fight by Acestës who is sitting beside him, reminding him of his glory of days gone by. Entellus decides he will fight and throws in a pair of gauntlets (leather gloves extending to the elbow) worn by Eryx who fought with Hercules against Alcidës on that very shore.[56] Entellus gets up to fight:

He threw the double mantel from his shoulders,
Bared his great arms and legs, all thew[57] and bone,
And took his stand, gigantic, in the arena.[58]

As the two fight the crowd watches. Entellus is huge but Darës is swift, able to evade some of Entellus's blows. At one point, Entellus looks to hit Darës with all of his might, but when Darës moves out of the way Entellus's momentum carries him on to the ground. Entellus is embarrassed and returns to the fight with a wild fury. He rushes Darës and throws him over the ring pounding him with blow after blow. Aeneas mercifully stops the fight and says to Darës, "Don't you feel/A force now more than mortal is against you ...?"[59] Virgil describes Entellus as "the old hero" as he battered the young Darës.[60]

After the battle, Entellus took his prize—an ox—and with one mighty blow to its forehead "smashed the skull/And fragmented the brains."[61] This was no ordinary feat by an ordinary man. No one really thought that Entellus was immortal, but he was a hero who was bigger and stronger than most, even as he showed signs of age.

What are we to make of these stories of the ancients? We should first remember that Homer wrote his story for Greeks while Virgil wrote his story for Romans. Obviously, Homer will focus on the history of their Greek ancestors and Virgil on that of the Roman ancestors. Reading or hearing these stories, then, provides a way for the common Greek or Roman person to connect to her or his past. We also should note that those reading or hearing these stories would have considered not only the main characters as heroes, but also the entire group of Achaeans or Trojans. Walter Burkert makes this point with regard to the Greeks, and it is not unreasonable to suggest that the Romans would have seen Virgil's Trojans *en masse* as well.[62] Someone raised in these cultures might think upon hearing these stories, "The ancestors of yore were amazing in what they could do, and I am connected to them because I am descended from them." Writing of the Greek heroes, Michael Grant says, "The Greeks of the eighth century BCE, and forever afterwards, saw something splendid and superhuman about what they supposed to be their lost past."[63] Grant goes on to say, "Yet, although [the hero] is no god, there is something about him which brings him not too far from heaven. ... Their mighty achievements inspired poets to suggest that human nature, far though it is from divinity, can yet come within reach of it."[64] Grant is suggesting that the heroes provided a connection between humanity and divinity. They are something of a bridge between the two.

This connection was provided by Homer and Virgil and others like them, but it reflected a desire common to many of their day and beyond. That is, if these ideas of Homer and Virgil were limited to these two writers, we probably would not have these works with us today. That they were accepted and preserved is an indication that they resonated at least with some of the people who heard the stories. Indeed, nationalism and/or ethnocentrism was as alive then as it is today, even if not universal.

Could Entellus have smashed the forehead of an ox with one blow? This is doubtful, but there is little doubt that hearing such a story would have made many Romans swell with pride to think that one of their ancestors was so strong. In this way, those hearing the story unite themselves to the image of Entellus by virtue of their (supposedly) having descended from him and thereby lift themselves above those who are not descended from such a mighty warrior.

Implied in this identification with the hero are two key points, two requirements, we might say, for a hero to be a hero. First, for identification with the hero to take place, the person must be able to identify with the hero. While this appears obvious, it cannot be overlooked. The point is that the hero has to be human enough for the human to be able to relate to him or her. The hero must also be more than human, though. That is, an ordinary human cannot be a hero, or that would mean that most of us are heroes, thereby negating the category completely. If the individual is to get close to divinity, the hero must be able to take her there and, so, must have a capability or divine quality that most humans do not have. If most humans had this capability, we would not need anyone but ourselves to raise ourselves to the level of the divine, again, negating the need for heroes.

In the stories of the games we have seen above as well as in accounts of Sargon, Moses, Karna, Oedipus, Cyrus the Great, Romulus and Remus, Theseus, Perseus, Zeus, Apollo, Jason, Dionysus, Joseph (of Genesis), Watu Gunung, and King Arthur (just to name a few), the heroes are able to afford the common people a measure of salvation by being both like them and unlike them. Indeed, Irenaeus said of the Christ that "what he has not assumed he cannot save," and later, Athanasius argued that for the savior to effect salvation he must be God. In the case of the Christian savior, then, he is both human and more than human.

Note, though, that the Greek and Roman heroes were not gods.[65] The gods certainly played a role in the affairs of the characters, but they were often seen as capricious and unapproachable by most. The gods of the Greeks and Romans were feared and honored so as to keep them away and happy; they were certainly not role models by most measures. Plato even calls for the banning of stories of the gods in his *Republic* because of their often shameful actions. The heroes, on the other hand—Odysseus, Hector, Priam, Achilles, Aeneas, and others—were seen primarily as human, though some had a divine parent to go with a human parent. Their connection to the divine, whether biological or simply through divine favoritism, meant that they could relate to humans as a human but also had the ability to raise up those around them because of their connection with the divine. While not immortal themselves, they could use their connection to the immortals to save or raise those around them. Grant puts it this way:

> The heroic outlook shook off primitive superstitions and taboos by showing that man can do amazing things by his own effort and by his own nature, indeed that he can almost rise *above* his own nature into strengths scarcely known or understood. As early as the Homeric poems themselves the great stories are held up as educational examples. … When we read the *Iliad*, we feel larger than life, freed from the compulsion of present realities. The epic heroes carry us with them in their struggles and their sufferings; they are not as we are, yet we follow after them. And so when they suffer or exult, so do we.[66]

While Grant dismisses the outright equality of the hero with the common person, he implies it when he indicates our ability to follow the heroes and to feel what they feel.[67]

Grant says that when "we read the *Iliad*, we feel larger than life." Though he suggests that this feeling frees us "from the compulsion of present realities," we suggest that reading the *Iliad*, or cheering for a particular athlete or team, lifts us out of the isolation we feel as individuals and unites us with that which is greater than we are. We feel a union with the hero who connects us with the divine, the eternal. We overcome our finitude through the mediating power of the athlete or athletes with whom we identify—individuals who, through their athletic excellence, are infinite.

The Hero and Contemporary Sports

This ability to follow the heroes and feel what they feel is as contemporary as today's box scores. Indeed, many feel a strong pull to align themselves with certain heroes and thus be raised to glory with them. This pull to align oneself with the hero or heroes takes at least two, closely related forms: alignment with a group of heroes normally referred to as a "team" and alignment with individual heroes. In the case of the former, many people become fans of a particular team. Fans buy paraphernalia related to the team to display their unity with the team. Such paraphernalia might include flags to attach to one's vehicle or to hang in front of one's home or in one's office. These flags are not unlike the standards borne by armies going to war. Indeed, it is common to see such "armies" going to the "battlefield" on game day with their flags attached to their "steeds," ready to make war against the opponent. Fans also dress in team colors and may color their bodies to announce their unity with the team. Some fans even decorate their bodies as though they were attempting to personify the team and what it stands for. There is clearly an attempt to identify with the team as a whole to the point that their lives can revolve around the successes and failures of the team.

One often hears this fan-team identification in the use of plural, personal pronouns in describing the team and its qualities and/or activities. "We won," "We lost," or, sometimes, "We were cheated." Emotions experienced at the victory or loss of a fan's team can be as intense as if the fan had actually participated in the game, sometimes even more so. Warren St. John notes the dejection University of Alabama college football fans feel after a loss.[68] Their whole personas change; they are sullen, depressed. Fights break out in the stands between drunken fraternity men.

St. John recalls his year of living with the RVers[69] who travel to all Alabama Crimson Tide football games in his *Rammer Jammer Yellow Hammer: A Journey into the Heart of Fan Mania*. St. John—a Crimson Tide fan—reveals how he rips open the wrapping of *Sports Illustrated*'s annual college football preview to see where his Tide is ranked. He says, "I open it with the anxious anticipation of a high school student ripping into a long-awaited letter from a college admissions office, eager to learn if we've been accepted or rejected."[70] St. John identifies with the team to the point where, in his mind, what others think of the team applies to him. The annual rankings are a reflection on St. John, and other fans, at least in their minds. St. John voices what is, most likely, common among fans of most sports, but especially true of American football.

One bit of evidence that indicates a heightened sense of self-identification with their football teams is that football fans tend to be more prone to dress in their team's garb than do fans of other sports. No doubt, other sports, such as baseball, basketball, hockey, and soccer, have their fans dressing in the team colors with authentic and replica jerseys and hats. Football fans more often tend to "go the second mile" when it comes to dressing in team colors. Going far beyond wearing a team jersey or painting one's face or body in team colors, National Football League (NFL) fans often wear complete football uniforms and sometimes replace the helmet with something that looks like the team's mascot or that symbolizes the character of the team. For example, it is not uncommon to see Oakland Raiders fans wearing skulls and spikes on their shoulders and helmets to symbolize the team's perceived "bad boy image." (See Fig. 4.1)

National Football League and other sports fans see themselves as part of the team and unite their self-image with that of the team for which they are cheering.

Fans tend to display their identification with their favorite team more often when the team is successful. St. John cites a 1970s study by psychologist Robert Cialdini who "found that fans were much more likely to wear their team's colors after a win than after a loss. Cialdini theorized that by wearing the colors of a winning team, fans were claiming a little of that superiority themselves, a phenomenon he called 'basking in reflected glory.'"[71] There is an identification of the self with the team so that the fan participates in the win as though he or she were actually on the field and actually feels herself or himself to be superior to the other team and anyone associated with that team.

It is telling that fans are willing to pay money to be able to identify with their teams. It is well known that sales of team merchandise and attendance at games rise significantly when a team is winning. When teams win championships or at least have very successful seasons, fans tend to buy merchandise associated with that team more

Fig. 4.1 Raiders fan with skull face.

than merchandise associated with other teams, and, usually, fans buy the replica jerseys of the stars of the team as representative of the team itself. In the NFL, this means fans tend to buy the jerseys of the quarterbacks more than of other players since quarterbacks get most of the media attention as well as "ball time" in the games. For example, the top five selling NFL jerseys from March 1, 2014, to February 28, 2015, all belong to quarterbacks on teams that made the playoffs and challenged for the Super Bowl title within the previous five years. The top two selling jerseys for that time period belong to Russell Wilson—quarterback for the Seattle Seahawks—and Peyton Manning—quarterback for the Denver Broncos. The Seahawks won Super Bowl XLVIII on February 2, 2014, beating the Denver Broncos.[72] So fans bought the jerseys of the "champions" of the two most recent teams to play for the overall championship for most of the year immediately following that championship.

Fans also show their desire to be associated with a winning team by attending the team's games and being present at the site of the competition to "participate" in the anticipated win. Attendance at games tends to be higher when teams win more games than they lose. The regular season-winning percentage of the top ten highest-attended Major League Baseball (MLB) teams for the 2014 season was 0.529 while the winning percentage of the lowest-attended MLB teams was 0.476. Even more telling, though, is a look at the history of one of the MLB teams as it began to win more games and then lose more games over roughly a ten-year period.

In 1991 the Cleveland Indians had a won-loss record of 57–105. They finished thirty-four games out of first place and were in last place in their division. Their total attendance for home games that year was 1.05 million. In contrast, the Toronto Blue

Jays led MLB in attendance that year with just over 4 million fans attending home games. In just a few years, Cleveland became a much-better team and began to win more games than they lost. In 1995, Cleveland finished their division in first place with a record of 100–44.[73] Their total attendance that year was 2.84 million, third-best overall in MLB. From 1996 to 2001, the Indians finished first in their division each year except for 2000 when they finished in second place, two games out of first place. During that six-year span, their average won–loss record was 92–70, and they averaged 3.4 million in attendance per year. In 2002, one year after finishing in first place in their division, the Indians posted a record of seventy-four wins against eighty-eight losses and finished 20.5 games out of first place. Attendance that year dropped to 2.6 million. In 2003, the club was even worse, finishing with a record of 68–94, twenty-two games behind the first-place team. Attendance that year was 1.73 million.[74]

Professional sports team owners know that more fans will buy team-related paraphernalia and attend games, thus raising revenue, when teams win more games than they lose. This is a large part of the reason owners fire coaches who do not produce enough wins or enough championships in the eyes of the owners. Besides wanting to win for the sake of winning, owners want their investments to make money, and they make money when they win.

Fans want to be associated with winners because this makes them feel like winners themselves. Being associated with a winning team, especially the championship team, allows fans to see themselves as part of something larger than their limited, finite selves. In the view of Michael Balint, the individual fan of a championship team is no longer a distinct individual, separated from everything else. He or she is part of a larger mass of championship fans who are all champions together. It is no wonder that when a team makes a good play or closes out a win that fans turn to each other to enjoy their championship together. They chest-bump and hug each other, they slap each other's raised hands, and sometimes home-team fans even rush the playing field at the conclusion of a winning game to be a part of the sea of winners.

In contrast, teams with losing records tend to have low attendance at their games, and their fans tend not to buy team-related merchandise. Sport is about competition and the goal of competition is to win. Cheering for a losing team (or player) at best indicates a poor judgment on the part of a fan (or, perhaps, undying devotion) and thus reflects negatively on the fan. More likely, because the fan has identified with the team, the fan's self-image is lowered when the team loses, especially vis-à-vis fans of the winning team. This concern for self-image is why fans of a losing team tend to display their association with that team less than they would if their team were a winning team. They do not want others to know they are associated with losers.

It seems clear, then, that people want to be associated with winners and will give up their hard-earned wages to buy merchandise and attend games that display their allegiance to and identification with their team, especially when their team is on the winning side. Making identification with a winner explicit in the form of wearing or displaying a team's colors and logo signals to others, especially those who are not identified with the winner but with an opponent, that the wearer of the jersey or other team paraphernalia is better than they are.

Wins feel better for the fans of the winning team because they know they will have "bragging rights" among their colleagues, family, and friends who support opposing teams. The phrase "bragging rights" itself reflects the idea that the winners "own" something as a result of their team's win, and this ownership/identification lasts as long as their team continues to win. They lose those rights when their team loses, and this serves as the basis for feelings of dejection. When a team loses, its fans immediately feel their self-image reduced vis-à-vis their colleagues, family, and friends who identify with a rival team, especially if the rival team has defeated the cheered-for team. In other words, when a fan's team wins, that fan sees himself as better than others, and when that fan's team loses, he is afraid that others will see themselves as better than he is. There is a sort of "competition" between the fans of opposing teams so that fans "battle" each other through their team's on-field competition.

American football is a sport that is based on conquering the other in a physical way. All sports have a physical component to them, but in most sports the physical component comes through self-exertion. Baseball, for example, can be extremely physical, but the physicality of the sport is not usually directed toward the opponents directly. The physicality of baseball comes in running, catching, hitting, and throwing *a ball*. Basketball is a very physical sport often including direct, physical contact between players. Hockey is also rather physical and involves direct contact between players, sometimes in the form of fistfights (though the fistfights are not actually part of the team competition and are not officially scored). In both basketball and hockey, however, the physical contact between players is incidental to the object of the game itself. Theoretically, basketball and hockey could both be played without players having significant contact between opponents. One may argue that they may not be played well, but physical contact between players is not essential to the sports being played. American football, on the other hand, is designed for hand-to-hand combat between players and may not be played at all if such contact does not occur. Football is a contact sport between opponents. It is about blocking, tackling, and even hitting for the effect of intimidation. Football demands personal contact between opponents.

Winning means conquering the other, defeating the opponent. These are terms often used when describing the outcomes of competitions. The sport of American football is especially illustrative of this language. The essence of football is physical contact between players that results in "marching up and down the field" like an army overrunning the enemy. In his article, "The Super Bowl as Religious Festival," Joseph Price illustrates the religious elements of the Super Bowl as played in 1984. There, Price points out that the object of the game is the conquest of territory, namely, the end zone of the other team.[75] Clearly, this has to do with control and power. One often hears announcers and coaches talking about controlling the line of scrimmage. The strongest, most physical line usually determines which team will win the game. The game is about control and defeat of the other through brute, physical force.

What does this have to do with the average, rabid fan? In football, especially, but also to some degree with other sports, there is a basic human desire to conquer the other for resources to survive. Controlling resources allows us to survive and overcome our finitude (even if for a brief period). Having limited resources might mean that we all cannot survive which puts us in conflict with each other. Sport allows us to enact this conflict without actually having to engage in mortal combat with another. We pretend that we have won and that we are better than our opponent when our team wins. We live vicariously through the actions of others. We claim a victory when our team wins and suffer a defeat when our team loses. As Grant says, we are following our heroes—who are very much alive in the realm of sports—through victory and defeat.

In addition to identifying themselves with a particular team, thus seeking to be united with the eternal through the team's winning the championship, there is another way for fans to align with the hero, and that is through individual athletes. Fan identification with their heroes can be seen in the area of sports memorabilia. While some fans seek autographs and other items that have come in contact with a famous athlete so they can sell them for a profit, most fans who seek contact with the hero will stand in long lines at autograph sessions just to have a few moments with the famous athlete. Some will arrive at sporting venues early or remain outside long after the games have been played hoping to get a glimpse of their favorite players as they arrive or leave the stadium or arena. Upon gaining such contact, the fan must share the experience with those he or she knows. It is practically impossible to have an encounter with a hero and keep quiet about it, especially if one engages in a conversation where such encounters are replayed. The fan has momentarily escaped his finitude and has had contact with the eternal. Remembering the episode allows the fan to relive the moment over and over again in his mind. Retelling the episode to others is a way of conquering the others by asserting one's superiority over the other in the same way the fan does when her team defeats the opponent.

So what does this have to do with religion? Staying with the theme of touching greatness in individual form, we know that religion seeks to allow the individual to ascend above the level of normal human existence and touch the divine in some way. As humans we want to rise above our finitude and touch the infinite, the eternal. According to Freud and others, we want to experience security, union with the eternal, and comfort in the face of threatening finitude. In Eastern mystical traditions, this may be attempted directly through mysticism, while in the West the mediator often plays a key role in trying to raise the finite to the level of the infinite.

The mediator may be a well-known, current religious leader like Billy Graham or the Pope. Both of these leaders draw crowds because of their supposed connection to the divine or to ultimate reality. Charismatic religious leaders much less well known spring up all the time and draw followers who are convinced that the leader has some connection with the divine that is not available to the common person. In both sport and religion, people want to connect with the eternal.

Conclusion

Athletic competition and religious practice offer much the same thing in the way of escaping finitude and uniting with the eternal, the infinite. In athletic competition, fans can "achieve" infinity when their team wins the championship. While most fans do not actually engage in athletic competition, they often align themselves with well-known teams that most people know and hope that they will experience victory along with the heroes with whom they have aligned themselves. Joining a religious community assures followers of the ultimate "win," because they believe they will escape their finitude by being a part of the true religious community.

Additionally, fans may lift themselves up individually (as opposed to communally by identifying with a team) and have direct contact with the heroes and relics of sports. Having some direct contact with a famous athlete or relic will raise them from their common finitude instantly, should they be so lucky (blessed?) to have some kind of contact. For those who are not so lucky, money will sometimes work to bring one into contact with the heroes by buying special tickets to events where the heroes will be present or by buying autographed memorabilia that has been in direct contact with the hero.

In the following chapter we consider the perspectives of social theorists and see how sport brings people together in much the same way that religion brings people together. We may be individuals, but we seek union with a larger group. We find community in both religion and sport.

Discussion Questions

1. Do you agree with Freud that dreams represent our wishes? Do you believe religion satisfies a basic human need? If so, what is that need? Could this need be satisfied in other ways besides formal religion?

2. If you have a favorite sports team or athlete, how does it feel when the team or player wins the championship? How does it feel to lose a championship game? Why is winning so important? What are some other ways we "win" or "lose" in life? How do you feel when you win or lose?

3. Have you ever had direct, personal contact with a famous athlete (or famous person in general)? What was that like? Did you keep the encounter to yourself or have you told others about it? What did it feel like to share that encounter with others? Did you feel a sense of superiority when telling the story?

Glossary

cosmos — the world as a whole.

finitude — the state of being limited. In the case of humans this means, among other things, that we have a definite beginning (birth) and a definite ending (death).

infinity — the state of being unlimited, usually associated with God and, perhaps, the universe.

narcissism — the psychological condition of focusing an inordinate amount of affection on the self to the detriment of others. The narcissist will ensure her or his own good above all others, even at the expense of others' good.

psychoanalysis — field of psychology developed primarily by Sigmund Freud in the early twentieth century; Freud sought to find causes of and influences on contemporary behavior in the very early stages of childhood, sometimes hidden in the person's subconscious memory.

relic — typically, a religious object considered sacred, often associated with a saint or holy place.

5   Come Together: A Sociology of Religion and Sport

When we think about religion, we often think of buildings where people gather to engage in collective religious activity. Churches, synagogues, temples, and mosques demonstrate an important function of religion—its ability to bring people together and to make them feel part of something greater than themselves. Religion gives people a sense of belonging, and this belonging helps to shape their identities.

In this chapter we explain some central ways in which we can think about the sociological function of religion—utilizing the seminal work of Emile Durkheim (supplemented at points by the likewise important work of anthropologist Victor Turner) to make the case that religion above all else is a phenomenon that has society as its roots and its object of worship. At various points we show how Durkheim's theories can be applied to sport. We then turn to the work of Johan Huizinga. He provides a sociological account of "play" that supplements Durkheim's analysis—especially when thinking about the sociological elements that sport shares with religion. In the second half of the chapter, we then look at two case studies that reveal how sport functions socially like a religion—through football in the United Kingdom and rugby Down Under (in New Zealand and South Africa, to be specific).

Durkheim's Sociology of Religion

Emile Durkheim (1858–1917) was a French scholar and one of the founding fathers of the discipline of sociology. His work covered a range of institutions and issues in society, from the division of labor to the social causes of suicide. He also wrote on religion, and much that he wrote on that subject continues to carry weight today.

Durkheim divides religious phenomena into two categories: beliefs and rites (rituals or practices).[1] These two categories are dependent on one another, though Durkheim certainly emphasizes the role of collective action as preeminent. As Robert N. Bellah concludes in regard to Durkheim's position, beliefs "arise from and express the homogeneous physical movements that constitute the ritual, not the other way around."[2] In other words, religion is as much about what we *do* as what we *think*.

Portions of this chapter are reprinted (with some revision) from Eric Bain-Selbo's *Game Day and God: Football, Faith, and Politics in the American South* (2009) by permission of Mercer University Press (Macon, Georgia).

Sacred objects, places, or times are not sacred because they have some special substance that makes them that way. They are sacred because human beings deem them to be sacred. Ann Taves makes this point when she argues that when we talk about religious experiences (what we might see as experiences of the sacred or holy), we really are referring to "experiences deemed religious"—and that such experiences in fact are "a subset of things people consider special."[3] The point, in part, is that we do not inhabit a world with preexisting sacred or religious things or experiences, but that such things or experiences are socially constructed. Taves concludes: "Whether people consider a special thing as (say) 'religious,' 'mystical,' 'magical,' 'superstitious,' 'spiritual,' 'ideological,' or 'secular' will depend on the preexisting systems of belief and practice, the web of concepts related to specialness, and the way that people position themselves in a given context."[4]

Taves draws explicitly from Durkheim in this regard, and her argument about specialness is instructive as we move forward. If things or experiences that are religious or sacred are simply a subset of things or experiences that human beings consider special, then other special things or experiences (such as a baseball caught in the stands at Wrigley Field in Chicago or the opportunity to watch a football World Cup final) may not be as different from religious or sacred things or experiences as many might think. The concept of "special" is useful as well in that it does not carry the same preconceptions and commitments that terms like "religious" or "sacred" carry. However, since "sacred" was the term utilized by Durkheim, we will stick with it in this chapter.

All religious beliefs, Durkheim notes, presuppose the dichotomy between the sacred and the profane. He argues that the sacred and profane are radical opposites and that a central aspect of the religious life is the continual separation of the sacred from the profane.

It is important to note that religious beliefs are not held and rites are not performed simply by individuals. Beliefs are held and rites are performed by individuals who are part of a group that holds the beliefs and performs the rites in common. Indeed, it is the holding of beliefs and the performance of rites in common that help to form the group itself.[5] Durkheim calls such a group a "Church" (though predominantly a Christian term, by "Church" he simply means any religious community). Thus he arrives at the following definition of religion:

> A religion is a unified system of beliefs and practices relative to sacred things, that is to say, things set apart and forbidden—beliefs and practices which unite into one single moral community called a Church, all those who adhere to them.[6]

While Durkheim believes that his definition of religion holds universally, his particular interest in *The Elementary Forms of Religious Life* is totemic religion in aboriginal Australia. In a sustained argument, Durkheim makes the case that the totem (e.g., a

The notion of society being the ultimate object of worship is worked out in the later half of the twentieth century in the idea of civil religion. Popularized by sociologist Robert Bellah, the point behind the idea is that societies have a set of beliefs and rituals by which they celebrate (worship) themselves. In the United States, for example, Independence Day (July 4) and Thanksgiving are special (sacred) days when Americans celebrate their history and culture—affirming the uniqueness of their country and the character of its people. In numerous ways, sport also plays a key role in civil religion. Again, in the American context, the Super Bowl in football and the World Series in baseball are key elements of the liturgical calendar of American civil religion. Later in the chapter we will look more extensively at rugby in New Zealand and South Africa as part of their civil religions.

particular animal, such as a kangaroo) of a tribe or clan is what is most sacred. It also is what represents the tribe or clan. For Durkheim, these are one and the same. Take a hypothetical example of a tribe with a kangaroo as its totem. What is most sacred may be the kangaroo, but the kangaroo simply represents the tribe. Thus, it is the tribe or clan that is most sacred and is the object of religious devotion—not directly but via the totem.

The totemic principle is that which comes to organize all people, animals, and things. It helps to designate the relative importance of everything by virtue of any particular thing's affinity or relatedness to the totem. For example, a particular field where kangaroos tend to congregate would be especially sacred, as would be the water in the stream that runs through the field. Stones from the field might be used in certain rituals, as will (of course) the kangaroos themselves (particularly in sacrifices). The result is a coherent system of beliefs (organized around the totem) about the world around the tribe or clan as well as a set of rituals that affirm and sustain those beliefs.

Of particular interest to Durkheim is how the totemic principle comes to organize human beings and other human-like beings such as great ancestors, gods, and goddesses. Gods and goddesses (culminating in the idea, eventually, of one god) developed from the idea of ancestors. The idea of ancestors living after the death of the body was inferred by the empirical evidence of the survival of the tribe or clan even as individuals pass away. In other words, the analogy goes that just as the spirit or essence of the tribe or clan persists even after the death of any individual, so the spirit or essence of the individual persists even after the death of the body. So, the idea of ancestors also can be understood as a consequence of our sense that we have something eternal and objective in us—separate from our bodies and idiosyncratic thoughts. For Durkheim, this eternal and objective thing is the soul.

The soul, Durkheim believes, is what is sacred about human beings, as opposed to the body that is profane. The soul is the spark or fragment of the divine (the totem) that connects human beings to ancestors, gods, and goddesses. It is our moral conscience that guides our thoughts and actions and somehow seems other than ourselves. This is why Durkheim writes of our "double nature." Any person is both an individual and something else—this something else is denoted by the idea of the soul. But this something else is not unique to the individual; it is what is shared in common with everyone else (or at least everyone else in the tribe or clan). Our soul then, according to Durkheim, is really a spark or fragment of the collective soul (as represented in the totem). Durkheim writes that "there truly is a parcel of divinity in us, because there is in us a parcel of the grand ideals that are the soul of collectivity."[7] In short, we are both individual and social beings, and though the soul is individual in us, it is part of a larger soul or spirit that is the society. Thus, Durkheim concludes: "[M]an is double. In him are two beings: an individual being that has its basis in the body and whose sphere of action is strictly limited by this fact, and a social being that represents within us the highest reality in the intellectual and moral realm that is knowable through observation: I mean society."[8]

The soul then represents what is transcendent. It is immortal—greater than any individual life. Durkheim observes:

> In sum, belief in the immortality of souls is the only way man is able to compre-
> hend a fact that cannot fail to attract his attention: the perpetuity of the group's
> life. The individuals die, but the clan survives, so the forces that constitute his
> life must have the same perpetuity. These forces are the souls that animate the
> individual bodies, because it is in and by them that the group realizes itself. For
> that reason, they must endure. Indeed, while enduring, they also must remain the
> same. Since the clan always keeps its characteristic form, the spiritual substance
> of which it is made must be conceived of as qualitatively invariable.[9]

The soul is identical to that which makes the ancestors, gods, and goddesses sacred, and it is what connects us to them. But the soul is nothing more nor less than society itself. The soul is our social nature, experienced by us as something other and greater than ourselves. Ultimately our soul is identified with some form of ultimate reality that is everlasting and the source or our being. Some call such an ultimate reality God, but for Durkheim the term "God" is only another word for society itself—for it is society that is everlasting and the source of our being.

For Durkheim, this idea of transcendence, represented by the concept of the soul as the psychological experience of the power of the collectivity (tribe or clan) within us, is central to understanding what rituals achieve. Rituals entail our participation in something greater than ourselves—that something greater being society itself. This is true for Muslims who gather for prayer, for Christians joining for communion, but also for people engaged in a wide variety of ritual activities—including, for our purposes, sports. Those who participate in sporting events, whether as athletes or spectators, are joining in something that transcends their individual egos and connects them with a greater reality. Fans and athletes alike often talk about the "spirit" of the team, and we should not take this wording as just a clumsy attempt by such people to describe their experience of this greater reality. The "spirit" of the team is the soul of the collectivity to which individual players and fans are bound inextricably—for their souls are the same as the team "spirit." The team "spirit" is a greater reality because it is the collective, the society, in which the individual is absorbed. In previous chapters we have considered this greater reality as the divine, the infinite, or the eternal. Here we draw from Durkheim to consider society as the referent of all these names.

Though critical of the notion that we should celebrate sport as religion, Robert J. Higgs and Michael C. Braswell claim that the "individual is called upon to surrender the ego, individual consciousness that is, to the group. He or she is asked to become a 'fan' and to take up all the totemic practices fandom entails, such as getting 'the spirit' or 'fever' and painting one's face."[10] The comparison to totemic practices should not be taken lightly here. What Higgs and Braswell note about the contemporary sports fan echoes what Durkheim sees in totemism in Australia:

> Those who conduct them [totemic rites], playing the role of celebrants—and sometimes even those who are present as spectators—always wear designs on their bodies that represent the totem. One of the principal rites of initiation, the one that initiates the young man into the religious life of the tribe, is the painting of the totemic symbol upon his body.[11]

Anyone who has been to a sporting event (particularly in major team sports) may be struck by how well Durkheim's account fits with what fans often do to themselves as part of their participation in the sporting experience. Whether it is wearing the totem (team mascot) on apparel or painting it on their faces or chests, fans seem to engage in the same kind of totemic representation that Durkheim identifies among totemic tribes and clans. Through apparel or paint, the fan is acknowledging in a very physical and public way his or her "double nature" as an individual and as part of the collective.[12] All of these, for good or ill, also are characteristic of the sporting experience for millions of fans across the globe.

Durkheim divides rituals into "negative cult" and "positive cult." The negative cult has to do with that which is prohibited—often those things that are associated with the totem. What is prohibited is considered taboo. Certain things associated with the totem, certain powerfully sacred things, are too great to be handled at will. They are taboo for most people. That is, most people are prohibited from touching them. Priests or others who conduct rituals may be allowed to handle taboo elements, but even they may have to go through rites of purification to do so. There are few elements of the sporting experience that are taboo in this sense, that people are prohibited from touching. There are, however, elements that *some* people at least are excluded from touching. For example, fans generally are excluded from touching or handling the balls and equipment necessary for the play of a sport that they are watching. They also are prohibited from being on the field or court.

More relevant for our purposes is what Durkheim describes as the positive cult. The positive cult is not about avoiding the sometimes-dangerous power of sacred elements, but bringing the participants of the ritual into communion with the sacred. Thus, it is a system of ritual practices that "regulate and organize" our relationship with the sacred.[13] So it is through the collective enactment of ritual that people are brought into contact with the sacred—the sacred ultimately being that very collective enactment itself (when properly performed and engaging the appropriate emotions).

A great example of the positive cult is the sacrificial feast. Here the power of the totem is released and incorporated by the tribe or clan through, as one example, the killing (sacrifice) and eating of a representative totemic animal. Remember, however, that the totem is a symbol for the society itself, and in this instance any particular totemic animal is like an individual. Just as a particular totemic animal may be sacrificed (and through its being consumed, its power is distributed throughout the members of the tribe or clan), so any individual in a society must be prepared to sacrifice himself or herself for the good of the whole. At the most extreme, one may be asked to sacrifice his or her life, but generally sacrifices involve the giving up of one's time, energy, or goods.

The sacrificial feast is not simply (or perhaps not even mainly) about consumption. It also entails renunciation—a giving up of some of the totemic animal and/or other goods to the gods. Sacrifice "always presupposes that the worshipper relinquishes to the gods some part of his substance or his goods."[14] But what is even more important as an offering in the sacrificial feast is the thought of the participants.[15] The ritual is performed to strengthen the society as a whole (albeit through the strengthening of individual members) through an act of communion. And while it is believed that this strength comes from oblation to the gods and/or the ingesting of the totemic animal, it really comes from the active participation of the community's members in the ritual—it comes from the care and concern that they demonstrate toward the whole as demonstrated by and as a consequence of their participation. So while it is believed that the ritual strengthens members of the tribe or clan, and through the offering strengthens the totem and/or the gods, according to Durkheim's analysis it is society itself that is preserved and revived by the ritual.

What happens to the participants in the sacrificial feast or other rituals of the positive cult is what Durkheim describes as "collective effervescence." He notes that the "state of effervescence in which the assembled faithful find themselves is translated outwardly by exuberant emotions that are not easily subordinated to ends that are defined too strictly."[16] In other words, the effervescence is not about achieving some other practical end. It is an end in itself. It is an end because it represents the social and psychological unity of the community itself—and the community is the highest good (and thus, is not a means to some other good). It is central to our collective lives. As Roger Friedland concludes: "Effervescent aggregation performs, expresses, mimes, indeed, is, the enabling powers of collective life, upon which not only does the finest within us depend, but from which we derive our meaning and our material existence, indeed which enables us to be."[17]

What Durkheim refers to as collective effervescence is similar to what Turner describes as *communitas*. *Communitas* refers to the direct meeting and interaction of concrete, particular individuals with one another. This interaction is not between, for example, a teacher and a student or a clerk and a customer; it is between two human beings stripped of their roles and statuses in society.[18] These roles no longer mediate our experience with another person. Such interaction between human beings, though the most fortuitous and beneficial of encounters, cannot be maintained indefinitely. All human societies need (or, at least, seem to need) some kind of division of labor, clearly understood power relations and duties/obligations for their citizens, and orderly and effective social institutions with accompanying hierarchies. All of this is what Turner calls "structure." Structure is "a more or less distinctive arrangement of mutually dependent institutions and the institutional organization of social position and/or actors which they imply."[19] Structure allows societies to function effectively. The "spontaneity and immediacy" of *communitas* inevitably gives way to structure.[20] But it is *communitas* that provides the powerful emotional bond to one another that human beings need as social creatures. It is through *communitas* that "*anomie* [the psychological distress caused by chaos in the social order; a term popularized by Durkheim] is prevented or avoided and a milieu is created in which a society's members cannot see any fundamental conflict between themselves as individuals and society. There is set up, in their minds, a symbiotic interpenetration of individual and society."[21] What we have then is a continual tension, a dialectic, between *communitas* (also called anti-structure) and structure. Both are necessary for human life, and our objective should be finding the appropriate balance between the two. Turner concludes:

> Spontaneous communitas is richly charged with affects, mainly pleasurable ones. Life in "structure" is filled with objective difficulties: decisions have to be made, inclinations sacrificed to the wishes and needs of the group, and physical and social obstacles overcome at some personal cost. Spontaneous communitas has something "magical" about it. Subjectively there is in it the feeling of endless power. But this power untransformed cannot readily be applied to the organizational details of social existence. It is no substitute for lucid thought and sustained will. On the other hand, structural action swiftly becomes arid and mechanical if those involved in it are not periodically immersed in the regenerative abyss of communitas. Wisdom is always to find the appropriate relationship between structure and communitas under the *given* circumstances of time and place, to accept each modality when it is paramount without rejecting the other, and not to cling to one when its present impetus is spent.[22]

The rituals of various sporting events, like religious rituals, contribute to the establishment of *communitas* and "collective effervescence." Durkheim notes that games originated in a religious context, and that recreation "is one form of the moral remaking [society itself] that is the primary object of the positive cult."[23] Games or recreation help to create *communitas*, for the players encounter one another directly — not mediated by the structures of the social order. In the end, there are numerous rituals — religious and apparently nonreligious — that allow *communitas* to occur. What Durkheim's work clearly indicates is the great need we have for all collective rituals. "There can be no society," he writes, "that does not experience the need at regular intervals to maintain and strengthen the collective feelings and ideas that provide its coherence and its distinct individuality."[24] There can be no society that does not engage in rituals to achieve "collective effervescence" or *communitas*. In this regard, religion and sport function very similarly in a society.

Homo Ludens

One of the earliest and still most prominent sociological treatments of sport is the work of Johan Huizinga (1872–1945). His book, *Homo Ludens: A Study of the Play Element in Culture*, allows us to understand sport through the concept of play. While all play is not sport (for example, childhood games, playing with one's dog, and bouncing a ball against a wall are play but not sports), play nevertheless is at the core of whatever we would identify as sport.

For Huizinga, play is a central element of human culture; it allows us to see the broader cultural context of sport. While Huizinga does not focus on religion per se, his argument nevertheless has affinities with that of Durkheim and others and helps in our inquiry concerning the relationship of religion and sport. While Durkheim looks at religion and finds a critical role for play (for example, in the energetic behavior of the celebrants in a festival), Huizinga looks at play and finds its critical role in religion.

Huizinga describes play in a number of ways. It is a "*significant* function" that "transcends the immediate needs of life and imparts meaning to the action."[25] He identifies the "primordial quality of play" as "this intensity, this absorption, this power of maddening" that play brings to its participants.[26] In the end, he argues for at least four main characteristics of play: (1) it is free; (2) it is not ordinary, it is "a stepping out of 'real' life into a temporary sphere of activity with a disposition all of its own"; (3) it is "'played out' within certain limits of time and place"; and (4) it "promotes the formation of social groupings."[27] All of these characteristics can be found in religion, particularly as explained by Durkheim.

While play is "non-seriousness," it nevertheless is critical to human life.[28] Play is critical to both the individual and social good—in fact, Huizinga finds it to have an important role in the development of culture or civilization. It permeates culture or civilization. "The spirit of playful competition is, as a social impulse, older than culture itself and pervades all life like a veritable ferment," Huizinga claims. "We have to conclude … that civilization is, in its earliest phases, played. It does not come *from* play like a babe detaching itself from the womb; it arises *in* and *as* play, and never leaves it."[29]

Huizinga recognizes that play pervades much of the religious activity that humans have engaged in through history. "Primitive society performs its sacred rites, its sacrifices, consecrations and mysteries," Huizinga writes, "all of which serve to guarantee the well-being of the world, in a spirit of pure play truly understood."[30] The activities always lead people "to participate in the sacred happening itself."[31] We have here a description of ritual that closely mirrors the one provided by Durkheim.

But play is not just part of religious activity. Play itself has a sacred quality in the sense that it is "set apart" from ordinary, profane existence. Like ritual in general, the "sacred activity" of play "contributes to the well-being of the group."[32] Though he does not emphasize the sacred/profane dichotomy in the same way Durkheim does, Huizinga clearly is referring to it in these claims about play.

Where play occurs, the physical space, also is sacred. "Formally speaking, there is no distinction whatever between marking out a space for a sacred purpose and marking it out for purposes of sheer play," Huizinga concludes. "The turf, the tennis-court, the chessboard and pavement-hopscotch cannot formally be distinguished from the temple or the magic circle."[33] He concludes that all of these places "are temporary worlds within the ordinary world, dedicated to the performance of an act apart [sacred activity]."[34] In this "set apart" world, order is created and sustained in contradiction to the chaos that holds sway in the ordinary, profane world.[35] Indeed, order is one of the distinguishing characteristics of what is holy, sacred, or religious.

In these sacred spaces, the participants in play test themselves mentally and phys-ically. The player even tests "his spiritual powers—his 'fairness'; because, despite his ardent desire to win, he must still stick to the rules of the game."[36] In this sense, winning or losing is not the definition of success. Here, success is the raising of the consciousness of the player in the sacrality of play. "In the form and function of play," Huizinga concludes, "man's consciousness that he is embedded in a sacred order of things finds its first, highest, and holiest expression."[37]

While we can make the distinction between play and religion for the purposes of analysis, in the end it is clear that Huizinga does not see them as fundamentally differ-ent. Play and religious practices serve the same fundamental function. In sum, both serve the common goal of uniting people in an activity that raises the consciousness of those involved—direct participants as well as spectators—to an order that tran-scends their everyday experience. We have here with Huizinga simply another way of talking about *communitas* and "collective effervescence."

On Belonging

If one of the primary functions of religion is the creation of community and thus the experience for the individual of belonging to something greater than himself or herself, then clearly sport functions like religion. According to sociologist Harry Edwards, fans "are members of the family [the team], and a loss by 'their sports family' affects them deeply and personally."[38] The team is the totemic tribe that provides the players and fans with their identity.

This sense of belonging to a family or community certainly is true in the United Kingdom in regard to football. Indeed, football (or soccer) is the sport that probably is most associated with the British—and many scholars and writers have noted how the game serves as a unifying function in the society. Simon Kuper and Stefan Szymanski observe that "big soccer tournaments provide some of the communal glue once supplied by trade unions, churches, and royal weddings. Possibly the best chance English people get to bond with each other nowadays … is during a World Cup."[39]

But Britons are not simply unified by their national team. They are united in hundreds of smaller groups around club teams all across the British Isles. Kuper

Fig. 5.1 Racially diverse Arsenal fans singing.

and Szymanski describe the British as a "rootless" people—citing the frequency with which they move, the decline of religion as a central element of communal life, and the absence of other institutions to ground the individual in the community.[40] Indeed, football perhaps can be seen as an institution that has taken on the social function that used to be the purview of traditional religion and other groups.

Evidence of the social function of football in England can be found in the popular memoir by Nick Hornby, *Fever Pitch*. It is the story of a boy who grows up as a fan of the Arsenal Football Club of London—and how the team became a permanent part of his life and identity. (See Fig. 5.1)

Hornby identifies a "sense of belonging" as critical to what it means to be a fan.[41] "I have learned the value of investing time and emotion in things I cannot control," he writes, "and of belonging to a community whose aspirations I share completely and uncritically."[42] Hornby describes Highbury, Arsenal's home pitch, as "the place I know best in the world, the one spot outside my own home where I feel I belong absolutely and unquestionably."[43] Highbury is sacred for Hornby, a place of comfort and acceptance. His experience undoubtedly is like that of many more stereotypical religious adherents in regard to their church, temple, or other spiritual home.

For Hornby, the pervasiveness of Arsenal in his life and the effects the team has on him are part of the reason that he insists that soccer is more than just a game—at least for him and fans like him. To describe soccer as just a game for someone like Hornby would be like describing religion as just a social club for a devout Catholic. As Hornby insists, soccer "is not an escape, or a form of entertainment, but a differ- ent version of the world."[44] It is a version of the world that makes sense of the fan's behavior and orients the fan to his or her environment. And though soccer, like most sports, has its winners and losers, for the true fan the results do not matter. Hornby makes clear that "it simply doesn't matter to me how bad things get ... results have nothing to do with anything," adding that for fans like him, "the quality of the product is immaterial."[45]

The world that revolves around Arsenal is one that shapes the attitudes and behavior of its fans. In terms of behavior, it is important to note that fans do not sit passively and watch games (either in person or on television). They very much are active participants. For Hornby, soccer "is a context where watching *becomes* doing."[46] The watching and the actions revolving around the watching are rituals that shape the experience. These rituals might be considered, to use Durkheim's terminology, part of a positive cult.

Hornby writes about how, for each game, he ritually bought a program from the same seller and entered the stadium through the same turnstile.[47] He remembers purchasing a new team shirt before a particularly important game "because I felt I had to do something."[48] Such rituals give us a sense of control in regard to events over which we have little or no control.[49] Which team wins the game is something that, ultimately, we *know* is out of our control. Indeed, sometimes it even seems like a complete mystery why one team wins and another loses—there are so many funny bounces of the ball, gusts of wind that come at inopportune (or opportune) times, and a myriad of other variables that are inexplicable. Thus, as Hornby explains, it is understandable that "we are reduced to creating ingenious but bizarre liturgies designed to give us the illusion that we are powerful after all, just as every other primitive community has done when faced with a deep and apparently impenetrable mystery."[50] Like most rituals, soccer rituals are performed at specific times. In particular, they follow the schedule of the teams. Indeed, the schedule comes to be a liturgical calendar for the fan, one that structures his or her year.[51]

The culmination of the soccer experience, like the culmination of many religious practices, is an ecstatic state of being that is both the product of the communal experience and a rejuvenation of the communal bond. At the end of a particularly dramatic and important victory, Hornby explains that his "delirium was such that I had no idea what I was doing" and that an "old man behind me grabbed me around the neck and wouldn't let go."[52] The experience described here is one that Hornby recognizes across the range of sporting events. He concludes:

> There is then, literally, nothing to describe it [the ecstatic or delirious experience].
> I have exhausted all the available options. ... So please, be tolerant of those who describe a sporting moment as their best ever. We do not lack imagination, nor have we had sad and barren lives; it is just that real life is paler, duller, and contains less potential for unexpected delirium.[53]

"Real life," in short, is profane. And what Hornby is talking about is sacred.

Hornby's ecstatic or delirious experience is much more than an individual experience; it is *communal*. Indeed, Hornby insists that his experience is one of "*communal ecstasy*."[54] It is communal because the fans are bound to one another in their common object of worship and prescribed rituals, and the fans are bound to their team as any group of people may be bound to their totem. Their souls are united in the great soul of the group. Hornby writes:

> The joy we feel on occasions like this [important team victories] is not a celebration of others' good fortune, but a celebration of our own; and when there is a disastrous defeat the sorrow that engulfs us is, in effect, self-pity, and anyone who wishes to understand how football is consumed must realize this above all things. The players are merely our representatives, chosen by the manager rather than elected by us, but our representatives nonetheless, and sometimes if you look hard you can see the little poles that join them together, and the handles at the side that enable us to move them. I am a part of the club, just as the club is a part of me. ...[55]

Given this kind of sense of identity, of belonging so strongly to something greater than oneself, it is not surprising that a fan like Hornby would want his ashes scattered in the stadium of his beloved team. He imagines being able then to "hang around inside the stadium in some form" to watch the team play. He says further, "[I] like to feel that my children and grandchildren will be Arsenal fans and that I could watch with them. It doesn't seem a bad way to spend eternity ..."[56] Here we have a dream of belonging forever—a dream and an urge that is distinctly religious.[57] We also have the attainment of the infinite or eternal and the sense of immortality that we described in previous chapters.

What Hornby so brilliantly describes is the social cohesion that football provides—a social cohesion that is critical for a meaningful life. In many if not most cases, the important thing is to belong. It matters little to what we belong (within certain socially accepted limits, of course). Simon and Szymanski cite data that show the incredible role that soccer can play in European countries.[58] The data clearly indicate that during periods in which the national team is competing in a major tournament (and regardless of whether the team wins or loses), suicide rates in the country go down. Simon and Szymanski attribute the decline to the social cohesion that the national football team creates—as the citizens experience a deep sense of belonging, a belonging beautifully expressed in Hornby's memoir.

Some may argue that sport cannot be religion because it is just play. But play can be serious and tremendously meaningful, as Huizinga indicates. When embodied in sport, play can lead to phenomena that are critical to our identities as individuals and as communities. And as Simon and Szymanski show, that identity can be a matter of life and death.

Rugby Down Under

One of the most popular sports in the Southern Hemisphere is rugby—particularly in places like South Africa, Australia, and New Zealand.

Rugby has been called a religion in New Zealand for a long time. New Zealand historian James Belich says that rugby "achieved prominence in the 1880s[,] precedence in 1890–1910, and dominance by the 1920s."[59] By the early 1920s "it was incontestably the national game ... with twice as many club members as the next most important sport (tennis) and four times as many as soccer."[60] The game became an important form of play in the rugged New Zealand culture—a means by which boys and men could gather in a collective activity to test their individual will and prowess (and, frankly, courage). In fact, the role of rugby in New Zealand might be a good example of what Huizinga describes as the cultural production function of play.

Belich notes that by the end of the 1920s, one prominent national publication already was describing rugby as "some type of pseudo-religious activity."[61] He concludes that while there was no state religion, there certainly was a state sport—and that sport was rugby. The sport very likely was and is more religious than Belich acknowledges.

The key to rugby's rise to prominence and then dominance, according to Belich, was "its role in collective identity"—from the local club teams on up to the national team.[62] He argues that "rugby acted as proxy for suppressed collective identities" and that the "history of New Zealand regionalism is probably better mapped through rugby unions than through official divisions such as land districts."[63]

Rugby served and continues to serve as a potent "metaphor for pluralist unity" in New Zealand—bringing together a wide range of people from different locales and ethnicities. "Clubs competed fervently, their best players uniting into regional and then island teams (for the annual North v. South match), and competing quite bitterly at these levels too," Belich claims. "All then united into the national team."[64] The national team is known as the All Blacks, because of the color of their uniforms. Rugby and the All Blacks "were confirmed as symbols of the nation by a triumphant All Black tour of Britain in 1905, in which a New Zealand team won 34 games and lost one, scoring 976 points in total, with only 59 points against it."[65] The All Blacks team is the totem by which many New Zealanders came to and continue to identify themselves.

Michael Grimshaw details how New Zealand writers and scholars have described the role of rugby in New Zealand culture—from the local club teams to the beloved All Blacks. He argues that "the oft-quoted phrase 'Rugby is New Zealand's religion' does, in fact, express a variety of experiences, at both a societal and an individual level, that can be included under the broad heading of 'religion.'"[66]

Two of New Zealand's prominent literary figures of the twentieth century were Alan Mulgan and his son John Mulgan. Both featured rugby significantly in their works. For them, rugby is a "substitutionary religion, a pagan, primitive faith that acts to bind together, to mythologize, to provide communal meaning and transcendence for a people, who, without either transplanted tradition or culture, recreate ritual, transcendence, and communal meaning in the religion of rugby."[67] In short, rugby serves as a common tradition that celebrates virtues of strength, perseverance, and courage—qualities that New Zealanders value in themselves. According to Grimshaw, rugby is "a religion of identity, of virtues, of culture and context expressed through intertwined rituals of action, masculinity, tribalism, and nationhood."[68] Rugby is *religare*, a binding together of "players, spectators, supporters, and society."[69] Durkheim certainly would see rugby as the cult of this tribe of New Zealanders, that which helps to create community and reflect back to itself its most treasured values.

While fans engage in a range of personal and collective rituals in support of their team, the All Blacks have one pre-game ritual that exemplifies the *binding* that Grimshaw describes. Before the game, the players gather in the middle of the field and perform the *haka*, a Maori dance/chant that warriors would perform before going into battle. It is meant to strike fear into the opponent. (See Fig. 5.2) Symbolically, the performance emphasizes the unity of the team members—both Maori (the indigenous population) and *pakeha* (the white population). Colonized and colonizers come together to go off to battle against the enemy (the Springboks from South Africa or the Wallabees from Australia). As Grimshaw concludes, rugby in New Zealand is "a key facet of nation building."[70]

A powerful example of the role of sport in nation building can be found in the case of the Springboks in South Africa and the amazing story of how Nelson Mandela used rugby to unite a very divided country. John Carlin tells the story in his best seller *Invictus: Nelson Mandela and the Game That Made a Nation* (originally published as *Playing the Enemy*)—a book that then was turned into a major motion picture.[71]

As the system of racial segregation known as apartheid was coming to an end in the 1990s, the first integrated and free elections were held in South Africa in 1994. Nelson Mandela, a leader of the African National Congress who had spent much of his adult life in South African prisons as an enemy of the state, was elected president. But while the country was legally united, it hardly was united politically or socially. Conservative Afrikaners (a white ethnic group) continued to threaten armed insurrection to return power to whites and to maintain segregation.

Fig. 5.2 All Blacks performing *haka*.

Into this heated context came the South African Springboks, the national rugby team. Rugby was not a sport that had previously united black and white South Africans. Blacks preferred football (soccer) and viewed rugby as a symbol of racist South Africa—beloved by Afrikaners who saw it as a symbol of cultural strength and courage. Rugby "was a white sport," Carlin writes, "and especially the sport of the Afrikaners, South Africa's dominant white tribe—apartheid's master race. The Springboks had long been seen by black people as a symbol of apartheid oppression as repellent as the old white national anthem and the old white national flag."[72] Carlin, in fact, describes rugby as the "secular religion" of the Afrikaners, and "the more right-wing the Afrikaners were, the more fundamentalist their faith in God, the more fanatical their attachment to the game."[73]

With the 1995 Rugby World Cup scheduled in South Africa, however, Mandela saw an opportunity to support the beloved sport of his staunchest opponents. At the same time, he needed to bring along his supporters and help them overcome their disdain for the sport and the team. Blacks so despised the South African team that they were accustomed to rooting *against* the Springboks when they played other national teams.

At the end of a string of brilliant and courageous political moves, Mandela was able to unite blacks and whites around the Springbok team. Some of these moves were particularly precarious, especially those connected with symbols and rituals. As we learned from Durkheim, symbols or totems (in this case, a Springbok, which is a type of antelope indigenous to South Africa) and rituals play powerful roles in our collective life. Some of Mandela's moves involved changes to some symbols (for example, the South African flag) and rituals (for example, the new national anthem sung before matches) while leaving other symbols (for example, the Springboks' uniform) and rituals (for example, the old national anthem sung alongside the new one) the same. All of these symbols and rituals were meant to represent the country and, for Mandela, *all* the people. Mandela even invented a slogan for the team, "One Team, One Country" that "not only captured the imagination of South Africans, it conveyed Mandela's purpose to perfection."[74] Indeed, by the time the Springboks faced off against the all-powerful All Blacks in the championship final, whites and blacks alike were rooting together for their team and their country. Carlin notes that blacks "were seen all over South Africa happily sporting the symbol [Springbok jersey] of the old oppressors."[75] Mandela led by example, proudly wearing the green Springbok jersey. Blacks and whites, at least temporarily, were part of the same tribe.

The Springboks squeaked out a victory to claim the Rugby World Cup. As the trophy was presented to the winning team, the culmination of Mandela's efforts to unite the country (at least for the moment) was reached. He was able to use the Springboks as a way of developing South African civil religion. "The gods at that moment were Mandela and [Francois] Pienaar [the Afrikaner captain of the team]," Carlin writes, "the old man in green, crowned king of all South Africa, handing the cup to Pienaar, the young man in green, anointed that day as the spiritual head of born-again Afrikanerdom."[76] (See Fig. 5.3) One player described going down to a

Fig. 5.3 Nelson Mandela and Francois Pienaar.

large public celebration the night after the match, where he found whites and blacks "hugging and laughing and crying, late, late into the night."[77] The symbols and rituals of sport, like many religions, had brought about the *communitas* and "collective effervescence" that is so critical to our living harmoniously with one another. The particularities of our individuality (our jobs, social standing, even our race) melt away as we join into a single, undifferentiated sacred community.

Conclusion

Sports are forms of play that bring people together in powerful instances of *communitas* and "collective effervescence." Individuals test themselves in these sports, but players and spectators alike transcend concerns with the self. Through that transcendence they have an experience of the sacred collectivity that is the very basis of their culture and defines who they are. While Durkheim, Turner, Huizinga, and others provide us with theoretical approaches to understand this phenomenon, it is stories like those of soccer in the United Kingdom and rugby "Down Under" that reveal the true power of the communal experience of sport.

Discussion Questions

1. Does sport create community in a way similar to religion? If not, what is the difference?

2. What do we lose about religion when we reduce it to its sociological function?

3. Are there other elements of popular culture that function sociologically like sport and religion?

Glossary

anomie—the absence or loss of order and meaning.

civil religion—a set of beliefs, practices, and attitudes that takes the society or nation as its object of worship.

collective effervescence—the ecstatic state resulting from participation in communal ritual activity.

communitas—the experience of the loss of individuality into the collective.

homo ludens—refers to the intrinsic element of play in human beings.

sacrifice—the relinquishing of time, energy, or property (sometimes even one's life) for the greater good of the collective.

soul—that which individuals have at the core of their being that results in an identity with others in their community.

taboo—that which is powerful and dangerous, and from which most individuals are prohibited from having contact.

totem—something that serves as a physical representation of a collective.

6 Sport and the Moral Life

When people think about religion, they often connect it with morality—and for good reason. Religious traditions across the globe and throughout history have provided ethical codes of conduct and models of the moral life. These codes of conduct have listed important prohibitions (acts we should not do) and prescriptions (acts we should do) that allow us to live a moral life. In the Western world, we think most immediately of the Ten Commandments in the Bible. Though several of the commandments are about the individual's relationship to God, most are about human relationships with one another. Buddhism has a similar list in the Five Precepts—shorter in part because there is no God (in the Western sense) in Buddhism, so there is no reason to have rules about our relationship to God.

In Hinduism, the *Bhagavad Gita* provides us with the story of Arjuna who struggles with the question of whether or not to go into battle against fellow countrymen and even family. Arjuna becomes a model for Hindus in terms of how to think about moral obligations to others (including how to think about warfare). Likewise, figures such as the Buddha, Muhammad, Abraham, and Jesus provide models for moral living even if clear rules are not available. No set of prescriptions and proscriptions can cover all moral dilemmas, so these exemplary models can help us imagine how we should conduct ourselves in various situations. We also have negative models, such as in the case of David in Hebrew scripture. He sends Uriah into battle (where he is killed) so that David can have Uriah's wife Bathsheba.[1] While David is otherwise a hero in the Abrahamic traditions, here he serves as a negative model of the consequences of lust and envy.

While being religious certainly does not make one moral (and vice versa), there clearly is a connection between the two. At a minimum, religious traditions provide ethical codes and exemplars for moral life. If, then, sport functions like religion, does sport also provide such codes and exemplars for moral life? In this chapter we answer that question in the affirmative and provide case studies to support that answer. But first, we look more closely at the various ways we can think about morality.

Approaches to Morality

Though human beings have been thinking about moral issues for millennia, there really are a limited number of theoretical approaches to moral life. Here we will summarize these approaches, with special attention to how they might look in a religious context.

First, there is the rule-based or deontological approach. The Greek root of the word "deontology" (*deon*) means duty. So how are duty and rules related? Think of it this way: We could say that a merchant has a duty to treat a customer fairly (in other words, not to cheat the customer in some way). We can formulate this duty as a rule by saying: A merchant should treat every customer fairly. Here we can see that the rule entails a corresponding duty (or, a duty has an implicit rule).

We can have many rules or duties—hundreds perhaps, or even thousands. But we also may be able to reduce these many rules or duties to a handful or perhaps even one. For example, there is the Golden Rule. The Golden Rule requires that you treat others as you would like to be treated. Or, in its negative formulation, do not treat others in ways that you do not want to be treated. It is a nice way of getting at the essence of so many of our rules or duties. The eighteenth-century philosopher Immanuel Kant famously provided an extensive philosophical defense of something like the Golden Rule—what he called the Categorical Imperative. While the Categorical Imperative has a number of formulations, the first is the most common: "*Act only on that maxim* [principle] *through which you can at the same time will that it should become a universal law.*"[2] Take the example of going into a store and stealing something just because you want it. The principle here or maxim is that a person should take whatever he or she wants—regardless of whether or not the item taken is someone else's property. Certainly we would not want this principle or maxim to become universal law (applicable to everyone). Such a universal law would make the concept of property rationally impossible (and, consequently, would make civil society impossible). The actions that it would promote also would treat others (those from whom one would be taking property) as a mere means to one's own ends (happiness, satisfaction, etc.). We should never treat others as merely means to our ends. This is the second formulation of the Categorical Imperative: "*Act in such a way that you always treat humanity, whether in your own person or in the person of any other, never simply as a means, but always at the same time as an end.*"[3]

Though few religious traditions rely on Kant to explain their moral teachings, these teachings often focus on rules or duties that the adherent must follow. Indeed, in a religious context there may not be any reasons for following the rules or fulfilling the duties other than because the sacred texts, foundational figures, or traditions tell you to do so. When the Bible says that you should not steal, there may be multiple reasons for the prohibition. But for many people, the primary and most important reason why you should not steal is because the text tells you not to do so. When Jesus says to love your neighbor as yourself, you need not reason through the Categorical Imperative to convince yourself to do as Jesus says. You follow the rule and fulfill your duty to your neighbor because Jesus says so. Still, it may be that some kind of Kantian justification lies behind our rational assent to religiously inspired moral rules and duties.

The second general approach to thinking about morality is consequentialism—a focus not on the nature or character of a rule or duty but on the consequences that may result from any particular action or set of actions. Utilitarianism is the classic example of a consequentialist approach to ethics. While nineteenth-century British philosophers Jeremy Bentham and John Stuart Mill are the most recognizable utilitarian thinkers, consequentialist thinking certainly is hardwired into the human mind. We all have thought about the consequences of our actions when trying to determine the moral merits of the actions themselves. What utilitarian theorists argue for, however, is that the consequences are the *only* means by which to determine moral value. In other words, regardless of how we may assess the moral worth of our actions (even if we believe ourselves to be Kantians), an assessment of the consequences is ultimately how we do it. And, to take it a step further, an assessment of the consequences is how we *should* assess the moral worth of our actions.

While utilitarians may state their most fundamental principle in slightly different ways, one formulation is fairly standard: A moral act is one that achieves the greatest happiness of the greatest number of people.[4] Much has been written about how to define happiness. Mill, for example, famously argues against the notion that it can be reduced to mere sensual pleasure—that, in fact, there are pleasures of emotion and intellect that would lead us to reject a base hedonism. Much too has been written about how much weight should be given to the happiness of the greatest *number* of people. For example (so the famous example goes), if it were the case that the torturing of one child brought great happiness to 100 people and nobody was disturbed or saddened (other than, of course, the child), would it be moral to torture the child? We often make trade-offs when making moral decisions and performing moral actions, but where do we draw the line between promoting the happiness of the greatest number of people and protecting the rights and dignity of individuals? Here is where the Kantians enter the picture again, insisting that the moral worth of an action cannot be based merely on its consequences—because such a moral perspective could lead to all sorts of horrendous moral decisions (e.g., the tortured child used as a mere means for the happiness of everyone else). On the other hand, utilitarians are puzzled by Kantians who insist on acting according to principle and from a sense of duty in spite of the consequence. The utilitarians counter with an example from Kant himself. Imagine that you are hiding an innocent person in your home. Someone comes to the door looking for the innocent person. This person is angry and has an ax—apparently for the purpose of killing the innocent person. Do you act according to principle, the universal law that we ought not to lie? Kant claims that you should *not* lie. But should you not consider the consequences and thus lie to the person at the door? Intuitively, we tend to think that lying in this case is okay and may even be *the* moral action in this case. Utilitarians thus claim that Kant's answer demonstrates a critical flaw in his theory.

The third general approach—virtue theory—is very different from the first two approaches. Whereas the first two approaches try to provide criteria by which we can evaluate whether or not an action is moral, virtue theory wants us to think about the kind of virtuous habits and capacities we might have in order to become the type of person we want to be. Even more, virtue theory asks the question of what constitutes human happiness and how a virtuous life can contribute to it.

Virtue theory is most associated with the ethics of Aristotle. He defined happiness as *the* good of life, for it is the only good that is pursued for its own sake and not as a means to another good.[5] For example, health is a good. But we seek health so that we can avoid pain or go for a bicycle ride. Health is good in itself, but it also is something we pursue for other goods. Such is the case too with money or food or shelter. Happiness, however, is different. We do not seek happiness in order to achieve something else. We seek happiness only in order to be happy.

Of course, identifying happiness as the good of life begs the question of what constitutes happiness. Like Mill, Aristotle is not advocating for any kind of hedonist version of happiness. Human happiness for him is connected with that which makes human beings distinct. And what makes human beings distinct from other creatures? Reason. So, for Aristotle, the good life is one lived according to reason and in pursuit of the goals or goods available to a human being. Virtues, then, are skills or capacities that allow us to live such a life, and vices are shortcomings or character flaws that get in the way.

What the goals or goods of life are may vary from culture to culture. In fact, contemporary ethicists often have treated Aristotle as a foundational figure of communitarianism—an approach to moral theory that grounds moral rules, goods, or virtues in the life of a community. From this perspective, there are no universal moral imperatives or duties (Kantians) or principles (utilitarians) that cut across cultures and time, because what constitutes the good life and the virtuous person will vary from community to community. What Aristotle provides, according to communitarians, is not a set of absolute moral rules, duties, or principles, but a general framework for thinking about how moral life works.[6]

The lack of specific criteria or principles helps to explain why it is so important to have exemplary models of the virtuous person so that a community can have an understanding of what a moral life is like. As mentioned previously, figures like Jesus, Muhammad, and the Buddha fill this role. Somewhat closer to ordinary human beings, saints also are exemplary models of the moral life. "Saints and moral exemplars," Lamin Sanneh notes, "define and demonstrate the hopes, desires, practices, and moral ideals of their community. The lives of these persons provide inspiration and guidance, typically providing devotees with help on complex moral demands and personal struggles."[7]

As one might expect, the lived experience of moral life hardly falls into these three distinct approaches. Moral life is much too complex. Any given moral situation can be understood and analyzed from multiple perspectives. Let us return to the story of Arjuna in the Indian classic *Bhagavad Gita*. As a member of the royal and warrior caste, Arjuna is faced with the difficult task of leading his men into battle. The task is all the more difficult because the battle is to be waged against an enemy that includes Arjuna's friends and family. How can he be part of such bloodshed? How can he harm or even kill those for whom he has affection? "Those I do not wish to slay," Arjuna says, "even if I myself am slain. Not even for the kingdom of the three worlds: how much less for a kingdom of the earth!"[8]

In the midst of his moral dilemma, Krishna (a manifestation of Brahman or God) appears to Arjuna to explain to him why he must go into battle. In the reasons that

Krishna provides, we can find all three of the approaches to thinking about moral action. First, Krishna emphasizes the fact that it is Arjuna's duty to go to war. There is an order to society and rules based on where one falls in that order. In response to Arjuna's claim that the righteous path would be to preserve life, Krishna insists that "to forgo this fight for righteousness is to forgo their duty and honour; is to fall into transgression."[9] He later adds that "he who does holy work ... because it ought to be done, and surrenders selfishness and thought of reward, his work is pure, and is peace."[10] One simply cannot allow negative consequences to get in the way of fulfilling one's duty. One simply cannot ignore his or her duty just because of the emotional anguish that duty may cause. To will that we do our duty unless it makes us feel bad would make the very concept of duty impossible (i.e., the very concept of duty makes no sense if we simply are going to act according to our feelings). Thus, Krishna here provides us with a deontological argument.

Second, Krishna argues that ultimately even the deaths of the enemy will produce the greater good. Those who may perish clearly have a karmic debt that they must pay. As a consequence of dying in battle, they compensate for or burn off bad karma, allowing them to be reborn in a more fortuitous situation in their next life. So, while Arjuna will see his enemies die, they do not really die. They simply are exchanging one life for another. Krishna says, "As a man leaves an old garment and puts on one that is new, the Spirit [the individual soul] leaves his mortal body and then puts on one that is new."[11] Despite what Arjuna sees as the negative consequences of going into battle, we find out that the consequences ultimately will be good. Clearly we have a kind of utilitarian calculus at work, with key religious concepts like karma and reincarnation helping us work through the calculation.

Finally, Krishna challenges Arjuna to think about what kind of person he would be if he neglected his duty in this case. He tells Arjuna of the honor that will be received from fighting in the battle, but also the shame if he does not fight. "The great warriors will say that thou hast run from the battle through fear," Krishna argues. "And thine enemies will speak of thee in contemptuous words of ill-will and derision, pouring scorn upon thy courage. Can there be for a warrior a more shameful fate?"[12] Certainly Arjuna does not want to be the kind of person shamed in this way. He wants to exhibit the virtue of courage, so that he can be the kind of honorable leader who is praised by his community. Happiness, then, will be achieved through such virtuous action.

In the end, we see that there are multiple reasons for Arjuna to join the battle. They are (at a minimum) duty (he *ought* to do so), utility (deaths are necessary in order to lead to new and better lives), and virtue (by acting courageously, he will be the kind of person he wants to be). We see here how religion can be a vehicle for moral reasoning—a very important one historically and still for many people today.

Morality and Sport(s)

Just as the morality in religion can be approached in different ways, so can sport be looked at from multiple ethical perspectives.

There certainly are a lot of rules in sports. Various prescriptions and proscriptions help to ensure that games or matches are played fairly by all involved and that victories and records are earned legitimately. In organized sporting events, officials are on hand to guarantee that the rules are followed. But even when officials are involved, the participants are expected to respect the game and their opponents—to realize that the game cannot be played and true competition engaged in unless the rules are followed. Consequently, they should feel morally obligated to abide by the rules. Of course, for many people who participate in sport, there are no officials to ensure that the rules are followed. In a "pick up" basketball game, players call fouls. In a friendly tennis match, each player determines if a hit ball is in or out. Millions of games or matches are played every year in which players regulate the games or matches themselves. In short, they feel a duty to play fairly.

Violating the rules of the game makes the game logically impossible to play. The cheater also treats his or her fellow players as simply means to his or her ends. In both senses, our duty to the rules of the game can be seen as an example of Kant's Categorical Imperative. Robert L. Simon puts it well when he writes:

> Thus, cheating, at least in paradigm cases, involves violating a public system of rules that every participant in an activity may reasonably assume will govern the activity in question in order to obtain benefits for oneself, one's teammates, or others for whom one cares. The cheating is wrong because it could not be reasonably accepted by other participants in the activity [could not be a universal law]. Cheaters disregard the legitimate interest that other competitors have in a fair contest and may use other competitors as mere means to an end or tools for their own benefit.[13]

When the rules are followed and a game or match is conducted fairly, we most likely will maximize the happiness of the participants and the spectators. Few people enjoy playing a game in which the rules are consistently and continuously violated. In addition, spectators enjoy contests that are played fairly by all those involved. Thus, the goal of promoting the happiness of participants and spectators is intrinsic to the rules of sport. In this sense, we can say that sport is subject to the principle of utility.

Perhaps the best way of thinking about the morality of sport, however, is from the Aristotelian perspective. Alasdair MacIntyre provides us with a useful Aristotelian framework for our purposes.[14] He notes that societies are made up of various practices that are critical to its proper functioning and to the lives of its members. Some practices are clearly indispensable for societies to function, such as those in the political arena. But practices also can be on a smaller scale—such as those involving religion, community organizations, and even sport. In order to succeed in any of these practices, a person needs to exhibit certain virtues. While we tend today to think of virtues in strictly moral terms, that need not be the case. Virtues may be simply excellences that allow someone to succeed in a particular practice. In short, virtues are particular skills and capacities that help us achieve our goals.

Perhaps an example from the sporting world can help. To be a good athlete, a person needs to exhibit a number of virtues. Among these (though this certainly is not a complete list) are perseverance, patience, courage (at times), dedication, and teamwork (and all the virtues associated with working well with other people). By cultivating these virtues in the context of a particular sport, a person is in a position (given that he or she has learned the basic skills of the sport) to succeed or even excel at that sport. In doing so, he or she achieves the *internal* goods of that sport. These internal goods are playing the sport well and the happiness or satisfaction one gets from playing the sport well. Of course, if one becomes really good at a sport, he or she also may receive various *external* goods—ranging from ribbons awarded to children to large financial rewards for exceptional professional athletes. But these external goods are not intrinsic to sport and should not be confused with the internal goods that can be obtained.[15]

Community is critical to our success in almost any practice. Take golf as an example. We need people in our community to teach us the basic physical skills to be successful at golf, but we also need them to help us learn and cultivate the kind of virtues that will allow us to excel. These mentors or experts often teach us just by being who they are. As excellent golfers, they become models for how we should conduct ourselves. Determining who is a worthy mentor or expert is a function of how well such individuals engage in certain practices—so, for a golfer, it will be someone who can shoot a very good score and, more importantly, shows respect for the game by conducting herself in a virtuous manner. But the standards or norms always are community generated and sustained. These standards or norms determine what participants can do in any particular practice and what the measures of success are. Practices like playing jazz or tending a garden may have more subjective measures of success (in particular, requiring experts to make judgments about the skill of the musician or the beauty of the garden), while practices like golf may have more objective measures of success (e.g., one's golf score). While it may seem like the former demands a larger role for the community in determining measures of success, the latter still includes a key role for the community that determines what makes a golf score very good and, more importantly, what makes someone a virtuous or honorable player of golf. Always playing the ball where it lies, always writing the correct score on your card, and always being gracious in victory or defeat are more than rules—they are community standards and norms.

The standards and norms as well as the measures of success that the community affirms are part of a tradition related to the practice in question. Golf has a tradition that dates back centuries (to fifteenth-century Scotland) that includes the development and history of rules of the game, changes in equipment (necessitating changes in the rules in some cases), great tournaments that have been staged every year for decades (and more), and exemplary (virtuous) players who serve as models for all golfers.

Again, when we think of practices and virtues, communities, and traditions, we need not view these in narrow moral terms. However, they *can* have a moral dimension. In fact, many people believe that sport has an intrinsic moral dimension and that it can contribute to the moral development of those who participate in a wide range of sports. Ethicist Randolph Feezell summarizes this MacIntyrean perspective well:

> Given the definitions of a practice and a virtue, it is easy to see why the character building view is so plausible. The young athlete needs to develop a keen sense of himself and his abilities in relation to the traditions of his sport. His development or simply his participation requires a certain honesty about himself, a respect for coaches who embody the tradition, a sense of who deserves or merits playing time, a feeling about the need for cooperation to achieve shared goals, courage in the face of failing to achieve standards, and persistence or determination in the attempt to achieve his goals. Since an athlete will participate in a variety of practices in life, if he really acquires or exercises justice, honesty, courage, and determination, because they enable him to achieve goods internal to his sport, he will benefit throughout life.[16]

This idea that sport prepares us for life may be as old as sport itself.

Sociologist Harry Edwards writes about what he calls the dominant creed in American sports, but much of what he says about sport is applicable in other countries. This creed has seven central themes: character development (cultivating loyalty, "clean living," altruism, and much more), discipline, competition, physical fitness, mental fitness, religiosity, and nationalism.[17] In helping the athlete develop these qualities, sport is seen to prepare him or her for life in the broader society. "In short," Edwards concludes, "competition in sport is claimed to be of value in *preparing the athlete for life*, and in *providing him an opportunity for personal advancement* in the greater society."[18]

Much like religion, sport in this perspective is an institution that prepares participants for a successful and moral life in society and promotes identification with and support for the nation. But like many institutions, its *promise* of results may differ from the *results* that are produced. As Feezell concludes, "The best that can be said for this view is that sport can help build a part of character, especially if coaches and parents are good moral educators."[19]

Of course, what Feezell concludes about sport can be applicable to many of our institutions—including religious institutions. They have a great capacity for moral education; however, their success will depend on those people who run the institutions. But even if sport is no better or worse than other institutions in this regard, it still is the case that sport plays an affirming or supporting role in regard to the dominant moral environment (the ethos) of a culture. Much of Edwards's work is directed toward making this case. In short, Edwards argues that sport reaffirms the dominant values of the culture in which it exists. He writes that "sport affords the fan an opportunity to *reaffirm the established values and beliefs defining acceptable means and solutions to central problems in the secular realm of everyday societal life*."[20] The fan confronts a world that often is difficult—with challenges and obstacles that can be extremely frustrating. But there is a kind of identity between the fan's life and the sports that he or she follows and loves. "Because fans *believe* these sports ... to be governed by the same values prescribing acceptable conduct for themselves in the larger society," Edwards claims, "these sports become microcosmic illustrations that this system of values continues to be effective in efforts toward goal achievement."[21] Thus, "the institution of sport ... serves a pattern—or value—maintenance function for the general society, and thus sustains the fan's belief in the viability of social values through his involvement."[22] Here is a communitarian perspective—with the rules and values of sport reflecting those of the community in which it is found and conversely helping to establish and support those rules and values.

While religion, like sport, reflects the values of the community, it also serves as a critique of society. Religion provides resources for challenging the dominant norms or ethos of a society. While someone like Karl Marx may have viewed religion as a mere instrument of the oppressors to maintain an unjust social order, it is impossible to deny the liberating role that religion can play in the beliefs and actions of those who have fought for justice. One need look no further than the role of religion in the thought and work of figures like Mahatma Gandhi or Rev. Dr. Martin Luther King, Jr. Even among ordinary religious adherents, their traditions provide resources for every-day critiques of the world around them—critiques that spur them to seek changes for the better.

Simon makes the case for seeing sport as a form of external critique of a culture. He rejects what he calls "reductionism," in which "values in sports are reflections and perhaps reinforcers of values in the broader society."[23] He argues that sport maintains some independence from the culture, and thus it (like religion) can be a resource for criticism of the dominant norms and ethos:

> For example, if dominant ideologies within a society were to devalue excellence and challenge, the values expressed in good sports contests, conceived of as mutual quests for excellence through challenge, would conflict with rather than reflect dominant social values. If so, sports might be an important source of moral values and even have a significant role to play in moral education ....[24]

We can imagine other instances in which the values of sport (loyalty, hard work, discipline, sportsmanship, etc.) may be resources to challenge the kind of values and behavior in the society at large. For example, the excessive individualism often associated with the culture of the United States might be critiqued by the loyalty and teamwork associated with sport. Thus, Simon concludes, "the values found in sport can conflict with those dominant in the wider society, and so are not mere reflections of prevailing social morality."[25] Simon even goes so far as to claim that the "inner morality of sports" can have "justificatory force independent of political ideologies and even provide grounds for their revision. Maybe sports, when properly conducted, rather than merely reflecting external social and political values, can provide a justification for changing such external values for the better."[26]

So sport, like religion, is an institution that includes many rules and duties and produces many positive consequences. It is an institution that may contribute to the moral development of athletes and even those who are spectators. It provides a wide range of practices in which participants and spectators can cultivate virtues—many of which are moral in nature. Like religion, sport plays a role in affirming the most important moral values of a society. Like religion, sport also can serve as a critique of those values and perhaps even be an agent for change. Perhaps Simon sums up our perspective best when he writes:

> [S]ports, properly conducted, express, illustrate, and perhaps reinforce values of enduring human significance. Through sports, we can learn to overcome adversity and appreciate excellence. We can learn to value activities for their own sake, apart from any intrinsic reward they provide, and learn to appreciate the contributions of others, even when we are on opposing sides. Through sports we can develop and express moral virtues and demonstrate the importance of dedication, integrity, fairness, and courage.[27]

Golf: Rules, Conventions, and Exemplary Actions

Following the Rules

Golf is a sport with many rules. When most participants (certainly 99 percent or more) go out to play a round of golf, there are no officials to enforce the rules. There are only the player and her playing partners. And golf is the kind of sport where the player can end up out of sight of her fellow players, and thus there are many opportunities for violating the rules. However, most players feel an obligation or duty to follow the rules—for doing so is part of what it means to play and to respect the game.

Sometimes professional golfers are put in a position where they must report violations of the rules on themselves, even when they may be the only person to witness the violation. A recent example involves Brian Davis. At the 2010 Verizon Heritage golf tournament, Davis ended up tied with Jim Furyk after seventy-two holes. In order to determine the winner, the players proceeded to a playoff. Whichever player could score better than the other one on the next hole would win the tournament. In the event of a tie, they would continue to play holes until there was a winner. On the first playoff hole, Davis missed the putting green on his approach shot and his ball ended up in the midst of grass, twigs, and reeds. As he began to hit his next shot, he thought he saw his club move a loose reed behind the ball. He immediately called over an official and asked that they review the shot on slow-motion video replay. The replay confirmed that the reed had been moved, and according to rule 13.4, Davis was assessed a two-stroke penalty. The penalty effectively ended Davis' chances, and Furyk went on to win the hole and the tournament.

Davis had never won a Professional Golfers Association (PGA) event. He certainly had powerful incentives to ignore the violation—attaining a life-long dream and a substantial financial reward being among them. As reporter Jay Busbee summarized the situation: "Imagine standing on the edge of achieving your life's dream. You make a small mistake that will cost you your dream—but if you don't say anything, you might just get away with it. Would you own up to the mistake, or would you keep quiet and hope for the best?"[28]

So, why did Davis call the penalty on himself? Like most people, Davis probably follows rules because those are the rules. We often do not even think about why the rules are the way they are. The official rulebook of the United States Golf Association, in this sense, is like a sacred text that golfers follow. Whatever that book says, that is what we must do. As Davis said, "The rules are the rules."[29] It is unlikely that Davis ever thought through a Kantian justification of the rules, but certainly there is one. It is clear that only by following the rules is a game like golf even possible, so following the rules places a certain burden (a duty or obligation) on every player who wishes to call himself or herself a golfer.

But Davis' commitment to the rules also extends to how he thinks about himself. As Davis said, "I could not have lived with myself if I had not [drawn attention to the violation]."[30] He would add: "I am proud to uphold the values that my parents taught me and I teach my kids the same stuff. Be honest in your sport and in your life and simply do your best. That's all you can do."[31] Here we see a concern not about following rules, but about being a person of a certain character—a person who can be a credit to his parents and an exemplary model for his children. Davis most likely is not a virtue theorist, but he nicely illustrates an important element of Aristotle's approach to ethics. He makes explicit the intertwining of sport with the ethos of the broader society, indicating values in the society that are reflected in sport and showing how sport can help to reinforce those values. His story also is an example of how the actions of an athlete can serve as a critique of the sporting world. As one writer notes, "Davis' self-imposed violation [is] something inconceivable in most other sports, where competitors take pride in getting every edge they can."[32] In fact, we can see Davis' act as an implicit critique of many cultures, where competing to get ahead often leads us to act immorally.

Players, officials, and reporters praised Davis for his action—using words like "respect," "admire," and "honor" to describe what he did. As Busbee concludes, "the guy gave away a chance at winning his first-ever PGA Tour event because he knew that in golf, honesty is more important than victory. It's a tough lesson to learn, but here's hoping he gets accolades … that more than make up for the victory he surrendered."[33] In short, there is a certain ethical code as a golfer, and in a very difficult situation Davis was able to live up to that code. He is a better golfer and person for having done so—and thus is an exemplary model not just for his children but also for all of us.

The "Concession"

Jack Nicklaus is one of the greatest players in the history of golf. But one of his greatest moments had nothing to do with a shot that he made, but with a shot that he prevented a fellow competitor from making.

In 1969, Nicklaus was in the prime of his career. In September of that year, he was in England with a team of American golfers to compete in the Ryder Cup—an annual competition between American golfers and British golfers.[34] On the British team was Tony Jacklin, who had become a national hero by winning the British Open only a couple of months before. The fierce competition between the two sides came down to the last match and the last hole—Nicklaus against Jacklin in front of a British crowd desperately rooting for its countryman to pull out the victory.

Nicklaus and Jacklin came to the last hole tied. On the green, Nicklaus faced a four-and-a-half foot putt for par. Jacklin had two feet left for par. Nicklaus stepped up to his putt, knowing that a miss very likely would give Jacklin an excellent opportunity to win the match and the Ryder Cup for the British. As Nicklaus said, "I was terrified. I wasn't just putting for me, I was putting for my country."[35] He made the putt, and this is where the story gets interesting. If Jacklin were to make his putt, the match with Nicklaus would end in a draw and both sides in the competition would finish with sixteen points. A tie. Ryder Cup rules, however, state that in the case of a tie the side that previously won the Cup would retain it. In this case, it would mean that the United States would retain the Cup. Of course, if Jacklin were to miss the putt, the United States would finish ahead of the British team and have a clear victory.

Fig. 6.1 Jacklin (left) and Nicklaus (right) shaking hands after Ryder Cup match in 1969.

Immediately after making his putt, Nicklaus picked up Jacklin's marker (a marker is used so that a player can pick up his ball while another competitor putts) and conceded Jacklin's putt. Nicklaus then went to Jacklin and reportedly said, "I was sure you would hole the putt. But I was not prepared to see you miss."[36] (See Fig. 6.1) In short, Nicklaus chose a tie rather than to have to watch Jacklin possibly miss the short putt in front of the British crowd. Years later Nicklaus recalled, "Jacklin had won the British Open, he was a national hero. I felt like the U.S. was going to retain the Cup either way. I didn't think it was in the spirit of the game to make Jacklin have a chance to miss a 2-footer to lose the matches in front of his fans."[37]

Nicklaus's act of sportsmanship was praised widely at the time, even if some of his teammates did not agree with the concession of the putt. Since then, Nicklaus and Jacklin have become friends, and the picking up of the marker has been referred to simply as "The Concession." By rule, Nicklaus could have made Jacklin attempt the putt. But the rules also allowed Nicklaus to concede the putt. By doing so, Nicklaus showed that sportsmanship is more important than winning at all costs and that being remembered as a good person is just as important as being remembered as a great golfer. In this way, Nicklaus honored the "spirit of the game."

Both Brian Davis and Jack Nicklaus show us that rules only get us so far. Just as in religious traditions, rules need to be embodied in the actions and attitudes of practitioners—particularly those who are faithful to the tradition or sport and who become exemplary models for all of us.

Sport and Living Together Morally

It should be clear that much of what sport can do (or is believed to be able to do) is moral in nature. Bringing people together, promoting teamwork and mutual respect, and creating peace are all moral endeavors. To this extent, sport functions much like many religions do. Even if the world's religions often are used by adherents to foster division and conflict, every religion posits peace and harmony as an ultimate aim. Many local, national, and international organizations explicitly promote sport as a way of achieving similar moral aims.

The United Nations, the International Olympic Committee, and beyond

The first International Day of Sport for Development and Peace was celebrated on April 6, 2014—a day established by the United Nations General Assembly (by consensus) the previous fall. The day probably went unrecognized by most countries and few people knew about it. But the establishment of the day certainly is significant in that a major international organization (in fact, the most important one) acknowledged the role that sport can play in creating a better, more peaceful world. As Vuk Jeremic, the president of the 67th session of the General Assembly, said, "Sport can be a powerful handmaiden for peace and reconciliation. It can bring us closer through shared celebration of achievements of universal appeal and attraction."[38]

The United Nations Office on Sport for Development and Peace (UNOSDP) was created at the beginning of this century with a mission to "promote sport as an innovative and efficient tool in advancing the United Nations' goals, missions and values. Through advocacy, partnership facilitation, policy work, project support and diplomacy, UNOSDP strives to maximize the contribution of sport and physical activity to help create a safer, more secure, more sustainable, more equitable future."[39]

The connection between sport and the aims and values of the United Nations was demonstrated further by an April 2014 agreement between the United Nations and the International Olympic Committee (IOC). The agreement affirmed that the two organizations "share the same values of contributing to a better and peaceful world through sport."[40] IOC President Thomas Bach remarked, "Sport can change the world, but it cannot change the world alone. When placing sport at the service of humankind, we need and we want partnerships with other players in society. The Olympic Movement is willing and ready to make its contribution to the most laudable efforts of the United Nations to maintain and build peace and to bring along social change."[41] UN Secretary-General Ban Ki-moon concurred with this estimation of the power of sport to bring about positive change in the world. He said, "Sport has great power to bring people together, improve public health and promote teamwork and mutual respect."[42]

Though not as powerful as the United Nations and the IOC, other examples of the ethical efficacy of sports organizations abound. PeacePlayers International (PPI), founded in 2001, is based on the premise that "children who play together can learn to live together....Through a groundbreaking peacebuilding-and-leadership development curriculum, PeacePlayers International uses basketball to bring children together and teach them proven tactics for improving their communities." PPI identifies its mission as "To unite, educate and inspire young people in divided communities through basketball."[43] Similarly, Football Beyond Borders (FBB) "uses the power of football [soccer] to inspire young people to achieve their goals and make their voice heard." More important for our point, FBB "also run[s] international exchange and football programmes focused on breaking down barriers between individuals from different and often antagonistic backgrounds."[44]

In reflecting on the UN agreement with the IOC, Secretary-General Ban noted that sport can "be used to bridge cultural, religious, ethnic and social divides."[45] The ability of sport to help people overcome cultural, religious, ethnic, and social divisions is well known. The Olympics certainly help to promote the overcoming of differences—differences that otherwise lead to misunderstanding, conflict, and even war. The World Cup in football (soccer) also achieves a similar aim. Perhaps no recent story illustrates this power of sport better, however, than the story of American Nick Pugliese and his soccer odyssey in Afghanistan.

An American Soccer Player in Afghanistan

The United States has a checkered history in Afghanistan. It has taken sides in numerous internal conflicts, and much of its rhetoric against Islamic extremism undoubtedly has offended many Muslims (even moderate ones). As a consequence, there are many people in Afghanistan who have a very negative opinion of the US government and its citizens—perhaps even hating them. But a recent story about one American athlete shows us how sport can counter and transcend the dominant ethos in a culture—even when that dominant ethos is very much shaped by the powerful passions of politics and religion.

Nick Pugliese was captain of his Williams College (United States) soccer team. After he graduated in 2012, he took a job with Roshan, a telecommunications company in Afghanistan. Desperately wanting to play soccer again, Pugliese sought out informal "pick up" games in Kabul—not an easy task for an American in Afghanistan. The security concerns of his company for an American walking around the streets of Kabul were significant. For Pugliese, however, playing soccer again was worth the danger involved.

While security concerns were an issue, finding games to play in was not. Soccer is incredibly popular in Afghanistan—both in terms of players and fans. With greater access to television and broadcasts of the game from around the world, many Afghans have become fans of Premier League (United Kingdom) and La Liga (Spain) teams. Fan loyalty has even rearranged more traditional divisions among the population. Pugliese reports one of his friends telling him, "We used to sit in our college classroom based on ethnicity. The Pashtun over here, the Tajik over there. Now we sit split by who is Real Madrid and who is Barcelona [two prominent teams in La Liga]."[46]

Pugliese quickly became a regular participant in many local matches. His skills soon led him to an amateur league team and then, through a teammate, to a spot on the Ferozi Football Club professional team in the Kabul Premier League. Once he joined the Ferozi FC team, he quit his job with Roshan so he could dedicate his time to soccer and his teammates.

Through his journey, Pugliese has experienced the ways in which sport can break down cultural, political, and religious walls that lead to suspicion and animosity on the individual level and violence and war on the social level. As he says, "I met people through football I never would have otherwise. Soccer opened the door."[47] He adds, "The interesting question to me is why I've been accepted as a member of the community in spite of or because of my status as an American. Through these soccer teammates, I've become part of the community."[48] Becoming part of the community includes hanging out with teammates and friends at their houses, sharing meals, and talking about cultural differences. The creation of community not only is an important sociological function of sport and religion (as we saw in the previous chapter), but the creation of community also is a moral project.

Pugliese joined his teammates and friends in rooting for the Afghanistan team in the South Asian Football Federation Championship—a tournament that the Afghans won in 2013. Pugliese says, "It was absolutely massive. I was watching it with my friends and as soon as they won we took to the streets, chanting and dancing, pretty much clogged the roads."[49]

As of the summer of 2014, it was unclear where Pugliese's soccer career was headed. But it is clear that the game provided him and the Afghans with an opportunity to see beyond the cultural, political, and religious differences that they had and to treat one another with tolerance and respect. The sport provided an important context in which people could develop more moral attitudes and behaviors toward one another. The respect that the players had for one another and the decency with which they treated one another were not a result of Kantian moral reflection or utilitarian calculus (though it would be easy to make a deontological or consequentialist argument here). It simply was part of the game. As a cultural practice, soccer for Pugliese and his teammates required them to see beyond skin color, religion, and nationality. The game required that they only see their teammates as teammates. It required them to see the other as a brother, ultimately part of one reality (the team) to which all are committed. In this sense, soccer functioned for Pugliese and his Afghan friends much like religion when religion functions at its best.

Conclusion

At the start of this chapter, we asked whether or not sport might function like religion in providing resources to guide us in our moral decision-making and to facilitate our moral development. The case studies provided here are just a very few that help to demonstrate that sport can indeed function like religion in this way. As with any institution, however, so much depends on those who work in and preserve these institutions. Famous cheaters like bicyclist Lance Armstrong can be found in any institution. Our point is simply that, at its best, sport can have a positive impact on our moral lives.

Discussion Questions

1. Are there universal moral principles or rules? Does religion teach these to us? Does sport teach these to us?
2. Do sports provide us with moral lessons? What are they?
3. How do we become morally good people? What role does religion play? Can sport play the same role?
4. Can sport lead to peace? To what extent is sport similar to or different from religion in regard to peace?

Glossary

categorical imperative—Immanuel Kant's famous formulation of the universal ethical principle; the first formulation is: *Act only on that maxim* [principle] *through which you can at the same time will that it should become a universal law.*

communitarianism—an approach to ethics that views rules and norms as relative to particular communities.

consequentialism—the general idea that acts are judged to be morally good or bad depending on their consequences.

deontological ethics—an approach to ethics that emphasizes duty and the determination of universal moral principles.

practices—social activities that are connected to the history and traditions of a society and that can be performed better or worse depending on the virtues embodied by the practitioners.

utilitarianism—an approach to ethics that claims that morally good actions are those that lead to the greatest happiness of the greatest number of people.

virtue theory—an approach to ethics that focuses on the moral development of the individual through the inculcation and practice of moral virtues.

virtues—excellences of conduct that allow one to achieve the good(s) of particular practices.

Thinking Critically about Religion and Sport

While religious beliefs, practices, and institutions have very positive impacts on the lives of individuals and societies, they also can work in destructive ways as well. Human history is filled with criticisms of the negative effects of religion—with the current "New Atheist" movement just the most recent manifestation.

If sport functions like religion, then sport might have negative effects like religion has. Sport then might be subject to the same kind of criticisms that have been leveled against religion. In this chapter we look at some modern (nineteenth century to today) criticisms of religion and sport and see how the ways in which sport functions like a religion can be the same ways that lead to problems for individuals and groups. In particular, we look at the difficult social problems connected with economic class and race to see how sport is implicated in both.

Marx and the Marxist Approach

Karl Marx (1818–1883) describes religion as the "*opium* of the people."[1] Along with his frequent coauthor Frederick Engels (1820–1895), he argues that the character of a society is fundamentally shaped by the way in which it produces what it needs and how it organizes people through those means of production. This fundamental economic base then gives rise to the superstructure. This superstructure is what we call culture. It includes art, religion, law, literature, and philosophy (social or political most importantly). In these various cultural manifestations we can find the dominant ideology of a culture, that core set of interconnected beliefs and values that shape a society. These beliefs and values are taken for granted by almost everyone in a culture. Rarely are they criticized, and thus rarely do they need to be defended.

Marx claims that the ideology of a culture is not neutral in regard to the various groups or economic classes in that society. Ideology tends to support or justify the unequal distribution of goods and wealth. In other words, ideology tends to justify the superior position of the "haves" (those with wealth) against the "have nots" (those without wealth). This makes sense because it is the "haves" who are in control of the means of production—not only for the most basic necessities of life, but also the means of cultural production. The "haves" control art, religion, literature, philosophy, and much

Portions of this chapter are reprinted (with some revision) from Eric Bain-Selbo's *Game Day and God: Football, Faith, and Politics in the American South* (2009) by permission of Mercer University Press (Macon, Georgia).

more. If all the elements in a culture tell people (in the newspaper, at the theater, on the radio station, etc.) that poverty is a natural part of any society, then a social order free from poverty seems like a fantasy. Such a notion is not even worth considering.

We might wonder, then, why the "have nots" put up with such a situation. The reason is that they too often fail to realize that the ideology and the elements of culture are simply human creations that serve some interests more than others. The "have nots" see the ideology and the elements of culture as natural and obvious parts of the universe—not subject to refutation or even questioning. "Alienation" is the word that Marxists use to describe this condition in which people create a culture (along with its accompanying ideology) that they then do not recognize as their creation. In short, they are alienated from the products of their consciousness.

From a Marxist perspective, religion is a classic example of such alienation and of how cultural institutions come to serve the hegemonic aims of the ruling class or classes. The claim here is that the overwhelming majority of people fail to see religion as a human construction that serves some people better than others. For them, the central elements of religion (supernatural realms like heaven and hell, the existence of God, etc.) are seen as essential parts of the universe. Moral laws (handed down by God or the gods) also are understood as constitutive elements of the universe. This is the process of reification. The moral laws of the universe are not simply socially constructed (imposed perhaps by the "haves") and thus subject to debate. Because they have a "supernatural" origin, these laws are "real" in a way that human laws can never be.

Let us look at the example of stealing in the Ten Commandments in the Jewish and Christian traditions. The Ten Commandments are not human law. They are God's laws, literally written onto stone tablets with God's own hand. No law could be more certain or more real than those laws carved into stone. The commandment against stealing protects the property of the "haves" because the "have nots" fear an eternity in hell if they break God's law (and, of course, the "haves" also have police and armies to guard their stuff). The threat of hell, however, still may not be enough for the "have nots" to accept economic and social disparity. Fortunately (in a sense), religion offers one important consolation. Despite the struggles of living as a "have not," as long as one passively accepts the status quo one at least can look forward to an eternal reward in heaven.

Another powerful example involves the caste system in India, a system that ceased to have great influence only in the twentieth century. In the caste system (as traditionally understood), people are born into one of four castes—Brahmins (the priestly caste), Kshatriya (the warrior and ruler caste), Vaisya (traders and skilled laborers), or Sudra (unskilled workers).[2] Brahmins are at the top of the hierarchy, and Sudras are at the bottom. Wealth and power in the society are more concentrated at the top of the hierarchy than at the bottom. Strict social rules govern the interactions between castes, including (as one example) the prohibition of marriage between castes. The law of karma determines the caste into which one is born. If you generate good karma in your life, you can move up the hierarchy; bad karma moves you down the hierarchy. The important point here, however, is that where you are in the humanly constructed social hierarchy is not arbitrary. It is the result of a fundamental law of the universe (the law of karma). Those who are Sudras should not revolt or otherwise seek to end the injustices of the system, because only by living through one's life as a Sudra can you "burn off" the bad karma that made you a Sudra in the first place. In short, karma comes to serve as a justification for a hierarchical social order and all the injustices it entails.

In compensation for the injustices of certain socioeconomic forms, Marxists see religion acting as an "opiate" to pacify the "have nots" and preserve the advantages of the "haves." Marx and Engels sought to reveal to their readers the alienation (human beings alienated from their own creations, in this case laws related to stealing or those about the caste system) and reification (human laws projected into the heavens as if God created them or understood as fundamental to the universe) in religious worldviews. As a consequence, the readers (particularly workers) could see how culture was being used against them (even if subconsciously) by the powers that be—allowing the readers (again, the workers) to rise up and eliminate the injustices perpetrated against them.

This Marxist approach to culture has been influential to the work of many scholars attempting to describe and evaluate contemporary popular culture. In a sense, they see popular culture or elements of popular culture functioning in society in much the same way that Marx and Engels saw religion functioning in society.

Guy Debord's *Society of the Spectacle* is a great example. Spectacles are cultural events that act upon the masses like an opiate—leading people through a life detached from the real processes of existence and from real relationships. While spectacles are a product of the entire culture, they nevertheless function to the benefit of the "haves" rather than the "have nots." This is because spectacles implicitly or explicitly support or justify the existing socioeconomic order. The spectacle thus functions in much the same way that religion does. In the society of the spectacle, the "illusory paradise that represented a total denial of earthly life is no longer projected into the heavens, it is embedded in earthly life itself."[3] The spectacle gives the illusion of "heaven on earth"—leaving people oblivious to the real world, particularly the world of capitalist exploitation, alienation, and general social injustice. Debord concludes that the "spectacle keeps people in a state of unconsciousness as they pass through practical changes in their conditions of existence."[4]

The consequence of the society of the spectacle for a worker or a "have not" is that the fundamental structure of the socioeconomic world remains outside of his or her control. He or she is simply a cog in the machine with little dignity or respect—except, Debord notes, as a consumer: "Once his workday is over, the worker is suddenly redeemed from the total contempt toward him that is so clearly implied by every aspect of the organization and surveillance of production, and finds himself seemingly treated like a grownup, with a great show of politeness, in his new role as a consumer."[5] He is the consumer of spectacles, ranging from the hottest concert experience to the newest technological gadget. These are all designed to usher the worker through life without ever confronting reality (for example, the socioeconomic structure itself and genuine human relations not distorted by that very structure). Thus, the spectacles are not real. "The real consumer has become a consumer of illusions,"

Debord argues. "The commodity is this materialized illusion, and the spectacle is its general expression."[6] Our desires for these commodities also are produced and sold to us. In other words, the manufacturing of commodities, of spectacles, goes hand in hand with the manufacturing of the desires for those commodities. We see here the "replacing [of] the satisfaction of primary human needs (now scarcely met) with an incessant fabrication of pseudoneeds."[7] Debord adds, "Consumers are filled with religious fervour for the sovereign freedom of commodities whose use has become an end in itself. Waves of enthusiasm for particular products are propagated by all the communications media."[8] This propagation is ubiquitous today, given the wide range of media vehicles for advertisers and marketers. The typical consumer in developed countries sees hundreds if not thousands of messages a day—all designed by the culture industry to create needs and sell products.

The creation of "pseudoneeds" by the advertisers and marketers who control the media occurs on a daily if not hourly basis. The need that is really being met, of course, is the need of the system or structure itself. The "pseudoneeds" all "ultimately come down to the single pseudoneed of maintaining the reign of the autonomous economy."[9] This need is met quite well, while the needs of the workers/consumers are met sporadically and unsatisfactorily. They devote themselves to the next big experience (the next concert in town, the next game against the archrival, etc.) without even recognizing their own impoverishment (economically, psychologically, socially, politically, etc.). Debord concludes: "The image of blissful social unification through consumption merely *postpones* the consumer's awareness of the actual divisions until his next disillusionment with some particular commodity. Each new product is ceremoniously acclaimed as a unique creation offering a dramatic shortcut to the promised land of total consummation."[10]

Of course, from a consumer perspective, twenty-first-century advanced capitalism seems to provide a cornucopia of wonderful commodities. The society of the spectacle indeed seems spectacular. But the incredible range of goods, entertainment, and services provides consumers with only choices among illusions, for they ultimately prevent us (even while obtaining our allegiance) from directly confronting or even seeing the real world. As Debord puts it:

> The false choices offered by spectacular abundance—choices based on the juxtaposition of competing yet mutually reinforcing spectacles and of distinct yet interconnected roles (signified and embodied primarily by objects)—develop into struggles between illusory qualities designed to generate fervent allegiance to quantitative trivialities. Fallacious archaic oppositions are revived—regionalisms and racisms which serve to endow mundane rankings in the hierarchies of consumption with a magical ontological superiority—and pseudoplayful enthusiasms are aroused by an endless succession of ludicrous competitions, from sports to elections.[11]

Even our sense of choice is illusory. We choose what we desire or need, yet the desire or need is not truly a matter of choice. All the choices are thrust upon us by the culture industry. We become enamored by "ludicrous competitions" that seem to determine the objective value of things (think here of the many entertainment awards shows), but the *real* value of these competitions is their role in the otherwise debilitating social order.

In short, the Marxist critique reveals that much of contemporary popular culture functions as religion functions—it provides us an escapist path to an illusory world, preventing us from genuinely engaging reality and thus stopping us from addressing injustices and changing the world for the better. This critique is an important element of contemporary approaches to the study of sport. Like other cultural productions, sport serves ideological purposes. Allen Guttmann lays out this case (though he is critical of it) in his 1978 work *From Ritual to Record: The Nature of Modern Sports.*[12] Authors like David L. Andrews have extended it more recently in *Sport-Commerce-Culture: Essays on Sport in Late Capitalist America.*[13] In Debord's terms, we can say that sport is a principal spectacle of twenty-first-century capitalist societies. It works like religion in fostering pseudoneeds (Do we *really* need to root for our particular team? Does it really matter who wins?) that dull our sensibilities to the real nature of the world and the people around us, preventing us from confronting the reality of the world and doing something to make it better.

One easily could argue that sport is the preeminent element of popular culture in many countries—perhaps even surpassing religion in attention, influence, and devotion. While almost everyone in a developed country watches television shows and movies and listens to music, none of these elements of popular culture receive the kind of media attention that sport receives (coverage of sporting events on television, television shows reporting on and analyzing those events, entire networks that cover only sports, magazines devoted to sport and to the individual sports, dedicated sections of newspapers that focus only on sport, etc.).

So just as Marx and critical theorists provide insights into the political and economic dimensions of religion and popular culture, so they provide insights into those same dimensions of sport. Like religion, sport can be an institution that perpetuates social injustices (intolerance and discrimination, economic inequality, etc.) or, at the very least, can lead us to ignore such injustices. In the case studies below, we will focus on two sports in two different geographical areas—American football (with special attention to college football in the American South) and soccer in the United Kingdom.

Economic Class in American Football and Soccer

If sport can function—like religion—as an ideological tool, then what are its key beliefs and values and does it also blind fans to some reality around them? What reality is obfuscated by American football and soccer in the United Kingdom?

The standard Marxist approach would be to look at issues of economic class—and this certainly would yield some insight. How does sport, as part of the social superstructure (culture), reflect and thus reaffirm the basic beliefs and values found in the economic base? And how does sport work to prevent us from seeing and addressing potential injustices of the economic order?

Let us take the case of a capitalist society. The kinds of beliefs and values that a capitalist society endorses will be those operative in its economic relations. Many of these beliefs and values seem intuitively right—particularly among individuals in those societies. Indeed, the beliefs and values are just assumed to be true. They are rarely questioned because they are so ingrained into the culture.

In a capitalist society, competition is fundamental to our economic relations. It then is reflected in the superstructure, in beliefs and values manifested in our literature, art, law, and so much more. It also is reflected in our religious wisdom, such as in sayings like, "The Lord helps those who help themselves." Of course, the value of competition also is reflected in sport. Other beliefs and values associated with capitalism, such as hard work, perseverance, loyalty, determination, and even courage, also are reflected in our various institutions, from schools to churches to sports.

The beliefs and values of a capitalist society both grow out of its economic relations and affirm the very nature of those relations. Economic relations and their attendant beliefs and values also give rise to a class structure that represents the division of wealth in the society. While the structure is critical to the functioning of the society, it nevertheless leaves individuals alienated from each other.

Anthropologist Victor Turner's concepts of *communitas* and *structure* could help here.[14] As we learned in Chapter 5, structure refers to the predominant social roles, relationships, and stratifications in the society. *Communitas* refers to the transcendence of this structure through powerful and emotional ritual behavior. It involves bringing people into community who otherwise would be separated by virtue of their positions or roles in structure. The rituals of sporting events give rise to *communitas*. There is nothing inherently wrong with this experience. Indeed, as argued earlier, it can be critical in creating social unity and allowing the society to function efficiently. Still, the experience may blind us to the persistent injustices in the social structure (for example, poverty, discrimination, etc.).

The typical stadium in the United States is the site of many rituals and the experience of *communitas*. As argued earlier, this experience is a social good. And certainly a limitation of a Marxist approach to this phenomenon is that it fails to fully recognize and account for the good achieved.[15] At the same time, the stadium is very much structured along the lines of economic class and social status. While fans may chat about the game and "high-five" one another as they enter the stadium (an example of *communitas*), they inevitably will head to separate seating sections. Some of these will be in the "nose bleed" sections in the upper deck, while others may be at a lower level on the 50-yard line. Others still will be in "luxury" or "sky" boxes. Clearly there is an economic and social structure within the stadium. Those lower level seats or box seats will be much more expensive than those in the upper deck, sometimes by hundreds of dollars a seat. There also is class division manifested in the simple fact that some people can afford tickets to the game but many cannot. And there is no guarantee that one can even get a ticket if he or she had the money. Many games "sell out," and the only way to be assured of getting a ticket for a game is to be a season ticket holder. And season tickets are *very* expensive and outside the financial means of many average fans.

When a season ticket holder talks football with a fellow fan working at the gas station, the genuine bond they may share also conceals (probably for the season ticket holder more than for the gas station worker) the economic structure that legitimates the disparity of wealth between them. The season ticket holder is perceived as a "winner" in the economic game and deserving of his or her wealth as a consequence of hard work (and, certainly, he may work very hard). The gas station attendant and other working poor are "losers" in the same game (though, of course, they probably work hard too). Nobody questions the structures that shape the rules of the game in favor of some groups (often based on race, ethnicity, gender, or some other designation) over others. Of course, this structure is irrelevant anyway when the team wins—for that certainly is "heaven on earth." And just as heaven is the great equalizer in most religions (everyone in heaven is equal; there are no more divisions), so do sporting victories make everyone (regardless of race, income, etc.) a winner.

Increasingly, middle and working-class fans (not to mention poor fans) are financially incapable of attending games. In the United States, the growing gap between the top of the economic ladder and the bottom works itself out in the crowds at sporting events—where only the wealthy can attend. As Dave Zirin concludes, "Sports, which once was a welcome diversion from economic crisis, now, at best, highlights the crisis and, at worst exacerbates it."[16] Just as one example, the average face value for a ticket to the first Super Bowl (the championship game of the National Football League) in 1967 was $12 or about $85.65 adjusted for inflation (in 2015 dollars). The average face value for a ticket to the 2013 Super Bowl was $1,050.[17] While $12 may have been a little expensive for the average fan in 1967, that fan still could have afforded to go. However, the average price of more than $1,000 probably excludes many average fans today.

A similar phenomenon is occurring in the United Kingdom. Simon Kuper and Stefan Szymanski note that poor or working-class migrants were the first devoted fans of many city soccer clubs in the early twentieth century. These migrants had moved from the countryside to burgeoning industrial cities in order to find jobs. Thrown together with people with whom they may have had little in common, these migrants gravitated toward the football clubs. Kuper and Szymanski surmise that football "must have given them something of the sense of the community that they had previously known in their village."[18] In this sense, the football clubs took the place of churches—places where disparate groups of people could come together under a common focus (object of worship perhaps) and form a community. What happened in industrialized cities like Manchester also happened in similar cities across Europe. Kuper and Szymanski identify Manchester, Turin, Milan, Istanbul, and Barcelona as "the European cities with the most flux, the fewest long-standing hierarchies, the weakest ties between people and place. Here, there were emotional gaps to fill."[19] While religion may have filled those gaps before, soccer started to fill them in the early twentieth century and continues to fill them today. Thus, Kuper and Szymanski observe that today "a midsize city in Europe derives its status less from its cathedral than from its soccer clubs."[20]

Despite the working-class roots of football in England, however, the sport is becoming increasingly expensive and perhaps creating a clear socioeconomic divide.

A recent BBC report notes that the cheapest tickets for English league football aver-aged approximately $35US, with some tickets as much as $200US.[21] The sport that once brought people together from a wide range of socioeconomic classes is now increasingly restricted (at its highest level) to people with higher incomes. But to the extent that loyalty to teams across classes tends to obfuscate the socioeconomic divide, football in England still may be functioning very much like a religion. While churchgoers may have attained a level of equality in the sanctuary, their lives outside the religious institution nevertheless were structured significantly by economic class.

In both the United States and the United Kingdom (and, frankly, just about every-where that prices have gone beyond the reach of the average fan), there are demands for more reasonable ticket prices. But because of the religious love and devotion that fans have for their sports, they often are not able to engage critically an economic system that makes such inequalities (as reflected in ticket prices and hierarchical stadiums) possible.

Race in Football and Football

Despite the many advances made in many countries in the last century, race continues to be a factor in the ways in which many societies are structured. Hidden biases and prejudices often are obstacles to racial minorities and even weave their way through what is called "structural racism." Sport, like religion, sometimes can give us a false sense of success in regard to race—making us think that we somehow have overcome racism.

Race is a social structure obfuscated by major college football in the American South.[22] The racial divide in major college football in the South will be apparent to anyone who has witnessed the pregame walks of the football players to the stadium. The play-ers make their way through the crowd, as it forms a pathway for the athletes—the fans reaching out for "high fives" or handshakes or simply to touch the players. The fans are overwhelmingly white, while the players are black. In the state of Alabama, approx-imately 26 percent of the population is African American. At the University of Alabama, the student body is only 12 percent black—less than half the state percentage. The football team, however, is at least 60 percent black (twice the percentage of the state population and five times the percentage of black students at the school). In the state of Mississippi, 37 percent of the population is African American. At the University of Mississippi (otherwise known as "Ole Miss"), the student body is only about 14 percent black—again, less than half the state percentage. The football team, however, is more than 60 percent black (again, almost twice the percentage of the state population and nearly five times the percentage of black students at the school).[23] (See Fig. 7.1)

In some ways, college football in the South helps to erase the distinctions between "us" and "them"—the rich and the poor, whites and blacks. College football creates unstructured *communitas*. It does this at individual campuses by creating a larger "us" that is pitted against another (sometimes even demonized) "them." In Alabama, "us" and "them" means the University of Alabama and Auburn University. The divide is intense. As one fan suggests, the intensity or passion that fans have for their teams can even divide families.[24] In Mississippi, the primary rivalry is between Ole Miss and Mississippi State University. Each year they play each other. As one Ole Miss official put it: "It's kind of like the situation in the Middle East. ... Fans of one grow up hating the other and really don't know why."[25] The fans, of course, are predominantly white (at least those who are able to attend the games) while the players are predominantly black. This creates a perplexing situation. Michael Lewis writes of the moments before one game:

> The circumstances were that the Ole Miss football team, like the Mississippi State football team, consisted mostly of poor black kids from Mississippi. When the Ole Miss defense gathered in a single room, the only white people were coaches. On the football field the players became honorary white people, but off it they were still black, and unnatural combatants in Mississippi's white internecine war.[26]

Fig. 7.1 Tailgating site at Ole Miss, with Confederate flag featuring (Southern) rock-and-roll icon Elvis Presley.

Source: Photograph by Eric Bain-Selbo.

This situation is seemingly inexplicable or at least paradoxical. But the approach described above might help. College football, as a social construction that supports the fundamental ideology of the society, temporarily blinds the white spectators to the problem of race. For an afternoon the players are not white or black or brown. The only colors that matter are the ones on their uniforms (which generally cover the entire body, thus concealing skin color). They simply are Ole Miss Rebels or Mississippi State Bulldogs. The *communitas* formed by the two fan groups allows them to ignore the problem of race. Yet, the very formation of these groups requires the exclusion of others. The formation of the supporters of the Rebels excludes all Bulldogs, though it includes black Ole Miss players. The same is true for the formation of the supporters of the Bulldogs. But when the game is over and the players are out of their uniforms, the Ole Miss player might be just another young black man to the Ole Miss fan—and now that young black man becomes the excluded one while the Ole Miss fan goes off to play golf at the country club with his white Mississippi State friend. Strangely constructed alliances also arise in cases of class here. Think of the two fans—a Rebel and a Bulldog—playing golf. On game day, they may sit in separate areas of the stadium, fraternizing with fellow Rebels and Bulldogs respectively and doing so regardless of income. However, once the game is over, the friends return to the country club where the lesser-income fans they fraternized with in the stands are excluded.

At the same time, college football in the South can provide an effective form of escape from the various problems of prejudices and social division. This is true of most sports, religions, and forms of entertainment. They can take our minds off the pressing problems of the day and allow us some peace of mind or at least diversion. A University of Tennessee (UT) fan writes that "going to UT games provides an escape for a few hours. It doesn't matter what is going on in the world, how bad the world is screwed up, who is fighting who [sic] in a war, when I am over there everyone gets along with everyone and for those few hours everything seems ok."[29]

The ability of sport, like religion, to divide as well as gather can be seen in the case of soccer in the United Kingdom. Racism has been a persistent problem in soccer around the globe, but perhaps nowhere worse than among the British. "The issues of race and racism continue to be at the heart of some of the most polarizing political battles in soccer, particularly in Europe," Zirin writes. "In Britain, soccer 'hooliganism' has a long and ugly history of commingling with hard right-wing forces."[30] He notes that while about 25 percent of European players are "of color," "only a minute fraction of that diversity is reflected in the stands, mostly because of fear for personal safety."[31] The demographics in this case resemble those found in college football in the American South.

In his classic memoir *Fever Pitch*, Nick Hornby recounts instances of fans throwing bananas and insults at black players on the field.[32] In his powerful investigation of British hooliganism, Bill Buford writes of "banana attacks" and hearing the "ape grunts"—"the barking sound that supporters make when a black player gets the ball."[33] He recounts going to a party that included Chelsea and West Ham supporters

Of course, the us/them dichotomy is an inherent aspect of human beings and human collectivities. Seeing it in college football should not be surprising, and, indeed, this is another point of contact with religion. Regina Schwartz explicates this dynamic in the context of the biblical traditions in her book, *The Curse of Cain: The Violent Legacy of Monotheism*.[27] She argues that a scarcity of resources (God's favor) culminates in violence, for example, in the biblical story of Cain's slaying of Abel. In a college football game, obviously only one team can win (college football's adoption of an overtime system in 1996 eliminated the possibility of ties). Even more, only one team can earn the honor and adulation that comes with victory. Only one team can have "bragging rights" (often until the teams meet again the following year) after the game. All this undoubtedly contributes to the fervor and violence of the game. Little wonder then that violence breaks out occasionally among fans (as it does, of course, with religious fanatics as well). It is not unusual to have stories like the one where the University of South Carolina fan shot his friend (a Clemson University fan) when they argued about a $20 bet on the game (the game having been won by South Carolina). One would imagine that it was not so much the sum of money that was in dispute, but what the money signified—victory, honor, superiority, etc.

The sort of partisanship that divides the world up into "us" and "them," Rebels and Bulldogs, may be particularly prominent in the American South. David Goldfield notes that "southerners are quite fond of flag-waving, from flags snapping from car antennae on football Saturdays, proclaiming, 'My college is going to cream yours,' to a mindless patriotism that, like most southern religion, asks no questions and generates no doubts."[28] This somewhat "mindless" devotion to one's team or region becomes particularly problematic when it blinds American Southerners to problems like racism, economic disparity, etc., that are right in front of their faces. The socially constructed divide between "us" and "them" obfuscates the fundamental injustices that lie at the very basis of our societies.

listening to White Power music[34]—an example of the race divide taking priority over the divide between Chelsea and West Ham fans.

Kuper and Szymanski claim that in English soccer throughout "the 1980s racism had been more or less taken for granted in the game."[35] They are suspicious of people who long for the "good old days" when going to a match was more affordable and thus more accessible to the working class:

Whenever people reminisce about the good old days, when ordinary working people could afford to go to soccer matches, it's worth scanning the photographs of the cloth-capped masses standing on the terraces for the faces you *don't* see: blacks, Asians, women. It's true that today's all-seaters in the Premier League exclude poor people. However, the terraces before the 1990s probably excluded rather more varieties of people.[36]

The stands, in this case, continue to reflect issues of social status, class, and/or race in English society.

And just as in the case of college football, where there are often predominantly white coaching staffs on teams with a large portion of black players, so it is the case in the United Kingdom and Europe. Indeed, Kuper and Szymanski note that breaking down the discrimination against black coaches has been even harder than against black players.[37]

The religious devotion of fans will continue to fuel the popularity of soccer in the United Kingdom. But their religious fervor also will blind many of them to the social issues and injustices that the game itself can reveal to them.

In summary, we see in soccer and American football examples of institutions that at worst perpetuate racist attitudes and discrimination or, at best, obfuscate those racist attitudes and discrimination. In this regard, sport is not unlike many religious institutions—for certainly religions have contributed greatly to intolerance and discrimination. We do not have to look far into our history to see the egregious ways in which religions have created us/them dichotomies fueled by stereotypes and prejudices—Catholics and Protestants, Hindus and Muslims, and many more. We also know of the terrible ways in which religion has been used to support and promote racism—such as white Christianity in the segregated American South and in apartheid South Africa.

Of course, religions also have worked to overcome racism. Sport too has sought to overcome racism and has made great advances in the past century. In part, sport is successful in this regard because it is a meritocracy. As Kuper and Szymanski note, the results on the field increasingly determine the racial makeup of a team.[38] Great players are coveted, regardless of skin color. Just as was the case in the American South, "competition drove white men to ditch their prejudices."[39] We certainly hope sport continues to drive society toward a more racially sensitive and understanding consciousness.

Conclusion

What we see with college football in the American South and English soccer is what we can see with sport in general around the world. While providing some measure of equal opportunity for all, sport paradoxically conceals and reveals the underlying injustices of society. As sport around the world continues to become a communal and emotional fixture in people's lives—as it has with so many college football fans in the South and soccer fans in Britain—it increasingly is becoming the new "opiate of the masses." Even when sport no longer perpetuates economic injustice or racism, it often prevents us from seeing or addressing these critical issues. It very much remains a spectacle that obfuscates the kind of injustices that we need to confront and remedy.

While it is important to assess sport critically, we also must acknowledge the role it can play in a more just society. Again, this is just like religion. Religious institutions for millennia have been just as much part of the solution (to inequality, violence, injustice, etc.) as part of the problem. Harry Edwards has spent much of his career as an activist for African-American rights and causes in the United States. He is the author of *Sociology of Sport*, an early and important work in the field. In thinking about his own efforts to bring about social change, he concludes:

> Sport is about the most sacred, deeply rooted, most important values, sentiments, and structures in the society, and if you can get to sports and you can get to the athletes, you're way up the road in terms of changing definitions or reality in the society as a whole.[40]

As with most social institutions (including religion), sport bears both costs and benefits. While sport often replicates social divisions, it also has the great promise of overcoming them.

Discussion Questions

1. Do religion and sport *create* an us/them divide, or does it *reflect* a natural, human propensity that is simply part of who we are?

2. Do religion, sport, and other social institutions prevent us from addressing the injustices in our societies? If so, how?

3. To what extent do economic-class issues pervade your society? How are these issues reflected in religion or sport?

4. To what extent do issues of race and ethnicity pervade your society? How are these issues reflected in religion or sport?

Glossary

alienation—a term used to describe the situation in which individuals or groups feel disconnected to fundamental ideas or beliefs that are created by them.

base and superstructure—in the Marxist sense, these refer to the economic foundation (base) and the cultural overlay (superstructure) of any society; the base creates or shapes the superstructure, and the superstructure justifies the base.

communitas and structure—two terms that are central to the theories of anthropologist Victor Turner; structure refers to the predominant social roles, relationships, and stratifications in the society; *communitas* refers to the transcendence of this structure through powerful and emotional ritual behavior.

ideology—the dominant viewpoint or worldview of a culture; usually is never questioned or critiqued.

spectacle—a cultural product (thing, event, etc.) that seemingly fulfills a desire or craving; distracts us from the issues and relationships that should be our focus.

8 Religion, Sport, and Secularism

In previous chapters we examined the many different ways to look at religious phenomena and how difficult it is even to define religion. Understanding secularism can pose similar challenges.

Secularism generally is understood as the opposite of religion, similar to seeing the profane as that which is not sacred. What is secular is not religious. Secularization then is the historical process of moving from the religious to the nonreligious. Unlike the profane, however, which is defined almost exclusively in negative terms (it simply is that which is not sacred), secularism has a positive dimension. Secularism is more like a worldview or trend that affirms the secular against the religious. Secularists affirm a nonreligious understanding of the world or at least want to defend a secular realm of human life against the intrusion of religion (particularly in areas of politics, law, education, etc.).

If sport can be understood as a religious phenomenon, then what is the relationship of sport to secularism? This chapter will seek to answer this question by looking at two interrelated possibilities—sport as a contributor to the process of secularization and sport as a religious alternative in an increasingly secular world.

Like many other elements of popular culture, sport has functioned (in part) to diminish participation in religious institutions and subsequently undermine religious faith. In many Western societies, the time and energy previously devoted to church activities and religious practices increasingly have been devoted to one's favorite team or preferred recreational activity. For example, some might skip the Sunday service in order to go to the big game or miss a church activity in order to go to practice for a sport they play. They also may donate less money to their religious organization because of funds diverted to participating in or watching sports. In this way, sport has facilitated the process of secularization. At the same time, part of the success of sport in this regard is due to the fact that it embodies certain characteristics of religious life and even functions theologically, psychologically, sociologically, and morally like religion. These functions have been the focus of the previous chapters. Thus, there seems to be an apparent paradox. On the one hand, sport promotes the process of secularization. On the other hand, sport sustains religious experience by embodying certain stereotypical religious characteristics and functioning in religious ways.

In this chapter we hope to work out this paradox. But first, let us look more closely at secularism and secularization.

Narratives of Secularization

Sociologist Peter Berger defines secularization as "the process by which sectors of society and culture are removed from the domination of religious institutions and symbols."[1] More broadly, it refers to a historical transition from a fundamentally religious worldview to a fundamentally secular worldview. As Berger puts it, "secularization has resulted in a widespread collapse of the plausibility of traditional religious definitions of reality."[2] Philosopher Charles Taylor, in his massive treatment of the subject in his *A Secular Age*, investigates the great historical change in the Western world from a situation in which people "lived naively" in a theistic framework to one (today) in which theism is simply one option among many.[3] As he puts the question: "[W]hy was it virtually impossible not to believe in God in, say, 1500 in our Western society, while in 2000 many of us find this not only easy, but even inescapable?"[4]

Scholars and theologians have proposed many sources for the secular impulse — at least as it appears in the Western world. Death of God theologians might point to the crucifixion of Jesus. After all, what more could indicate the end of religion (at least institutional religion) than the death of God? The Protestant Reformation in the sixteenth and seventeenth centuries is seen as a turning point as well. To the extent that secularism is connected with the primacy of the individual and with individualism, the Reformation's emphasis on the individual's salvation through his or her faith as opposed to salvation through the corporate body of the Catholic Church helped to create the conditions for secularism. The eighteenth-century philosophical movement known as the Enlightenment also was critical. While Enlightenment thinkers generally defended religion, they nonetheless advocated that people think for themselves and not simply accept what traditions (including religious traditions) have handed down. This emphasis on reason would become a cornerstone of secularism.

There are numerous narratives about secularization. For our purposes, we will look at particular European and American narratives from the nineteenth and early twentieth centuries that continue to be held widely today. Many proponents of these narratives view the transition from the religious to the secular to be very positive. They conceive of it as a transition from superstition and irrationality (the religious) to reason and objectivity (the secular). They also see an impenetrable barrier between the two, and, in fact, advocate for such a barrier.

Secularism Triumphant

Karl Marx provides a classic example. As we saw in the previous chapter, he describes religion as the "*opium* of the people."[5] It is an institution used by those in power to justify economic and political inequalities and placate the impoverished and powerless masses with dreams of eternal bounty in heaven. Marx constructs a historical narrative that runs from feudalism to capitalism to the dictatorship of the proletariat and eventually to a communist utopia. At the end of history, private property is abolished and the guiding principle is "From each according to his ability, to each according to his needs!"[6] As humanity goes through these revolutionary changes, and as a condition of these changes, humanity will embrace reason and science and discard the dogmas and practices of religion. Indeed, given the equality and brotherhood (and sisterhood we assume) of the communist future, people no longer will need the solace of religion anyway. This radical antireligious position would dominate Marxist political movements and governments for much of the twentieth century.

Sigmund Freud provides a psychological perspective on secularization, though one informed greatly by sociological considerations. He views religion as an early stage in the development of humanity—designed to manipulate and placate individuals vis-à-vis society. The history of humanity then is the story of its growing maturity. Its ability to form successful societies will be based on reason and science without the crutch of religion. Just as a child must grow out of his or her fairy tales and fantasies, so must humanity grow out of religion. Indeed, our continuing reliance on religion is not only a sign of immaturity but of neurosis. Religion represents a fundamental inability of human beings to cope with psychological demands posed by the threats of nature (death being the most significant) and the necessary constraints that society must put on our freedom (especially in regard to sexual behavior). Take the example of the heavenly afterlife. Such a promise makes death more bearable, since death is not our final end. Indeed, not only will we continue to exist in some other realm, but our existence will be qualitatively better than our current existence. According to Freud, the promise of heaven also makes it easier to make the kinds of sacrifices that are necessary to live in a society. We all must curb our desires, our selfishness, in order to live with others. But in heaven all our desires are fulfilled or (to the same effect) we are liberated from all those desires. Either way, we exist in joyful satisfaction unlike our current existence.

While religion may have been helpful to individuals and societies in the past, we no longer need it. So, Freud argues, "the time has probably come, as it does in an analytic treatment, for replacing the effects of repression by the results of the rational operation of the intellect."[7] Liberating ourselves from religion consequently promises to make our lives better or at least more psychologically healthy. "By withdrawing their expectations from the other world and concentrating all their liberated energies into their life on earth," Freud claims, "they will probably succeed in achieving a state of things in which life will become tolerable for everyone and civilization no longer oppressive to anyone."[8]

The narratives of Marx and Freud tell a story of reason and science triumphing over religion—the former coming to dominate how we think about the world and act in it while the latter slowly withers away. Liberated from religious illusions, people are free to direct their attention to other projects and diversions. From this perspective, sport might be simply a form of entertainment that people spend time doing or watching in place of activities they otherwise might have done in a religious setting. In this way, sport contributes to secularization. However, many other thinkers provide more subtle theories of secularization that view the barrier between religious and secular worldviews as much more permeable.

Secularism and Religion Intertwined

From a sociological perspective, we can look at figures like Auguste Comte in the nineteenth century as well as Max Weber and Emile Durkheim in the twentieth century.[9] While these thinkers champion reason and science, they nevertheless acknowledge a critical, positive, and continuing role for religion (or, at least, certain aspects or dimensions of religion) in a society.

Comte's positivist sociology and philosophy is a kind of model of empiricism, scientism, and secularism. But he understands that traditional religion, while wrong or misguided in so many ways from an empirical perspective, nevertheless has an important function to play in maintaining the cohesiveness of society. Thus, in his "religion of humanity," he includes a role for worship, festival, and commemoration. He even devises a positivist calendar with "holy days" (celebrating great discoveries, advances in science, etc.) like the Catholic liturgical calendar. In short, his positivist future has many religious features.

As we learned in Chapter 5, Durkheim argues that God ultimately is a "stand in" for society—that when we worship God we in fact are worshipping ourselves, at least in our collective nature. This claim about worship applies just as much to contemporary society as it does to the ancient religious beliefs and practices of our ancestors. So, there is little difference between the modern worship of God and the "primitive" worship of the tribal totem. In fact, the latter is the evolutionary seed of the former. Both represent the collectivity, and the worship of them simply is the worship of that which is greater than any of us individually. It is the worship of society.

As people across millennia have gathered to worship, they have engaged in rituals that would work them into states of "collective effervescence"—an ecstatic state that provides an escape from the drudgery of everyday life and strengthens the bonds among the members of the group. While Durkheim certainly sees significant development from totemism to polytheism to monotheism, he nevertheless sees fundamental continuity in religious life—for people today need to experience this "collective effervescence" just as their distant ancestors needed to experience it. This continuity not only will continue into the future but *must* continue. Toward the end of his influential work, *The Elementary Forms of Religious Life*, Durkheim writes of his sense that his era (early twentieth century) was a "period of transition and moral mediocrity," but that a "day will come when our societies once again will know hours of creative effervescence during which new ideals will again spring forth and new formulas will emerge to guide humanity for a new time."[10] No matter how "modern" or "secular" we become, we always will need to engage in collective activity that fundamentally is religious in nature. This collective activity is both a product of our solidarity with one another and the way in which that solidarity is achieved. Such solidarity is critical to the future of all societies, but particularly critical in our highly complex modern societies. "The Durkheimian lesson is that if we want to achieve social and economic justice, whether we are living among civic or global diversity,"

Mark S. Cladis concludes, "we must remain committed to some form of solidarity. To neglect solidarity is to risk having our most cherished ideals ... drained of their capacity to shape our lives, institutions, and communities."[11]

Max Weber's *The Protestant Ethic and the "Spirit" of Capitalism* is a classic of Western scholarship. He argues that certain Protestant beliefs (e.g., predestination, asceticism, and the "calling") facilitated the growth of capitalism in many Western societies and even shaped its character. Consequently, as the explicit exercise of religion ebbs in the West, one can find remnants of Protestant beliefs in the economic behavior of otherwise "secular" individuals. For example, he writes of the ascetic impulse:

> Christian asceticism, which was originally a flight from the world into solitude, had already once dominated the world on behalf of the Church from the monastery, by renouncing the world. In doing this, however, it had, on the whole, left the natural, spontaneous character of secular everyday life unaffected. Now it would enter the market place of life [via the upheaval of the Reformation and the subsequent development of Protestant beliefs], slamming the doors of the monastery behind it, and set about permeating precisely this secular everyday life with its methodical approach, turning it toward a rational life *in* the world, but neither *of* this world nor *for* it.[12]

The ascetic life might include such characteristics as hard work, a disregard for one's pleasure, and a willingness to forego immediate gains for long-term goals. While people at the beginning of the capitalist-industrialist world did not live in monasteries, they nevertheless still viewed these characteristics as virtuous or noble. They may not have connected these characteristics with any theological teachings, but they still found them valuable. As Weber writes, though the "dogmatic roots of ascetic morality" may have died, the "dogmas left clear traces in later 'undogmatic' ethics."[13]

All of these classic sociological theories see certain fundamental religious impulses as persisting in society with or without stereotypical religious institutions. This notion of religious beliefs and practices continuing in seemingly secular ways also is affirmed from a psychological perspective.

Carl Jung represents an interesting break from Sigmund Freud (Jung's colleague and mentor)—not the least of which in his approach to secularization. Jung argues for the existence of archetypes of the collective unconscious. These archetypes— such as the trickster, the Mother, the hero—can be found in all cultures throughout human history. They typically appear in religious texts, legends, and folklore. They work implicitly through our collective unconscious, impacting our most basic beliefs and practices. They find expression in the imaginative creations that make up our culture. The sacrificial heroes of religious texts can be found in numerous novels and films as well as on the fields of play. While the process of secularization may impact how we assess the authority of our cultural creations (texts may be viewed today as humanly created, rather than provided by God), the archetypes nevertheless will continue to impact how we view the world and act within it.

When we think about religion, Jung would have us think of these archetypes and how they function in our psychic or spiritual life. No amount of secularization will change this basic psychological fact. Jung concludes:

> The living spirit grows and even outgrows its earlier forms of expression; it freely chooses the men in whom it lives and who proclaim it. This living spirit is eternally renewed and pursues its goal in manifold and inconceivable ways throughout the history of mankind. Measured against it, the names and forms which men have given it mean little enough; they are only the changing leaves and blossoms on the stem of the eternal tree.[14]

The archetypes and the collective unconscious are the "eternal tree." The "changing leaves and blossoms" merely are the expressions of the "eternal tree." These expressions may be explicitly religious, but they also may be secular—at least stereotypically secular.

The work of Jung provides a fitting segue to that of Mircea Eliade, the twentieth-century historian of religion who shaped the comparative study of religion perhaps more than any other figure. Eliade also used the concept of archetypes, though he insisted that his use of the concept was different from how Jung used it. For example, in *Patterns in Comparative Religion*,[15] Eliade looks at an incredible array of religious symbols, from the sun to mountains, from the moon to vegetation and animals. These enduring symbols may or may not be structures of our collective unconscious, but they nevertheless constitute distinct patterns throughout human cultures. The power and meaning of these symbols are relayed through communities and history by myth—and myth is enacted by ritual. Myths, symbols, and rituals will continue to persist even if not in explicitly religious contexts.

In addition to his analysis of myth, symbol, and ritual, Eliade provides extensive analysis of sacred space, sacred objects, and sacred time. These obviously are bound up with myth, symbol, and ritual as we saw in Chapter 2. For example, the ritual of communion takes place in a sacred space (church), is dependent on certain symbols/objects (the cross, bread, and wine), reenacts an important myth (the Last Supper), and generates a sacred time (the service itself, which transports participants back to the original event).

Eliade provides substantial conceptual tools for analyzing the religious character of seemingly secular phenomena. Indeed, his claim that we are *homo religiosus* means that we are innately religious regardless of how we might choose to describe our beliefs and practices. An obvious area in which to apply these Eliadean tools is sport.[16] It is hard to imagine any sport devoid of myth, symbol, and ritual, let alone sacred space, sacred objects, and sacred time. For example, American baseball has a rich mythology, a plethora of symbols, and many distinct rituals. All of these help to transform certain spaces, objects, and times into sacred spaces, sacred objects, and sacred times—raising them in quality from the mundane or profane to the holy. Few baseball devotees would deny the sacred quality of Yankee Stadium or Wrigley Field (or wherever their team plays), a home run ball caught in the stands, or the sweet passing of the nine-inning game.

While the survey we have provided above is far from exhaustive, let us draw one important conclusion. There are many people who naively embrace a kind of triumphalist secularism, but there are more good reasons to side with those who view the relationship between secularism and religion in a much more complex and subtle way. In short, the secularization hypotheses of Marx, Freud, and others are inadequate in light of the permeable and shifting nature of the categories "religion" and "secular."

In assessing recent scholarship, sociologist Niklas Luhmann claims that the "secularization thesis with its predetermined direction is therefore replaced by the much more open (but highly vague) question of religious transformation in our time."[17] Vincent P. Pecora adds, "[W]e seem increasingly compelled to acknowledge that traditional religion has not really disappeared in anything like the wholesale way this version of the secularization thesis predicts."[18]

"If anything is agreed upon," anthropologist Talal Asad writes, "it is that a straightforward narrative of progress from the religious to the secular is no longer acceptable."[19] In *Formations of the Secular*, Asad significantly problematizes the religious/secular dichotomy. He argues that the secular "is neither continuous with the religious that supposedly preceded it (that is, it is not the latest phase of a sacred origin) nor a simple break from it (that is, it is not the opposite, an essence that excludes the sacred)."[20] In postmodernist fashion, Asad rejects any essentializing of the categories "religious" and "secular." Discerning the permeable and shifting meanings of these categories requires subtle historical, archaeological, and genealogical analyses of concepts and their uses in the Western world in the last two centuries. In describing his project, Asad writes:

> The analyses that I offer here are intended as a counter to the triumphalist history of the secular. I take the view, as others have done, that the "religious" and the "secular" are not essentially fixed categories. However, I do not claim that if one stripped appearances one would see that some apparently secular institutions were *really* religious. I assume, on the contrary, that there is nothing *essentially* religious, nor any universal essence that defines "sacred language" or "sacred experience." But I also assume that there were breaks between Christian and secular life in which words and practices were rearranged, and new discursive grammars replaced the previous ones.[21]

In general, Asad is correct. We ought not to essentialize our categories. Indeed, the practical uses of these categories in our societies in the last 200 years demonstrate that we cannot essentialize them. It also is true that changes in our use of words as well as our beliefs and practices are significant. The world has *not* remained essentially the same in the last few hundred years. But it is precisely the nonessential character of the concept "religion" that gives us license to apply it to seemingly "secular" phenomena. Not all such phenomena are secretly religious. Again, Asad's point is well taken. But when we hear sports fans talk about their experiences participating in or watching sports, observe their rituals, and witness their ecstatic experiences, we believe we are fully justified in using the category "religious" to describe these phenomena.[22] Indeed, it is the *best* way to describe the phenomena.

Play in Sacred and Secular Contexts

The permeable and shifting uses of terms like "religion" and "secular" also can be seen in the work of scholars who focus on sport or play. In Chapter 5 we learned about the work of Johan Huizinga and the importance of play in human culture. Play is a constant element in human culture; in fact it is at the very foundation of human culture. Play is found in our rituals and wars and games and more. "The spirit of playful competition is, as a social impulse, older than culture itself," Huizinga writes, "and pervades all life like a veritable ferment."[23]

Though we never are free from the play element in culture, Huizinga nevertheless thinks there has been a transformation in the last few centuries. The most important development involved the way in which games of play were taken over by sport. Huizinga argues that "with the increasing systematization and regimentation of sport, something of the pure play-quality is inevitably lost."[24] He describes play as having "undergone almost complete atrophy."[25] There is a seriousness now about sport that threatens play. "In the case of sport we have an activity nominally known as play," Huizinga concludes, "but raised to such a pitch of technical organization and scientific thoroughness that the real play-spirit is threatened with extinction."[26] His point here is familiar to anyone who has had children in sports leagues. Often the passion of parents and coaches (who usually are parents) to see the sports played well and for their children's team to win is so strong that the children no longer have fun playing. Children often adopt their parents' seriousness about the sports, and their play turns into work.

Huizinga's fears about systematization and regimentation are reminiscent of those of Weber and Durkheim—both concerned about how modern dependence on reason alone, along with the systematization and bureaucratization of society, would impact human psychology and our connectedness with one another. In short, we might say that the process of secularization for Huizinga is one in which we increasingly lose the play element that has been so foundational for happy individual and social lives. This process culminates in professional sports, where the play actually becomes work.

That said, Huizinga nevertheless affirms the constant role of play in our lives. Despite its current obstacles, play remains central to our culture and continues to provide "happy inspiration."[27]

Roger Callois's *Man, Play and Games* extends Huizinga's work. Like Huizinga, Callois sees sport as based on play—a fundamental human drive. Though Callois does not use the language of secularization, he nevertheless describes an important historical transition from play primarily as *ilinx* (activity, like dancing, that leads to vertigo and ecstasy) and *mimicry* (the adoption of illusory roles and the suspension of reality) to *agon* (competition that rewards effort, skill, and strength) and *alea* (when outcomes depend on chance or fortune). *Ilinx* and *mimicry* are characteristic of what a secularist might describe as religiously primitive activity. Callois asks (and answers in the affirmative): "May it be asserted that the transition to civilization as such implies the gradual elimination of the primacy of *ilinx* and *mimicry* in combination, and the substitution and predominance of the *agon-alea* pairing of competition and chance?"[28] With this transition, "it is seen that all of collective life ... from the moment when *mimicry* and *ilinx* have been suppressed, rests on a precarious and infinitely variable equilibrium between *agon* and *alea*, or merit and chance."[29]

One might imagine that today *agon* is more prominent than *alea*. Because *alea* is associated with the gods (their favor, fortune, and good or bad luck), the move to modern society (a seemingly secular move) could entail a shift in primacy to *agon*. Indeed, much of modern society seems dominated by competition and an obsession with rewarding merit and rejecting chance. The primacy of *agon* can be found in many areas, including business, politics, and sports. But regardless of our fixation on *agon*, *alea* remains a powerful element in our everyday lives and in our sports and games. We recognize our inability to control the outcome of events in the world, regardless of our knowledge, skill, or strength. In sport, for example, we feel helpless against the odd bounces of the ball, the game-changing wind gust that suddenly arises, and the many other random events that can alter the outcome of a game or match (though, of course, for many people these are not matters of chance, but of the capricious actions of God or the gods).

Callois provides an interesting perspective to see the ways in which sport has changed through the centuries yet maintains perennial characteristics. *Agon* and *alea* are not new. They are as old as recorded history. They have roots in our ancient religious history. Their survival in contemporary sport points to the trace of our religious nature manifested in seemingly secular activities. Callois writes: "To the degree that he is influenced by play, man can check the monotony, determinism, and brutality of nature. He learns to construct order, conceive economy, and establish equity."[30] Overcoming nature and constructing order may not exhaust the functions of religion, but they nevertheless are critical functions in the history of religion. Sport, no longer an adjunct of our religious lives, continues to function in these ways. Sport is a social construct that brings order and consequently meaning to the world around us. The annual sports calendar and the rhythm of a season provide fans with order, and their personal identity with a team, and a fan community provides them with often powerful meaningful experiences. Thus, play (through sports) not only shares important characteristics with religion, it also functions like religion.

Today, many people share the concerns that Huizinga and Callois have about play and sport. Perhaps no writer has been more vociferous than Dave Zirin. One of his primary concerns is on the role of money and the behavior of owners in modern professional sports—particularly in the United States. For Zirin, professional sports are headed for a financial and moral crisis, and the "fault for this coming crisis [lies] at the feet of the political economy of twenty-first-century ownership."[31] In his book *Bad Sports: How Owners Are Ruining the Games We Love*, Zirin makes a powerful case against treating sports franchises *merely* as businesses—where the only goal is making money. He is critical of owners not only because making money tends to be their primary concern, but because they use the loyalty of fans and the ambitions of politicians to extract huge subsidies from taxpayers to support the owners' economic interests.[32]

When money intrudes on our sports, it corrupts the spirit of play that is central to our enjoyment of the games. This intrusion really is the intrusion of the profane into the sacred, the secular into the religious. Most religious traditions have an uneasy relationship with money and frequently condemn our obsession with it. These religious traditions are particularly uncomfortable with the role that money may play *in* the religion. An analogous situation can be found in sports. Robert L. Simon writes of what he calls the "corruption thesis"—the claim that "the commercialization of sport, the transformation of elite sport into a product that can be bought and sold, corrupts sport" by violating the goods or values that are internal to it (honesty and fairness in play being among the most important).[33] We know that money is part of the secular world, but when it becomes too prominent in sport we are uncomfortable and feel like our games are being ruined.

In their book *Soccernomics*, Simon Kuper and Stefan Szymanski argue that professional soccer clubs should not be seen as businesses in the normal sense. First of all, they often do not do very well *as* businesses—struggling to make profits on a very regular basis. More importantly, they have a different role in society than most businesses. Kuper and Szymankski argue that soccer clubs "are like museums: public-spirited organizations that aim to serve the community while remaining reasonably solvent."[34] The key here is "public-spirited organizations." It is public-spiritedness that embodies the sacred quality of play that we crave in our sports. As Simon concludes, the governance of sport "should reflect more than commercial interests concerned with generating wealth from the game. Governance should also give voice to and reflect the concerns of those whose allegiance is to the basic principles of competitive sport."[35]

If part of the secularization process is a tendency to boil human life down to a rational choice calculus that is dominated by economic self-interest, then sport is under threat by secularization. The intrusion of money undoubtedly will come to strip sport of the sacrality that draws us to it. Strangely, secularization then comes to be seen as just as much of a threat to the spirit of sport as it is to the spirit of institutional religions.

Conclusion

This chapter has highlighted a particular trend line, a transition in the recent religious history of humanity—from a rigid dichotomy in which religiosity is restricted to institutional traditions and stereotypical beliefs and practices to a steady decline of those traditions, beliefs, and practices and a recognition that religiosity is diffused through our lives to greater and lesser degrees. We see no reason to doubt the continuation of this trend. The "return of religion" that sometimes is proclaimed in the Western world (primarily the United States, and primarily referring to fundamentalist movements) is not a reversal of the trend but a reaction to the decline of stereotypical religious institutions, beliefs, and practices.

In light of this trend, sport will continue to play a critical role as a site for the expression of our religious impulses. Indeed, as stereotypical religious institutions, beliefs, and practices continue to decline in influence, sport will become even more important.

Many observers, particularly theological apologists with a vested interest in maintaining the cultural influence of religion, have expressed grave concerns about the demise of religion—imagining a future in which the social order crumbles under the weight of cultural anomie. Durkheim, for example, was concerned with the effects of meaninglessness on individuals and society at large. Berger more recently writes that "[p]robably for the first time in history, the religious legitimations of the world have lost their plausibility not only for a few intellectuals and other marginal individuals but for broad masses of entire societies."[36] Given that secularization (as stereotypically conceived) delegitimizes religion as an effective defense against anomie, one reasonably could suppose that a secular society would fall prey to anomie and all the despair and violence that might follow. But the decline of religion and the rise of sport have occurred during a period mostly of increasing tolerance and the preservation of order. Certainly it has been a period of significant violence (much of the twentieth century still was a disaster in this regard), but one would be hard-pressed to make the case that there was more violence (at least per capita) than in previous centuries. In fact, Steven Pinker makes a strong argument that the data indicate a decline in violence over the last two millennia—continuing even through the twentieth century.[37]

While the Olympic movement is the most obvious example of how sport spreads good will throughout the world, we can add to it the soccer World Cup, the rugby World Cup, golf's Ryder Cup, yachting's Americas Cup, and numerous other international competitions that bring people of different ethnicities, religions, and political systems into competition. Perhaps the competitors and fans will come to renounce the war and violence of their fathers. For in these competitions the athletes and fans participate in a sort of "like-mindedness" that transcends divisions of religion, race, and nationality. As Luhmann writes:

> Like-mindedness is an exception in modern society, a surprising and gratifying experience that can lead the individual to join a group where he might count on repeating the experience. There are fundamentalisms of the most diverse kind, revivalisms, remystifications, renewals of faith in sacred stagings, and so forth. And each of these, in their attentive intensity, might be said to oppose secularization, while at the same time being conditioned by it.[38]

While Luhmann probably has more stereotypically religious activities in mind, his comment nonetheless could be applied to the "sacred stagings" and "attentive intensity" we find at many sporting events. Pecora concurs when he writes that

> the secularization through which magic or myth is eliminated by reason may never in fact be complete. This is not simply a function of language or geography

but is perhaps something to be acknowledged as a result of an irreducible set of needs in human and group psychology. One might then conclude that the society that produces Enlightenment never fully outgrows its desire for religious sources of coherence, solidarity, and historical purpose, and continually translates, or transposes, them into ever more refined and immanent, but also distorted and distorting, versions of its religious inheritance.[39]

As we have learned, sport draws heavily from this religious inheritance. In this way, sport provides new venues for religious expression.

Discussion Questions

1. Do you think your society is becoming more secular? If so, why? If not, why not?
2. Do forms of popular culture like sport lead to the secularization of societies? If so, how?
3. Are certain forms of popular culture like sport signs of secularization or simply new avenues for religious expression?

Glossary

anomie—a lack of order or that which is counter to order; describes the meaninglessness and resultant anxiety and depression that many thinkers imagined would result from the decline of religion.

play—a fundamental element of the human condition; manifests itself in numerous activities, leading to an experience of transcendence from the mundane world.

postmodernism—a term that broadly describes a number of trends in contemporary culture, particularly Western culture; among its primary ideas are the rejection of any grand narrative about history or particular peoples and a rejection of any essentializing of peoples, ideas, etc.

secularism—a worldview or trend that affirms the secular against the religious.

secularization—the historical process of moving from the religious to the nonreligious.

Epilogue

In his seminal work *Sociology of Sport*, Harry Edwards describes sport as "a secular, quasi-religious institution. It does not however, constitute an alternative to or substitute for formal sacred religious involvement."[1] We clearly disagree. In fact, as we argued in the previous chapter, sport may be becoming an alternative or substitute for involvement in more stereotypically religious institutions.

While most people for the last few centuries have made a clear distinction between religion and sport, there have been times and places where that distinction would have been hard to make. Perhaps the most famous time and place was ancient Greece, and nowhere was the line between religion and sport more blurred than at the festival of games that we now call the Olympics. H. D. F. Kitto notes, "[I]t is sometimes made a reproach that a man 'makes a religion of games'. The Greek did not do this, but he did something perhaps more surprising: he made games part of his religion."[2] (See Fig. E.1)

While the festival certainly changed over the course of a thousand years, at its most vibrant the participants (whether athletes or observers) continuously were engaged in activities that we would identify as religious in nature. "The Games were introduced as a religious ceremony in honour of Zeus," Judith Swaddling writes, and the "ideology behind the Games reached its zenith in the fifth century BCE."[3] It is the Games at this zenith and even their slow decline that provide us with important insights into the relationship between religion and sport. We also find here lessons about the relationship between sport and the political-economic world.

David Stuttard describes the Olympic Festival (at least around the fifth century BCE) as the "most significant religious event in the panhellenic (Greek) calendar," adding that "people flocked in their tens of thousands from all over the Greek-speaking world. The closest (but still wildly dissimilar) modern parallel is perhaps the annual Hajj pilgrimage to Mecca [in the Islamic tradition]."[4] Or, we might add, just about any major sporting event today.

The image of pilgrimage certainly is an appropriate way to imagine the procession of Greeks from all directions streaming to the "most sacred place," Olympia, a "site combining a sports complex and a centre for religious devotion."[5] It was a place where Greeks from many different towns and islands came together to form and affirm their common identity and belief system. "The shivered atoms of Greek society, the divided communities of Hellas, were here beautifully and harmoniously blended for a few days in moonlit Olympia," James A. Harrison writes, "in the exercise

Fig. E.1 Greek vase with runners.

of religious worship and the display of the splendid physical and mental gifts natural to the race."[6] Here we see quite clearly the "binding" function of religion working through the festival of the Games, providing opportunities for individuals to perform before the gods.

The center of religious focus was the magnificent Temple of Zeus. Inside, a massive statue of the greatest of all Greek gods sat on a throne awaiting oblations and sacrifices. It was here in the temple that Greek unity was formed and celebrated. As Stuttard observes:

> With its prayers and hymns and incense, the great hecatomb to Zeus was, for the briefest moment, an affirmation of unity among Greek-speaking states—an acknowledgement of a common heritage and shared beliefs. It was one of the few times when men from every city-state from the entire Greek world could stand truly shoulder to shoulder in a communion of purpose, as they acknowledged the supremacy of the greatest god whose worship they all shared, Olympian Zeus.[7]

The games were contested all around the temple, athletes and spectators alike always aware of its presence and that of Zeus himself.

During the five days of the festival, numerous ceremonies and sacrifices took place in and around the temple.[8] In addition to the great sacrifice to Zeus (one that included the killing of 100 oxen), all around Olympia there were numerous temples and altars providing athletes and spectators with plenty of opportunities for prayers and sacrifices.[9] "The gods were believed to bestow on athletes the physical prowess that enabled them to take part in the Games," Swaddling writes, "and accordingly athletes prayed to the relevant deity and promised offerings should they be victorious."[10] Of course, with all the offerings and sacrifices of animals came wonderful feasts—ritual meals that concluded the days and provided one last opportunity before sleep for Greeks to celebrate their victories and mourn their losses.[11]

Certainly there was a lot of activity going on that today we easily would identify as religious. But the more interesting fact is that the athletic competition itself was *explicitly* a religious activity. The participation in the games was seen as an act of religious devotion. In regard to the boxing that took place in the shadows of the temple and other shrines, Stuttard notes, "[I]t was a contest to see whose strength was the more pleasing to the god. The more blood was shed and damage caused in the process, and the harder the outcome was to reach, the more honour was paid to the god."[12] It is not a stretch at all for us to conclude that the spilt blood was a kind of offering to the gods—that it indeed was a sacrifice.

To the victors, who both honored the gods and were helped by them, went the spoils. The winners were crowned with a wreath made of an olive branch from "the most holy of all trees" in the vicinity.[13] "Each victor's wreath," Stuttard observes, "was formed from a single branch of this tree—a ring of unending power which would link its wearer in a mystic union with the god."[14]

As a consequence of their success and their connection with the gods, many victors were celebrated not just as heroes but also as demigods or gods themselves. Recall Homer's and Virgil's depictions of athletes as we saw in Chapter 4. Upon returning to their hometowns, they would visit the temple or shrine of their god and dedicate their wreath in the god's honor. There was then a banquet and much celebration.[15] Statues might be erected in the athlete's honor, awards (monetary and otherwise) provided, and upon his death a grand burial might occur.[16] (See Fig. E.2)

Fig. E.2 Marble statue of discus thrower.

Myths and legends even arose around the athletes. Perhaps the greatest wrestler of all time was Milo, whose prowess fostered stories about eating a whole heifer, drinking large quantities of wine, and dying tragically in the forest.[17]

As the centuries went along, the explicitly religious dimensions of the festival seemed to fade away. Stuttard notes that political intrigue and a "win-at-all-costs" attitude (buttressed by the prospect of financial gain) contributed to the change in the games. Even a new building program that separated some of the sporting venues from the religious heart of the area meant that the "sacred had been removed from the secular. The Games had lost their soul."[18] Whatever the causes, it was clear that something had changed. "The Games were introduced as a religious ceremony in honour of Zeus, but as time went by, belief in the traditional religion faded, and the Games lost their religious significance," Swaddling concludes. "Although the sanctity of the Olympic Games was preserved for a little longer [after the fifth century BCE], men were beginning to usurp the sovereignty of the gods; the athletes credited themselves and not Zeus with their victories."[19] Still, Johan Huizinga claims that the Hellenic games always "remained closely allied with religion, even in later times when, on a superficial view, they might have the appearance of national sports pure and simple."[20]

The ancient Olympics show us how sport and religion can be so intertwined as to make distinguishing them nearly impossible. They also show us how politics and corruption can eat away at the very spirit of our games.

When we erode the spirit of our games, we do so at our peril. Sport produces neither saints nor sinners—though its emphases on hard work, fair play, and self-discipline may have many positive consequences. Like most social institutions, sport has its costs (financial and human resources that could be used in other ways, corruption, cheating, etc.) and benefits (providing a means to orient ourselves in the world, giving us resources for individual and social identity, teaching us important life lessons, etc.). The latter, we argue, certainly outweigh the former. And we believe sport will continue to provide social benefits because it taps into our fundamental religiosity without being bound to dogmatic beliefs that lead to discrimination, violence, and war. Many wars have been started because of ethnic, racial, or political differences. Many have been started because of religious differences as well. And though sport can give rise to violent activity both on the field and in the stands (think of soccer hooligans), sport does not lead us into war.

Indeed, events like the Olympics or the World Cup (soccer) bring together people from around the world—transcending socially constructed borders based on nationality, religion, ethnicity, and more. Dave Zirin notes that the "World Cup is by sheer numbers the most important sporting event on earth, creating the closest thing we have to a united global audience. More than one in four human beings viewed the final game in 2006. That means, outside the United States, just about anyone with access to a television tuned in."[21] A number of news agencies reported that approximately one billion people watched the 2014 final. Rarely does humanity collectively engage in an activity in these numbers where the celebration of human possibility and the expression of collective identities are so powerful. If, indeed, sport functions like religion, then the World Cup may well be considered the world's largest religious event.

Our hope is that citizens in many countries will understand the important role of sport in their culture and use the power of the state to protect it. Just as money and power can have and have had a corrupting influence on religion, so they have a corrupting influence on sport. The ancient Greeks teach us that lesson.

"The principle of play has become corrupted," Roger Callois wrote more than fifty years ago. "It is now necessary to take precautions against cheats and professional players, a unique product of the contagion of reality."[22] To the "cheats and professional players" we now can add owners, marketers, and media moguls whose interests in sport diverge from the genuine play that is at its core.[23] It is critical that nations see sport as a public good that cannot be left to the corrupting influence of the market.

Recognizing the public good of sport involves using the power of the state to control and regulate sport. For many people (particularly conservatives in the United States), such a conclusion will sound socialist. But it is important to note that many sports leagues function very much in a socialist manner already.

In the United States (perhaps the world's greatest advocate of capitalism), many of the professional sports leagues operate along principles that could be described as socialist — including revenue sharing, caps on team salaries, and a commitment to making sure even the smallest market teams can do well financially and have a chance to compete. In fact, even Roger Goodell, commissioner of the National Football League in the United States, has described the league's approach as a "form of socialism."[24] While the owners may not be too concerned about the common good, their approach to their business (American football) really does help to promote the common good.

Again, the ancient Greeks may provide us with a model. The Olympic games were just one of many examples in which games were part of broader civic and religious (the ancient Greeks did not separate these as we do) festivals. As Nancy Evans observes in *Civic Rites: Democracy and Religion in Ancient Athens*, these festivals were important markers on the calendar. The ancient Greeks understood the importance of these festivals for building community and promoting good citizenship. They not only were public events, but they were publicly funded.[25] While the world has changed greatly in 2,500 years, humans have not; the Greeks provide us with an important lesson here. If our sports are to fulfill their civic and spiritual promise, they must be operated by and for the public.

Writing about primarily the American context, Zirin makes a compelling argument for the public ownership and provision of sports teams. He describes a professional sports culture that is corrupt and increasingly only tenuously connected to the common good. He is outraged by owners (most of whom are multimillionaires) who use money and fan loyalty to extort billions of dollars from local governments to build new stadiums and arenas. This situation often leaves local governments in financial peril while owners reap the benefits. As Zirin would say, we have "collectivized the debt and privatized the profit."[26] Instead, he argues for public ownership of teams. The point is to preserve the public good of sport by putting ownership in the hands of the people. The point is to put the teams and their fans first — to put the spirit of sport before profits.

The public ownership of teams would prevent the all-too-common practice in the United States of sports franchises moving from one city to another. "In a just universe, there would be a constitutional amendment preventing sports franchises from moving to other cities," Zirin writes. "Sports teams operate on an entirely different emotional, or even spiritual, plane than any other corporate entity."[27] Here Zirin is referring to the "powerful, even magical connection"[28] between fans and their teams—a connection that we learned is indeed quite religious.

There are a few good examples of the public asserting its rights over its games. Zirin provides an account of a group called Share Liverpool FC (Football Club) that attempted a few years ago to get 100,000 fans to become shareholders of the team by wresting it away from its unpopular owners.[29] Though the owners eventually sold to the Fenway Sports Group (United States), the Share Liverpool effort still was a heartening affirmation of fan loyalty and an effort to gain control over the team that means so much to its fans. Around the same time, the Football Supporters' Federation was formed to advocate on behalf of fans. Current initiatives include getting maximum prices set for visiting fans' tickets and various measures to promote fan safety.

The best example, however, of what Zirin wants and what all fans should want for their teams, is the Green Bay Packers (members of the National Football League in the United States). The Packers are a publicly owned team. Their home is a city of only a bit more than 100,000 residents, easily the smallest city of any major professional sports team in the United States. "The nonprofit team is financially solvent, competitive, and deeply connected to the community," Zirin writes. "It has created something beautiful: a throwback that is also forward-looking. It deserves to be replicated."[30]

As we saw in Chapter 8, the role of money can be problematic for preserving the spirit of play in sport. In part, this is because money is an intrusion of the profane into a sacred world. Such intrusion led Jesus to overturn the tables of the moneychangers and the sellers of goods in the temple.[31] Similar intrusions are why televangelists in the United States and elsewhere often develop bad reputations—for they seem to be in the "religion business" for the money that they constantly are seeking to raise. Such intrusion is why sports fans often feel uncomfortable talking about money as it relates to their teams or their sports—why they want to talk about the games, teams, and players instead.

Like the ancient Greeks, whose games also came to be corrupted by politics and money, we need to recognize the critical importance of our games as well. Our games are not "just" play. Play is an intrinsic and critical human quality that is manifested through sport. It should not be taken lightly. And while sport may be "secular" in some sense, it nevertheless is "sacred secular." We should treat it as carefully as we should treat all that is "holy."

Discussion Questions

1. Is sport in the modern world like sport in ancient Greece? Why or why not?
2. Is sport religion? Is sport religious?
3. In sum, is sport mostly good for society or bad for society? What can be done to make sure that sport is the most beneficial institution in society that it can be?

Notes

Chapter 1

1 Michael Novak, *The Joy of Sports: Endzones, Bases, Baskets, Balls, and the Consecration of the American Spirit* (Lanham, MD: Madison Books, 1976, 1988, 1994).

2 Joseph L. Price, "The Super Bowl as Religious Festival," *The Christian Century*, February 22, 1984, 190.

3 Joseph L. Price, *From Season to Season: Sports as American Religion* (Macon, GA: Mercer University Press, 2001).

4 For a good overview of the scholarship over the last few decades, see Nick Watson's "Introduction," in *Theology, Ethics, and Transcendence in Sports*, edited by Jim Parry, Mark Nesti, and Nick Watson (New York: Routledge, 2011), 5–9.

5 Tracy Trothen, "Better Than Normal?: Constructing Modified Athletes and a Relational Theological Ethic," in *Theology, Ethics, and Transcendence in Sports*, edited by Jim Parry, Mark Nesti, and Nick Watson (New York: Routledge, 2011), 64–81.

6 The Greek notion of "perfection" had more to do with wholeness, or completeness, than it did with flawlessness. In this sense, Matthew's Jesus can urge his followers to be perfect as their heavenly Father is perfect (5:48) and it would not seem absurd as it would if to be perfect meant to be without flaw.

7 Robert J. Higgs and Michael C. Braswell, *An Unholy Alliance: The Sacred and Modern Sports* (Macon, GA: Mercer University Press, 2004).

8 Ibid., 18 (emphasis in original).

9 Ibid., 41–48.

10 Ibid., 81.

11 Ibid., 47–48 (emphasis in original).

12 Ibid., e.g., 16, 56–58, 62–63.

13 Ibid., 48.

14 Ibid., *x*.

15 Ibid., 156.

16 The irony (and ignorance) of their quoting the *Book of Job* (*Unholy*, 48) as though Job were a historical person is not lost on us.

17 John 3:3.

18 Augustine, *Confessions*, 1.1.

Chapter 2

1   Ninian Smart, *Dimensions of the Sacred: An Anatomy of the World's Beliefs* (Berkeley, CA: University of California Press, 1996).

2   Ibid., 10.

3   Ibid.

4   Mircea Eliade, *The Sacred and the Profane: The Nature of Religion* (Orlando, FL: Harcourt, Inc., 1987), 70.

5   Mircea Eliade, *The Myth of the Eternal Return: Or, Cosmos and History* (Princeton, NJ: Princeton University Press, 1991), 21.

6   Genesis 2:18–25.

7   Smart, *Dimensions*, 73.

8   Ibid., 109.

9   Ibid.

10 Ibid.

11 Joseph L. Price, "Conjuring Curses and Supplicating Spirits: Baseball's Culture of Superstitions," chap. 4 in *Rounding the Bases: Baseball and Religion in America* (Macon, GA: Mercer University Press, 2006), 106.

12 *Major League*, Dir. David S. Ward, Perf. Tom Berenger, Charlie Sheen, and Corbin Bernsen, Mirage Enterprises, 1989.

13 Warren St. John, *Rammer Jammer Yellow Hammer: A Road Trip into the Heart of Fan Mania* (New York: Three Rivers Press, 2004), 54.

14 The authors do not hold this philosophy of test-taking, by the way.

15 Smart, *Dimensions*, 46.

16 Eliade, *The Sacred and the Profane*, 30 (emphasis in original).

17 First People: The Legends, "Apache Creation Legend," accessed January 5, 2015, http://www.firstpeople.us/FP-Html-Legends/ApacheCreationLegend-Apache .html.

18 Richard Erdoes and Alfonso Ortiz, eds., *American Indian Myths and Legends* (New York: Pantheon Books, 1984), 88–93.

19 Genesis 1:1–2, New Revised Standard Edition. An alternative reading of the Hebrew is: "In the beginning, when God began to create the heavens and the earth, the earth was a formless void." This is an even clearer image of God bringing order to chaos.

20 Genesis 2:18–20.

21 Genesis 3:22–24.

22 James Gels, "Basketball Coaching Philosophy," The Coaches Clipboard, accessed January 17, 2015, http://www.coachesclipboard.net/BasketballCoachingPhilosophy .html.

23 Ibid.

24 Ibid.

25 Bob Griese and Dave Hyde, *Perfection* (Hoboken, NJ: John Wiley & Sons, 2012), 75–76, Nook edition.

26 Ibid., 78, Nook edition.

27 We should note that since the goal of the coach is to win games, some evidence of the truth of her or his philosophy can be seen in the coach's win–loss record. However, because there tend to be many aspects that go into the success or failure of a team (e.g., player talent, training facilities, quality of the competition), a coach's win–loss record may not be the result of the coach's philosophy alone.

28 Smart, *Dimensions*, 133.

29 There is little doubt that Jesus of Nazareth was, in fact, crucified by the Roman government for insurrection. There is no reason to doubt that Jesus shared a last Passover meal with his closest followers. The reason Smart includes the Last Supper is because of the way the story is told. For Smart, the story is mythicized to serve as a guide for the ritual that became Communion.

30 Smart, *Dimensions*, 133.

31 Ibid.

32 Smart, *Dimensions*, 136.

33 Genesis 32:22–32.

34 Babe Ruth, *The Babe Ruth Story: As Told to Bob Considine* (New York: E. P. Dutton and Co., 1948), 191.

35 Ibid., 191–192.

36 Ibid., 193–194.

37 Tom Meany, *Babe Ruth: The Big Moments of the Big Fellow* (New York: A. S. Barnes and Company, 1947), 127.

38 Ibid.

39 Robert W. Creamer, *Babe: The Legend Comes to Life* (New York: Simon and Schuster, 1974), 363.

40 Ibid., 365.

41 Ibid.

42 Ibid., 366–367.

43 Ibid., 367.

44 Ibid.

45 See, for example, Jerry Brondfield's hagiography, *Rockne: The Coach, The Man, The Legend* (New York: Random House, 1976), 16–17.

46 Murray Sperber, *Shake Down the Thunder: The Creation of Notre Dame Football* (New York: Henry Holt and Company, 1993), 353.

47 Andrew Hughes, "Birth of a Mythology," *South Bend Tribune* (South Bend, IN), November 21, 2008.

48 Sperber, *Shake Down the Thunder*, 328–332.

49 Ibid., 330.

50 As quoted in Sperber, *Shake Down the Thunder*, 360.

51 Sperber, *Shake Down the Thunder*, 360.

52 John Carlin, "Most Bonito," *New York Times Magazine*, June 2006.

53 Ibid.

54 Ibid.

55 K. V. Venugopal, "World Cup Football—Will Brazil Regain Its Glory?," *Alive* 380 (June 2014): 70–73.

56 Carlin, "Most Bonito."

57 Ibid.

58 Ibid.

59 Smart, *Dimensions*, 166.

60 Rudolf Otto, *The Idea of the Holy: An Inquiry into the Non-rational Factor in the Idea of the Divine and Its Relation to the Rational*, Second Edition, trans. by John W. Harvey (London: Oxford University Press, 1952), 5.

61 Ibid.

62 D. P. Simpson, *Cassell's Latin Dictionary* (New York: MacMillan Publishing Company, 1968), 398–399.

63 Otto, *Idea of the Holy*, 7.

64 Ibid., 10.

65 Ibid., 11.

66 Ibid., 25–26.

67 Ibid., 19–20.

68 Huston Smith, *The World's Religions* (New York: HarperSanFrancisco, 1991), 85–86.

69 Diarmaid MacCulloch, *Christianity: The First Three Thousand Years* (New York: Penguin Books, 2010), 209–210.

70 This was a dangerous term given that Gnostic Christianity was condemned in the second and third centuries and was still having an effect on Christianity when Evagrius wrote in the fourth century.

71 Augustine, *Confessions*, 9.10.

72 Smart, *Dimensions*, 178.

73 Ibid.

74 Ibid. 179.

75 Ibid., 182.

76 YouTube, "Best Fan Reactions to Patriots' Game-Winning Interception vs Seahawks! (Super Bowl XLIX)," accessed February 5, 2015, https://www.youtube.com/watch?v=smwmgZViC0g.

77 Ibid.

78 Ignacio Götz, *The Psychedelic Teacher* (Philadelphia, PA: Westminster Press, 1972), as quoted in Ignacio Götz, "Spirituality and the Body," *Religious Education* 96, no. 1 (Winter 2001): 10.

79 Götz, "Spirituality and the Body," 10–11 (emphasis in original).

80 Henning Boecker, et al., "The Runner's High: Opioidergic Mechanisms in the Human Brain," *Cerebral Cortex* 18 (November 2008): 2523.

81 A. Dietrich and W. F. McDaniel, "Endocannabinoids and Exercise," *British Journal of Sports Medicine* 38, no. 5 (October 2004): 536–541.

82 Robert R. Sands and Linda R. Sands, "Running Deep: Speculations on the Evolution of Running and Spirituality in the Genus *Homo*," *Journal for the Study of Religion, Nature and Culture* 3, no. 4 (December 1, 2009): 566.

83   Jeffery Summers, et al. "Middle-Aged, Non-elite Marathon Runners: A Profile." *Perceptual and Motor Skills* 54, no. 3, Pt 1 (June 1982): 967–968.

84   Sands and Sands, "Running Deep."

85   Smart, *Dimensions*, 197.

86   Ibid., 213.

87   Ibid., 201.

88   Ibid.

89   Philly.com, "Crew Chiefs Suspended, Drivers Docked Points for Cheating," last updated February 14, 2007, http://articles.philly.com/2007-02-14/sports/25238720_1_riggs-and-sadler-kenny-francis-chad-knaus.

90   Ibid.

91   Jeff Owens, "Knaus Not Fretting Reputation, but He Should Be," *Sporting News*, last updated March 2, 2012, http://www.sportingnews.com/nascar/story/2012-03-02/chad-knaus-cheater-not-worried-about-reputation-jimmie-johnson-hendrick-motor-spo.

92   Ibid.

93   Ibid.

94   The Archery Hall of Fame and Museum, Inc., "Our Mission," accessed February 9, 2015, http://www.archeryhalloffame.org/.

95   M. R. James, "Dr. Dave Inducted into Archery Hall of Fame," *Bowhunter* 37, no. 4 (January 2008): 38.

96   AJC.com, "John Smoltz: Becoming a Hall of Famer 'Just Incredible'," last modified February 3, 2015, http://www.ajc.com/ap/ap/georgia/john-smoltz-becoming-a-hall-of-famer-just-incredib/nj347/.

97   Smart, *Dimensions*, 216.

98   Ibid., 217.

99   Ibid.

100   Ibid., 219.

101   Ibid., 223.

102   Ibid., 225.

103   Ibid., 215.

104   Irv Moss, "Colorado Sports Hall of Fame Mentors Fill Class of '08 April 8 Inductees" (abbreviated title), *Denver Post* (Denver, CO), October 10, 2007.

105   See, for example, Doug Gillon, "Sports Focus Burn Out: Celebrity Status Should Not Cost So Much," *The Herald*, October 23, 1998, http://search.proquest.com/docview/332594024?accountid=2193.

106   Sharon Robb, "A Resurrection, Bela Style: Romanian Gymnastics Coach Rushes Back in to Save the Day for the U.S.," *The Ottawa Citizen*, September 13, 2000.

107   Smart, *Dimensions*, 275.

108   Ibid.

109   Ibid., 277.

110   Eliade, *The Sacred and the Profane*, 22.

111   Ibid., 26.

112 Ibid., 30 (emphasis in original).

113 Ibid., 31.

114 Ibid., 33.

115 Ibid.

116 Ibid., 44–45.

117 K. C. Hanson, "Transformed on the Mountain: Ritual Analysis and the Gospel of Matthew," *Semeia* no. 67 (January 1, 1994), 149.

118 Eliade, *The Sacred and the Profane*, 37.

119 Joseph L. Price, *Rounding the Bases: Baseball and Religion in America* (Macon, GA: Mercer University Press, 2006), 75–76.

120 Mary Gail Hare, "Retailer Eyed as Buyer of Ripken Ball; Local Promoter Wants to Sell Game Souvenir to Wal-Mart Chain; Price Set at $1 Million; Liberty Road Store Will Display Item, Other Memorabilia," *The Sun*, January 07, 1997, http://search.proquest .com/docview/406955232?accountid=2193.

121 Price, *Rounding the Bases*, 81–82.

122 Ibid. Price points out in a footnote that two Major League stadiums now have portions of the outfield raised, also. See his p. 81 n. 15.

Chapter 3

1 "Perfection" can refer to being without flaw, being complete, or even both of these.

2 We should note that the two main branches of Buddhism, Mahayana Buddhism and Theravada Buddhism, see the ideal human condition in slightly different ways. Theravada Buddhism has as its ideal the *arhat*. The *arhat* is the individual who has achieved Enlightenment primarily through her individual effort. Mahayana Buddhism, on the other hand, emphasizes more the role of the community in the achievement of Enlightenment. The ideal human in this type of Buddhism is the *bodhisattva*, one who, on the brink of escaping *samsara*, turns back to help others achieve it until all have achieved it.

3 Robert C. Gregg, trans., *Athanasius: The Life of Antony and Letter to Marcellinus*, The Classics of Western Spirituality (New York: Paulist Press, 1980), 31ff.

4 Ibid., 42–43.

5 Thomas À. Kempis, *The Imitation of Christ*, trans. by William C. Creasy (Macon, GA: Mercer University Press, 2007), 2.11.

6 We should note that Jews and Muslims interpret the story of Abraham, Sarah, Hagar, Ismael, and Isaac differently. In the Hebrew Bible, Ishmael, born first, is the product of Abraham and Sarah's slave, Hagar. Isaac is the product of Abraham and Sarah, Abraham's wife. With God's blessing, Sarah kicks Hagar and Ishmael out of the family thus securing the position and inheritance of her son, Isaac. However, just as God promised Abraham that he would be the father of a great nation, so God promised Hagar that Ishmael would be the father of a great nation. In the Qur'an, Hagar is not Sarah's slave but is Abraham's second wife, thus making Ishmael the legitimate first-born of Abraham's line.

7 Murray Chass, "Age Is No Deterrent to Perfection: Johnson Faces 27 Braves, and Retires Them All," *The New York Times*, May 19, 2004.

8 In this case, the concept of perfection includes both the fact that Comaneci had a *complete* routine and that it was *without flaw*.

9 Matt Rendell, "The Perfect Ten: Great Athletes Relish Their Achievements; Nadia Comaneci Wants to Forget Hers," *The Observer* (London, UK), July 4, 2004: 46.

10 William Wallace, Special to the New York Times, "Miami Wins in Bowl for Perfect Season," *The New York Times* (New York, NY), January 15, 1973: 1.

11 Leonard Shapiro, "1972 Dolphins Want to Remain the Big Fish: Team That Finished 17–0 Roots against 13–0 Broncos of 1998," *The Washington Post*, December 10, 1998.

12 Amy K. Nelson, "Searching for Meaning in the Mistake," ESPN, last updated January 9, 2011, http://sports.espn.go.com/espn/otl/news/story?id=5993137.

13 Ibid.

14 Simon Barnes, "Perfect Comaneci Keeps Her Sense of Balance," *The Times* (London, UK), October 17, 2009: 84.

15 William Wallace, Special to the New York Times, "Miami Wins in Bowl for Perfect Season," *The New York Times* (New York, NY), January 15, 1973: 1.

Chapter 4

1 Sigmund Freud, *The Interpretation of Dreams*, James Strachey, trans. (London: The Hogarth Press, 1958), 21.

2 Ibid., 550–551.

3 Ibid., 569 (emphasis original).

4 Sigmund Freud, *Civilization and Its Discontent*, James Strahey, trans. (New York: W. W. Norton and Company, 1961), 19.

5 Ibid., 21.

6 Michael Balint, *The Basic Fault* (New York: Bruner/Mazel, 1979), 14.

7 Ibid., 16–17.

8 Ibid., 14–15.

9 Ibid., 58.

10 Ibid., 64–65.

11 Ibid., 65.

12 Ibid., 66.

13 Ibid., 67.

14 Ibid.

15 Heinz Kohut, *Self Psychology and the Humanities: Reflections on a New Psychological Approach*, Charles B. Strozier, ed. (New York: W. W. Norton & Company, 1985), 454.

16 Ibid., 455.

17 Ibid., 456.

18 Friedrich Schleiermacher, *The Christian* Faith, ed. by H. R. MacIntosh and J. S. Stewart (Edinburgh: T&T Clark, 1989), 1.4.4.

19 Ibid., 1.19.2.

20 Ludwig Feuerbach, *The Essence of Christianity*, trans. by George Eliot (Amherst, NY: Prometheus Books, 1989), 7.

21 Ibid., 33.

22 Ibid., 26.

23 Paul Tillich, *The Courage to Be* (New Haven, CT: Yale University Press, 1980), 35.

24 Ibid., 35–36.

25 By "the God of theism" Tillich means the God that people imagine when they think of God as a supernatural being. This God is tied to a particular culture and is the key player in religious mythology, often the Creator and divine Parent and Judge of humans. The God above this culturally shaped God is beyond any limits of the human imagination. Tillich often speaks of this God as the "Ground of Being" or "Being itself." This God is experienced as the courage to be in the face of non-being.

26 Tillich, *Courage*, 186–190.

27 Reinhold Niebuhr, *Moral Man and Immoral Society* (New York: Charles Scriber's Sons, 1960), 42.

28 Homer, *Iliad*, 23:306–7.

29 Ibid., 23:290.

30 Ibid., 23:354.

31 Ibid., 23:293–294.

32 Ibid., 23:355.

33 Ibid., 23:528.

34 Ibid., 23:302.

35 Ibid., 23:360.

36 Ibid., 23:448.

37 Ibid., 23:643–645.

38 Ibid., 23:659.

39 Ibid., 23:664–665.

40 Ibid., 23:677–678.

41 Ibid., 23:700–739.

42 Ibid., 23:753–756.

43 Ibid., 23:773–783.

44 Ibid., 23:811–812.

45 Ibid., 23:836–838.

46 Ibid., 23:859–860.

47 Ibid., 23:884–897.

48 Homer, *Odyssey*, 8:104–119.

49 Ibid., 8:164.

50 Ibid., 8:186–198.

51 Virgil, *Aeneid*, 5:141–368.

52 Ibid., 5:291–293.

53 Ibid., 5:379–380.

54 Ibid., 5:381–382.

55 Ibid., 5:473–485.

56 Ibid., 5:518–545.

57 "muscle"

58 Virgil, *Aeneid*, 5:546–548.

59 Ibid., 5:603–604.

60 Ibid., 5:595.

61 Ibid., 5:621–622.

62 Walter Burkert, *Greek Religion* (Cambridge, MA: Harvard University Press, 1985), 203.

63 Michael Grant, *Myths of the Greeks and Romans* (New York: Penguin Books, 1962), 45.

64 Ibid.

65 See Burkert, *Greek Religion*, 205.

66 Grant, *Myths*, 46 (emphasis his).

67 It is also interesting to note that, in the cult of the hero—the honoring of dead heroes with shrines and monuments built at the graves of heroes—the cult is specific to one locality. As Burkert says, "An important difference between the hero cult and the cult of the gods is that a hero is always confined to a specific locality; he acts in the vicinity of his grave for his family, group or city. The bond with a hero is dissolved by distance …" (*Greek Religion*, 206). The hero is local and tied to a specific community, an indication of the necessity of the hero to be like those for whom he or she is a hero. This is why teams and athletes tend to find the largest concentration of their fans in the area they represent. Due largely to nationally and internationally televised games, however, some teams have fans who live far outside of the area formally recognized by the team (e.g., the New York Yankees, Manchester United). Sometimes, towns or cities will recognize a local athlete who has become nationally famous for her or his play. The small town of Pierson, Florida (USA), for example, has signs along the main road at the city limits noting that it is the home of MLB star, Chipper Jones.

68 Warren St. John, *Rammer Jammer Yellow Hammer: A Road Trip into the Heart of Fan Mania* (New York: Three Rivers Press, 2004), 96.

69 That is, those who travel in recreational vehicles (RVs) that can be anything from a small camper to a large, tour bus-like vehicle with nearly all of the amenities of a home. RVers tend to arrive at game sites days ahead of the actual game day for fellowship and partying with other RVers.

70 St. John, *Rammer Jammer*, 30.

71 Ibid., 47.

72 ESPN, "NFL History—Super Bowl Winners," accessed May 25, 2015, http://espn .go.com/nfl/superbowl/history/winners.

73 Teams played only 144 games (instead of the usual 162) that year due to the continuation of a strike begun in 1994.

74 Baseball-Reference.com, "Team Wins," accessed May 22, 2015, http://www.base -ball-reference.com/leagues/MLB/.

75 Joseph L. Price, "The Super Bowl as Religious Festival," in *From Season to Season: Sports as American Religion* (Macon, GA: Mercer University Press, 2001), 138.

Chapter 5

1 Emile Durkheim, *The Elementary Forms of Religious Life*, trans. by Karen E. Fields (New York: The Free Press, 1995), 34.

2   Robert N. Bellah, "Durkheim and Ritual," in *The Cambridge Companion to Durkheim*, edited by Jeffrey C. Alexander and Philip Smith (Cambridge, UK: Cambridge University Press, 2005), 184.

3   Ann Taves, *Religious Experience Reconsidered: A Building-Block Approach to the Study of Religion and Other Special Things* (Princeton, NJ: Princeton University Press, 2009), 14.

4   Ibid., 162–163.

5   Durkheim, *The Elementary Forms*, 41.

6   Ibid., 44 (italics in original).

7   Ibid., 267.

8   Ibid., 16.

9   Ibid., 271.

10 Robert J. Higgs and Michael C. Braswell, *An Unholy Alliance: The Sacred and Modern Sports* (Macon, GA: Mercer University Press, 2004), 211.

11 Durkheim, *The Elementary Forms*, 116.

12 Anthropologist Victor Turner also writes about the following characteristics of the religious rites or rituals that he observed or studied: "singing, dancing, feasting, wearing of bizarre dress, body painting, use of alcohol or hallucinogens." Victor Turner, *Dramas, Fields, and Metaphors: Symbolic Action in Human Society* (Ithaca, NY: Cornell University Press, 1974), 55.

13 Durkheim, *The Elementary Forms*, 330.

14 Ibid., 347.

15 Ibid., 350.

16 Ibid., 385.

17 Roger Friedland, "Drag Kings at the Totem Ball: The Erotics of Collective Representation in Emile Durkheim and Sigmund Freud," in *The Cambridge Companion to Durkheim*, edited by Jeffrey C. Alexander and Philip Smith (Cambridge, UK: Cambridge University Press, 2005), 243.

18 Victor Turner, *The Ritual Process: Structure and Anti-structure* (New York: Aldine de Gruyter, 1995), 131–132.

19 Turner, *Dramas*, 272.

20 Turner, *Ritual Process*, 132.

21 Turner, *Dramas*, 56.

22 Turner, *Ritual Process*, 139 (italics in original).

23 Durkheim, *The Elementary Forms*, 386.

24 Ibid., 429.

25 Johan Huizinga, *Homo Ludens: A Study of the Play Element in Culture* (Boston: The Beacon Press, 1955), 1 (italics in original).

26 Ibid., 2–3.

27 Ibid., 8, 9.

28 Ibid., 5.

29 Ibid., 173 (italics in original).

30 Ibid., 5.

31 Ibid., 15.

32 Ibid., 9.

33 Ibid., 20.

34 Ibid., 10.

35 Ibid.

36 Ibid., 11.

37 Ibid., 17.

38 Harry Edwards, *Sociology of Sport* (Homewood, IL: The Dorsey Press, 1973), 157.

39 Simon Kuper and Stefan Szymanski, *Soccernomics: Why England Loses, Why Spain, Germany, and Brazil Win, and Why the US, Japan, Australia, Turkey—and Even Iraq—Are Destined to Become the Kings of the World's Most Popular Sport*, revised and expanded edition (New York: Nation Books, 2012), 218.

40 Ibid., 250–252.

41 Nick Hornby, *Fever Pitch* (New York: Riverhead Books, 1992), 56.

42 Ibid., 62.

43 Ibid., 207.

44 Ibid., 156.

45 Ibid., 142. It should be noted, however, that Kuper and Szymanski report data that show that spectators *do* alter behavior based on their team's performance. Home crowds increase when the team does well and decrease when the team does poorly. See Kuper and Szymanski, *Soccernomics*, 240. We also provide data on this phenomenon in the previous chapter.

46 Hornby, *Fever Pitch*, 178 (italics in original).

47 Ibid., 102.

48 Ibid., 220.

49 Such seeking of control is a phenomenon we described in Chapter 2.

50 Hornby, *Fever Pitch*, 103.

51 See ibid., 108.

52 Ibid., 173.

53 Ibid., 223.

54 Ibid. (our italics).

55 Ibid., 179.

56 Ibid., 64.

57 Kuper and Szymanski challenge Hornby's account. They do not deny his experience but argue that his experience is not typical. In other words, Hornby is the *unusual* football fan in England—rooting for and sticking with one team through thick and thin. See Kuper and Szymanski, *Soccernomics*, 244, 248–252.

58 Kuper and Szymanski, *Soccernomics*, 253–266.

59 James Belich, *Paradise Reforged: A History of the New Zealanders: From the 1880s to the Year 2000* (Auckland, NZ: Allen Lane/The Penguin Press, 2001), 381.

60 Ibid., 381.

61 Ibid., 388.

62 Ibid., 385.

63 Ibid., 386.

64 Ibid.

65 Ibid.

66 Michael Grimshaw, "The Oval Opiate?: The History and Analysis of an Idea and Claim," *International Journal of Religion and Sport* 2 (2013), 57.

67 Ibid., 71.

68 Ibid., 76.

69 Ibid., 83.

70 Ibid., 73.

71 John Carlin, *Invictus: Nelson Mandela and the Game That Made a Nation* (New York: Penguin Books, 2008).

72 Ibid., 11.

73 Ibid., 42.

74 Ibid., 172.

75 Ibid., 209.

76 Ibid., 242–243.

77 Ibid., 249.

Chapter 6

1 2 Samuel 11:1–21.

2 Immanuel Kant, *Groundwork of the Metaphysic of Morals*, trans. by H. J. Paton (New York: Harper & Row, 1964), 88 (italics in original).

3 Ibid., 96 (italics in original).

4 The best and most famous defense of this ethical approach is probably John Stuart Mill's *Utilitarianism* (New York: Macmillan Publishing Company, 1957).

5 See Book I of Aristotle's *The Nicomachean Ethics* (New York: Oxford University Press, 1998) for the best account of the argument to follow.

6 While Aristotle may not have considered himself a cultural relativist, many contemporary theorists (including communitarians) have used his moral framework in that way.

7 Lamin Sanneh, "Saints and Exemplars," in *The Blackwell Companion to Religious Ethics*, edited by William Schweiker (Malden, MA: Blackwell Publishing, 2008), 94.

8 *The Bhagavad Gita*, trans. by Juan Mascaro (New York: Penguin Books, 1962), 46.

9 Ibid., 51.

10 Ibid., 115–116.

11 Ibid., 50.

12 Ibid., 51.

13 Robert L. Simon, *Fair Play: The Ethics of Sport*, 3rd edition (Boulder, CO: Westview Press, 2010), 56.

14 The best resource is probably MacIntyre's influential *After Virtue: A Study in Moral Theory* (Notre Dame, IN: University of Notre Dame Press, 1981).

15 To return to the work of Johan Huizinga, we can say that the internal goods derive from the true "play" quality of the sport, while the external goods are in some sense irrelevant or can even be a threat to that play quality.

16 Randolph Feezell, *Sport, Play & Ethical Reflection* (Chicago: University of Illinois Press, 2004), 129.

17 Harry Edwards, *Sociology of Sports* (Homewood, IL: The Dorsey Press, 1973), 69.

18 Ibid., 169 (italics in original).

19 Feezell, *Sport*, 141.

20 Edwards, *Sociology*, 243 (italics in original).

21 Ibid., 270 (italics in original).

22 Ibid., 271.

23 Simon, *Fair Play*, 193.

24 Ibid., 195.

25 Ibid., 197.

26 Ibid., 214.

27 Ibid.

28 Jay Busbee, "Davis calls penalty on himself, gives up shot at first PGA win." Yahoo Sports (yahoo.com), April 18, 2010.

29 "Brian Davis has no regrets for calling two-shot penalty on himself." *The Guardian* (theguardian.com), April 19, 2010.

30 "Jim Furyk wins Verizon Heritage after Brian Davis calls penalty on himself." *Golf* (golf.com), April 18, 2010.

31 "Brian Davis has no regrets for calling two-shot penalty on himself." *The Guardian* (theguardian.com), April 19, 2010.

32 "Jim Furyk wins Verizon Heritage after Brian Davis calls penalty on himself." *Golf* (golf.com), April 18, 2010. Recall our discussion of NASCAR crew chiefs in Chapter 2.

33 Jay Busbee, "Davis calls penalty on himself, gives up shot at first PGA win." Yahoo Sports (yahoo.com), April 18, 2010.

34 Today, the contest has been expanded to pit the Americans against European golfers.

35 Gwilym S. Brown, "Ryder Cup 1969: A Tie May Be Like Kissing Your Sister …" *Golf* (golf.com), August 19, 2008.

36 Bob Harig, "Jacklin fondly recalls the '69 Cup." *ESPN.com*, February 21, 2014.

37 Ibid.

38 United Nations Office on Sport for Development and Peace (UNOSDP), *Annual Report 2013* (Geneva: UNOSDP, 2014), 11.

39 Ibid., 5.

40 International Olympic Committee (IOC), "IOC and UN Secretariat agree historic deal to work together to use sport to build a better world." *Olympic.org*, April 28, 2014.

41 Ibid.

42 Ibid.

43 PeacePlayers International Web site, www.peaceplayersintl.org.

44 Football Beyond Borders Web site, www.footballbeyondborders.org.

45 UN News Centre, "UN, Olympic Committee sign formal agreement on role of sport in development, peace." *UN.org*, April 28, 2014.

46 "From NY to Kabul: Pugliese ponders Premier League move … to Afghanistan." *The Guardian* (theguardian.com), February 6, 2014.

47 Ibid.

48 Grant Wahl, "American Nick Pugliese breaking barriers by playing in Afghanistan." *Sports Illustrated* (si.com), June 27, 2013.

49 "From NY to Kabul: Pugliese ponders Premier League move … to Afghanistan." *The Guardian* (theguardian.com), February 6, 2014.

Chapter 7

1 *Karl Marx: The Essential Writings*, Second Edition, edited by Frederic L. Bender (Boulder, Colorado: Westview Press, 1972), 46.

2 There also are the "outcastes," people so low in the hierarchy that they are not in one of the respectable castes.

3 Guy Debord, *Society of the Spectacle*, trans. by Ken Knabb (London: Rebel Press, 1983), 12.

4 Ibid., 14.

5 Ibid., 22.

6 Ibid., 24.

7 Ibid., 25.

8 Ibid., 33.

9 Ibid., 25.

10 Ibid., 34.

11 Ibid., 30.

12 Allen Guttmann, *From Ritual to Record: The Nature of Modern Sports* (New York: Columbia University Press, 1978).

13 David L. Andrews, *Sport—Commerce—Culture: Essays on Sport in Late Capitalist America* (New York: Peter Lang, 2006).

14 See, in particular, chapters three and four of Victor Turner's *The Ritual Process: Structure and Anti-Structure* (New York: Aldine de Gruyter, 1969).

15 A fuller account of this argument, especially as it applies to the American South, can be found in Bain-Selbo's *Game Day and God: Football, Faith, and Politics in the American South* (Mercer University Press, 2009).

16 Dave Zirin, *Bad Sports: How Owners Are Ruining the Games We Love* (New York: The New Press, 2010), 29.

17 "Super Bowl ticket prices: Average cost for each year's game," SI.com (http://www.si.com/nfl/2015/01/29/super-bowl-ticket-price-history), January 29, 2015.

18 Simon Kuper and Stefan Szymanski, *Soccernomics: Why England Loses, Why Spain, Germany and Brazil Win, and Why the US, Japan, Australia, Turkey—and Even Iraq—Are Destined to Become the Kings of the World's Most Popular Sport* (New York: Nation Books, 2012), 166.

19 Ibid., 171.

20 Ibid., 176.

21 "Is football still affordable for the working classes?" BBC Consumer (http://www.bbc .co.uk/consumer), August 16, 2013.

22 See Bain-Selbo's *Game Day and God: Football, Faith, and Politics in the American South* (Mercer University Press, 2009) for a more thorough presentation of the subsequent argument.

23 Data for school enrollments and racial make up of the teams is from a 2014/15 review of institutional Web sites and a review of photographs of players on the Web sites or in the football media guides. While a review of photographs is not the best way to gather data about race, we were unable to find such data on either of the teams' Web sites. We are confident, however, that any errors we have made in the racial identity of players are negligible and would not affect the percentages significantly. State population percentages are from the 2010 US Census.

24 E-mail correspondence received October 10, 2006.

25 Quoted in Michael Lewis' *The Blind Side: Evolution of a Game* (New York: W. W. Norton & Company, 2007), 272.

26 Ibid., 280.

27 Regina Schwartz, *The Curse of Cain: The Violent Legacy of Monotheism* (Chicago: The University of Chicago Press, 1997).

28 David Goldfield, *Still Fighting the Civil War: The American South and Southern History* (Baton Rouge, LA: Louisiana State University Press, 2002), 84.

29 E-mail correspondence, August 28, 2006.

30 Zirin, *Welcome to the Terrordome: The Pain, Politics, and Promise of Sports* (Chicago: Haymarket Books, 2007), 94.

31 Ibid.

32 Nick Hornby, *Fever Pitch* (New York: Riverhead Books, 1992).

33 Bill Buford, *Among the Thugs* (New York: Vintage Books, 1990), 233, 136.

34 Ibid., 153.

35 Kuper and Szymanski, *Soccernomics*, 83.

36 Ibid., 87.

37 Ibid., 101–120.

38 Ibid., 84.

39 Ibid., 93.

40 Quoted in Zirin, *Terrordome*, 192.

Chapter 8

1 Peter Berger, *The Sacred Canopy: Elements of a Sociological Theory of Religion* (New York: Anchor Books, 1967), 107.

2 Ibid., 127.

3 Charles Taylor, *A Secular Age* (Cambridge, MA: Harvard University Press, 2007), 14.

4   Ibid., 25.

5   Karl Marx, *The Portable Karl Marx*, edited by Eugene Kamenka (New York: Penguin Books, 1983), 115.

6   Ibid., 541.

7   Sigmund Freud, *The Future of an Illusion*, trans. by James Strachey (New York: W. W. Norton & Company, 1961), 44.

8   Ibid., 50.

9   Vincent P. Pecora notes that "on the heels of the Enlightenment, the French Revolution, and a range of nationalist upheavals leading to 1848, the year of so many failed European rebellions, numerous thinkers of quite different religious and political persuasions were convinced that people needed to worship some transcendent force or idea if civilization was to survive the crises of legitimacy that afflicted it" (*Secularization and Cultural Criticism: Religion, Nation, & Modernity*, Chicago: The University of Chicago Press, 2006, 108).

10 Emile Durkheim, *The Elementary Forms of Religious Life*, trans. by Karen E. Fields (New York: Free Press, 1995), 429.

11 Mark S. Cladis, "Beyond Solidarity?: Durkheim and Twenty-first Century Democracy in a Global Age," in *The Cambridge Companion to Durkheim*, edited by Jeffrey C. Alexander and Philip Smith (Cambridge, UK: Cambridge University Press, 2005), 404–405.

12 Max Weber, *The Protestant Ethic and the "Spirit" of Capitalism and Other Writings*, translated and edited by Peter Baehr and Gordon C. Wells (New York: Penguin Books, 2002), 104–105 (italics in original).

13 Ibid., 68. In a recent study entitled *The Protestant Ethic and the Spirit of Sport*, Steven Overman finds these traces not only in the economic behavior of citizens of the United States in the twentieth century, but in the development and nature of sports in that country (Macon, GA: Mercer University Press, 2011).

14 C. G. Jung, *Modern Man in Search of a Soul*, trans. by W. S. Dell and Cary F. Baynes (New York: Harcourt Brace & Company, 1933), 244.

15 Mircea Eliade, *Patterns in Comparative Religion* (New York: Sheed & Ward, 1958).

16 Several essays in *From Season to Season: Sports as American Religion* (2001), edited by Joseph L. Price, utilize an Eliadean perspective. Also, see Chapter 1 of Eric Bain-Selbo's *Game Day and God: Football, Faith, and Politics in the American South* (2009).

17 Niklas Luhmann, *A Systems Theory of Religion*, trans. by David A. Brenner with Adrian Hermann (Stanford, CA: Stanford University Press, 2013), 202.

18 Pecora, *Secularization*, 26.

19 Talal Asad, *Formations of the Secular: Christianity, Islam, Modernity* (Stanford, CA: Stanford University Press, 2003), 1.

20 Ibid., 25.

21 Ibid.

22 While Asad does not take up the issue of sport, his chapter "Secularism, Nation-State, Religion" grapples with the question of whether or not the contemporary nation-state

can be represented as religious. While we do not agree with his conclusion (he argues that the nation-state generally should not be represented as religious), the chapter offers a strong counterargument to the kind of move we are making here. See Asad, 2003, 181–201.

23 Johan Huizinga, *Homo Ludens: A Study of the Play Element in Culture* (Boston: The Beacon Press, 1950), 173.
24 Ibid., 197.
25 Ibid., 198.
26 Ibid., 199.
27 Ibid., 211.
28 Roger Callois, *Man, Play and Games*, trans. by Meyer Barash (Chicago: University of Illinois Press, 1961), 97.
29 Ibid., 110.
30 Ibid., 58.
31 Dave Zirin, *Bad Sports: How Owners Are Ruining the Games We Love* (New York: The New Press, 2010), ix.
32 We will return to Zirin's point in the Epilogue.
33 Robert L. Simon, *Fair Play: The Ethics of Sport* (Boulder, CO: Westview Press, 2010), 168.
34 Simon Kuper and Stefan Szymanski, *Soccernomics: Why England Loses, Why Spain, Germany, and Brazil Win, and Why the US, Japan, Australia, Turkey—and Even Iraq— Are Destined to Become the Kings of the World's Most Popular Sport* (New York: Nation Books, 2012), 70.
35 Simon, *Fair Play*, 191.
36 Berger, *Canopy*, 124.
37 Steven Pinker, *The Better Angels of Our Nature: Why Violence Has Declined* (New York: Penguin Books, 2012).
38 Luhmann, *Systems*, 213.
39 Pecora, *Secularization*, 22.

Epilogue

1 Harry Edwards, *Sociology of Sport* (Homewood, IL: The Dorsey Press, 1973), 90.
2 H. D. F. Kitto, *The Greeks* (Baltimore, MD: Penguin Books, 1951), 173.
3 Judith Swaddling, *The Ancient Olympic Games* (London: The British Museum Press, 2011), 99.
4 David Stuttard, *Power Games: Ritual and Rivalry at the Ancient Greek Olympics* (London: The British Museum Press, 2012), 10.
5 Swaddling, *The Ancient Olympic Games*, 7.
6 James A. Harrison, *The Story of Greece* (New York: G. P. Putnam's Sons, 1898), 159.
7 Stuttard, *Power Games*, 115.
8 See Swaddling, *The Ancient Olympic Games*, 53, for an example of the "programme."
9 Swaddling, *The Ancient Olympic Games*, 55.

10 Ibid., 12.

11 Stuttard, *Power Games*, 128.

12 Ibid., 67.

13 Ibid., 168.

14 Ibid.

15 See ibid., 177–178.

16 See Swaddling, *The Ancient Olympic Games*, 93.

17 Ibid., 74–75.

18 Stuttard, *Power Games*, 206.

19 Swaddling, *The Ancient Olympic Games*, 99.

20 Johan Huizinga, *Homo Ludens: A Study of the Play Element in Culture* (Boston, MA: The Beacon Press, 1950), 73.

21 Dave Zirin, *Welcome to the Terrordome: The Pain, Politics, and Promise of Sports* (Chicago: Haymarket Books, 2007), 91.

22 Roger Callois, *Man, Play and Games*, trans. by Meyer Barash (Chicago: University of Illinois Press, 1961), 45. He adds: "Outside of the arena, after the gong strikes, begins the true perversion of *agon*, the most pervasive of all the categories. It appears in every conflict untempered by the rigor or spirit of play. Now competition is nothing but a law of nature" (46).

23 Callois identifies six key characteristics of play: Free, Separate, Uncertain, Unproductive, Governed by rules, and Make-believe. For a description, see Callois, 1961: 9–10. See our Chapters 5 and 8 for more about play.

24 60 Minutes, January 30, 2012, cbsnews.com (www.cbsnews.com/news /the-nfl-commissioner-roger-goodell/).

25 Nancy Evans, *Civic Rites: Democracy and Religion in Ancient Greece* (Berkeley, CA: University of California Press, 2010).

26 Dave Zirin, *Bad Sports: How Owners Are Ruining the Games We Love* (New York: The New York Press, 2012), xvi.

27 Ibid., 57.

28 Ibid., 58.

29 Ibid., 178.

30 Ibid., 183.

31 Matthew 21:12.

Bibliography

"1972 Perfect Season: Miami Dolphins 17–0." http://www.72dolphins.com/. Accessed March 22, 2013.

Alderman, R.B. *Psychological Behavior in Sport*. Philadelphia, PA: W. B. Saunders Company, 1974.

Andrews, David L. *Sport—Commerce—Culture: Essays on Sport in Late Capitalist America*. New York: Peter Lang, 2006.

Archer, Michael, et al. *The International Book of Soccer*. New York: A&W Publishers, Inc., 1977.

"Archery Hall of Fame and Museum." http://www.archeryhalloffame.org. Accessed February 9, 2015.

Arenofsky, Janice. "What Mentors & Role Models Can Do for You." *Career World* 27, no. 3 (November, 1998): 6–11. http://search.proquest.com/docview/209769292?accountid=2193.

Aristotle. *The Nicomachean Ethics*. Translated by David Ross (New York: Oxford University Press, 1998).

Arthurs, Brian J. "Pele Gave Soccer a Champ's Kick." *Investor's Business Daily*. Los Angeles. September 16, 2008.

Asad, Talal. *Formations of the Secular: Christianity, Islam, Modernity*. Stanford, CA: Stanford University Press, 2003.

Athanasius. *The Life of Antony and the Letter to Marcellinus*. Translated by Robert C. Gregg. The Classics of Western Spirituality. New York: Paulist Press, 1980.

Atkinson, Tommy R. "Spot in Nationals Fulfills Dream for Huntington Gymnast." *The Charleston Gazette,* August 10, 2009. http://search.proquest.com/docview/331574987?accountid=2193.

Augustine. *Confessions*. Translated by R. S. Pine-Coffin. London: Penguin Books, 1961.

Bain-Selbo, Eric. *Game Day and God: Football, Faith, and Politics in the American South*. Macon, GA: Mercer University Press, 2009.

Balint, Michael. *The Basic Fault*. New York: Brunner/Mazel, 1979.

Banier, Antoine. *The Mythology and Fables of the Ancients, Explain'd from History*. Google Books. http://books.google.com.

Barnes, Simon. "Perfect Comaneci Keeps Her Sense of Balance." *The Times* (London, UK), October 17, 2009: 84.

Basketball HQ. "Coach James Gels Interview." http://basketballhq.com/coach-james-gels-interview. Accessed January 17, 2015.

Belich, James. *Paradise Reforged: A History of the New Zealanders: From the 1880s to the Year 2000*. Auckland, NZ: Allen Lane/The Penguin Press, 2001.

Bellah, Robert N. "Durkheim and Ritual." In *The Cambridge Companion to Durkheim*, Edited by Jeffrey C. Alexander and Philip Smith. Cambridge, UK: Cambridge University Press, 2005.

Berger, Peter. *The Sacred Canopy: Elements of a Sociological Theory of Religion*. New York: Anchor Books, 1967.

"Best Fan Reactions to Patriots' Game-Winning Interception vs Seahawks! (Super Bowl XLIX)". *YouTube*. https://www.youtube.com/watch?v=smwmgZViC0g. Accessed February 5, 2015.

The Bhagavad Gita. Translated by Juan Mascaro (New York: Penguin Books, 1962).

Boecker, Henning, et al. "The Runner's High: Opioidergic Mechanisms in the Human Brain." *Cerebral Cortex* 18, no. 11 (November 2008): 2523–2531. *PsycINFO*, EBSCO*host*. Accessed February 5, 2015.

"Brian Davis has no regrets for calling two-shot penalty on himself." *The Guardian* (theguardian.com), April 19, 2010.

Brondfield, Jerry. *The Coach, the Man, the Legend*. New York: Random House, 1976.

Brown, Gwilym. "Ryder Cup 1969: A Tie May Be Like Kissing Your Sister "…" *Golf* (golf.com), August 19, 2008.

Buford, Bill. *Among the Thugs*. New York: Vintage Books, 1990.

Burke, T. Patrick. *The Major Religions: An Introduction with Texts*. Cambridge, MA: Blackwell Publishers, 1996.

Burkert, Walter. *Greek Religion*. Cambridge, MA: Harvard University Press, 1985.

Busbee, Jay. "Davis calls penalty on himself, gives up shot at first PGA win." Yahoo Sports (yahoo.com), April 18, 2010

Buswell, Jr., Robert E., and Donald S. Lopez, Jr. *The Princeton Dictionary of Buddhism*. Princeton, NJ: Princeton University Press, 2014.

Callois, Roger. *Man, Play and Games*. Translated by Meyer Barash (Chicago: University of Illinois Press, 1961).

Carlin, John. *Invictus: Nelson Mandela and the Game that Made a Nation*. New York: Penguin Books, 2008.

Carlin, John. "Most Bonita." *The New York Times Magazine* (June 2006): 56–61.

Carmody, Denise L., and T. L. Brink. *Ways to the Center: An Introduction to World Religions*, Sixth Edition. Belmont, CA: Thomson Wadsworth, 2006.

Chapman, J. Harley. *Jung's Three Theories of Religious Experience*. Studies in the Psychology of Religion, Vol. 3. Lewiston,NY: The Edwin Mellen Press, 1988.

Chass, Murray. "Age Is No Deterrent to Perfection: Johnson Faces 27 Braves, and Retires Them All." *The New York Times*. May 19, 2004.

Cladis, Mark S. "Beyond solidarity?: Durkheim and Twenty-First Century Democracy in a Global Age." In *The Cambridge Companion to Durkheim*. Edited by Jeffrey C. Alexander and Philip Smith. Cambridge, UK: Cambridge University Press, 2005.

Covington, James W. *The Seminoles of Florida*. Gainesville, FL: University Press of Florida, 1993.

Creamer, Robert W. *Babe: The Legend Comes to Life*. New York: Simon and Schuster, 1974.

"Crew Chiefs Suspended, Drivers Docked Points for Cheating." *Philly.com* http://articles.philly.com/2007-02-14/sports/25238720_1_riggs-and-sadler-kenny-francis-chad-knaus. Accessed February 14, 2007.

Cross, F. L., ed. *The Oxford Dictionary of the Christian Church*. Third Edition. Edited by E. A. Livingston. Oxford: Oxford University Press, 1997.

Debord, Guy. *Society of the Spectacle*. Translated by Ken Knabb (London: Rebel Press, 1983).

Doniger, Wendy. *The Hindus: An Alternative History*. New Delhi, India: Penguin Books, 2011.

Durkheim, Emile. *The Elementary Forms of Religious Life*. Translated by Karen E. Fields (New York: The Free Press, 1995).

Eason, Christianne M., Stephanie M. Mazerolle, and Ashley Goodman. "Motherhood and Work-Life Balance in the National Collegiate Athletic Association Division I Setting: Mentors and the Female Athletic Trainer." *Journal of Athletic Training* 49, no. 4 (July 2014): 532–539. http://search.proquest.com/docview/1561540048?accountid=2193.

Edwards, Harry, *Sociology of Sport*. Homewood, Illinois: The Dorsey Press, 1973.

Eliade, Mircea. *Patterns in Comparative Religion*. New York: Sheed & Ward., 1958.

Eliade, Mircea. *The Myth of the Eternal Return: Or, Cosmos and History*. Princeton, NJ: Princeton University Press, 1991.

Eliade, Mircea. *The Sacred and the Profane: The Nature of Religion*. San Diego, CA: Harcourt, Inc., 1987.

Erdoes, Richard, and Alfonso Ortiz, eds. *American Indian Myths and Legends*. New York: Pantheon Books, 1984.

Evans, Nancy. *Civic Rites: Democracy and Religion in Ancient Greece*. Berkeley, CA: University of California Press, 2010.

Feezell, Randolph. *Sport, Play & Ethical Reflection*. Chicago: University of Illinois Press, 2004.

Fenton, John Y., et al. *Religions of Asia*, Third Edition. Boston, MA: St. Martin's Press, 1993.

Ferguson, John. *The Religions of the Roman Empire*. Aspects of Greek and Roman Life. Ithaca, NY: Cornell University Press, 1970.

Feuerbach, Ludwig. *The Essence of Christianity*. Translated by George Eliot. Amherst, NY: Prometheus Books, 1989.

Finley, M. I. *The World of Odysseus*, Revised Edition. New York: The Viking Press, 1965.

"Fisher DeBerry." *AF Athletics Football*. http://www.goairforcefalcons.com/sports/m-footbl/mtt/deberry_fisher00.html. Accessed February 11, 2015.

Freud, Sigmund. *The Future of an Illusion*. Translated by W. D. Robson-Scott (New York: Liveright Publishing Corporation, 1953).

Freud, Sigmund. *The Interpretation of Dreams*. Translated by James Strahey (London: The Hogarth Press, 1958).

Freud, Sigmund. *Civilization and Its Discontent*. Translated by James Strahey. New York: W. W. Norton and Company, 1961.

Freud, Sigmund. *The Future of an Illusion*. Translated by James Strachey (New York: W. W. Norton & Company, 1961).

Friedland, Roger. "Drag Kings at the Totem Ball: the Erotics of Collective Representation in Emile Durkheim and Sigmund Freud." In *The Cambridge Companion to Durkheim*. Edited by Jeffrey C. Alexander and Philip Smith. Cambridge, UK: Cambridge University Press, 2005.

"From NY to Kabul: Pugliese ponder Premier League move ... to Afghanistan." *The Guardian* (theguardian.com), February 6, 2014.

Gardner, Paul. *The Simplest Game: The Intelligent American's Guide to the World of Soccer*. Boston, MA: Little, Brown and Company, 1976.

Gels, James F. "Basketball Coaching Philosophy." The Coaches Clipboard. Accessed January 17, 2015. http://www.coachesclipboard.net/BasketballCoachingPhilosophy .html.

Gillon, Doug. "Sports Focus Burn Out: Celebrity Status Should Not Cost So Much." *The Herald*, October 23, 1998. http://search.proquest.com/ docview/332594024?accountid=2193.

Gooding, Susan Staiger. "Interior Salishan Creation Stories." *Journal of Religious Ethics* 20, no. 2 (Fall, 1992): 353–387.

Goldfield, David. *Still Fighting the Civil War: The American South and Southern History*. Baton Rouge, LA: Louisiana State University Press, 2002.

Götz, Ignacio L. "Spirituality and the Body." *Religious Education* 96, no. 1 (December 1, 2001): 2–19. *ATLA Religion Database with ATLASerials*, EBSCOhost. Accessed February 7, 2015.

Grant, Michael. *Myths of the Greeks and Romans*. New York: Penguin Books, 1962.

Griese, Bob, and Dave Hyde. *Perfection: The Inside Story of the 1972 Miami Dolphins' Perfect Season*. Hoboken, NJ: John Wiley & Sons, 2012. Nook edition.

Grimshaw, Michael. "The Oval Opiate?: The History and Analysis of an Idea and Claim," *International Journal of Religion and Sport*, 2, (2013): 57–83.

Guttmann, Allen. *From Ritual to Record: The Nature of Modern Sports*. New York: Columbia University Press, 1978.

Hackfort, Dieter, and Charles D. Spielberger, eds. *Anxiety in Sports: An International Perspective*. New York: Hemisphere Publishing Corporation, 1989.

Hamilton, Edith, and Huntington Cairns, eds. *The Collected Dialogues of Plato Including the Letters*. Bollingen Series LXXI. Princeton, NJ: Princeton University Press, 1961.

Hanson, Kenneth C. "Transformed on the Mountain: Ritual Analysis and the Gospel of Matthew." *Semeia* no. 67 (January 1, 1994): 147–170. *ATLA Religion Database with ATLASerials*, EBSCOhost. Accessed February 18, 2015.

Hare, Mary Gail. "Retailer Eyed as Buyer of Ripken Ball; Local Promoter Wants to Sell Game Souvenir to Wal-Mart Chain; Price Set at $1 Million; Liberty Road Store Will Display Item, Other Memorabilia." *The Sun,* January 07, 1997. http://search.proquest .com/docview/406955232?accountid=2193.

Harig, Bob. "Jacklin fondly recalls the '69 Cup." *ESPN.com*, February 21, 2014.

Harrelson, Walter, gen. ed. *The New Interpreter's Study Bible*. New Revised Standard Version with the Apocrypha. Nashville, TN: Abingdon Press, 2003.

Harrison, James A. *The Story of Greece*. New York: G. P. Putnam's Sons, 1898.

Higgs, Robert J., and Michael C. Braswell. *An Unholy Alliance: The Sacred and Modern Sports*. Macon, GA: Mercer University Press, 2004.

Holtzclaw, Mike. "Couple Puts Stock in Ripken Memorabilia Collection Stays Ahead of the Game." *Daily Press,* September 03, 1995. http://search.proquest.com /docview/342788254?accountid=2193.

Hornby, Nick. *Fever Pitch*. New York: Riverhead Books, 1992.

Hughes, Andrew S. "Birth of a Mythology." *South Bend Tribune* (South Bend, IN). November 21, 2008.

Huizinga, Johan. *Homo Ludens: A Study of the Play Element in Culture*. Boston: The≈Beacon Press, 1950.

"Image of Mary Beckons Few Now." *St. Petersburg Times Online*. http://www.sptimes
.com/2002/09/28/NorthPinellas/Image_of_Mary_beckons.shtml. September 28, 2002.
Viewed June 3, 2015.

International Olympic Committee (IOC). "IOC and UN Secretariat agree historic deal to work
together to use sport to build a better world." *Olympic.org*, April 28, 2014.

"Is football still affordable for the working classes?" BBC Consumer (www.bbc.co.uk),
August 16, 2013.

James, M. R. "Dr. Dave Inducted into Archery Hall of Fame." *Bowhunter* 37, no. 4 (January,
2008): 38. http://search.proquest.com/docview/200118866?accountid=2193.

"Jim Furyk wins Verizon Heritage after Brian Davis calls penalty on himself." *Golf* (golf.com),
April 18, 2010.

Jung, C. G. *Modern Man in Search of a Soul*. Translated by W. S. Dell and Cary F. Baynes
(New York: Harcourt Brace & Company, 1933).

Kant, Immanuel. *Groundwork of the Metaphysic of Morals*. Translated by H.J. Paton (New
York: Harper & Row, 1964).

Kempis, Thomas À. *The Imitation of Christ*. Translated by William C. Creasy. Macon, GA:
Mercer University Press, 2007.

Kitto, H. D. F. *The Greeks*. Baltimore, MD: Penguin Books, 1951.

Kohut, Heinz. *Self Psychology and the Humanities: Reflections on a New Psychological
Approach*. Edited by Charles B. Strozier. New York: W. W. Norton & Company, 1985.

Kuper, Simon and Stefan Szymanski. *Soccernomics: Why England Loses, Why Spain,
Germany, and Brazil Win, and Why the US, Japan, Australia, Turkey—and Even Iraq—
Are Destined to Become the Kings of the World's Most Popular Sport*, Revised and
Expanded Edition. New York: Nation Books, 2012.

Lage, Larry. "Blown Call Costs Gallaraga Perfect Game in the 9th." Yahoo Sports
(http://sports.yahoo.com/mlb/recap?gid=300602106). Accessed March 22, 2013
. Originally posted June 3, 2010.

Lattimore, Richmond. *The Iliad of Homer*. Chicago: University of Chicago Press, 1951.

Lattimore, Richmond. *The Odyssey of Homer*. New York: HarperCollins, 1967.

Lee, Hyun-Woo, Young Do Kim, Joshua I. Newman, and Yukyoum Kim. "Group Emotion
in Spectator Sport: An Interdisciplinary Approach to Affective Qualia." *Journal of
Multidisciplinary Research* 5, no. 2 (Summer, 2013): 53–70. http://search.proquest.
com/docview/1492267816?accountid=2193.

Lewis, Michael. *The Blind Side: Evolution of a Game*. New York: W.W. Norton & Company,
2007.

Luhmann, Niklas. *A Systems Theory of Religion*. Translated by David A. Brenner with
Adrian Hermann (Stanford, CA: Stanford University Press, 2013).

MacCulloch, Diarmaid. *Christianity: The First Three Thousand Years*. New York: Penguin
Books, 2010.

MacIntyre, Alasdair. *After Virtue: A Study in Moral Theory*. Notre Dame, IN: University of
Notre Dame Press, 1981.

"Malcolm Butler's Goal-Line Interception Gives Pats Super Bowl XLIX title." *ESPN NFL*.
http://scores.espn.go.com/nfl/recap?gameId=400749027. Accessed February 5, 2015.

Mantzaridis, Georgios I. *The Deification of Man*. Crestwood, NY: St. Vladimir's Seminary
Press, 1984.

Marx, Karl. *Karl Marx: The Essential Writings*, Second Edition, edited by Frederic L. Bender.
Boulder, Colorado: Westview Press, 1972.

Marx, Karl. *The Portable Karl Marx*, edited by Eugene Kamenka. New York: Penguin Books, 1983.

Maslow, Abraham H. *Religions, Values, and Peak-Experiences*. New York: Penguin Books, 1978.

Matthews, Warren. *World Religions*, Fifth Edition. Belmont, CA: Thomson Wadsworth, 2007.

Meany, Tom. *Babe Ruth: The Big Moments of the Big Fellow*. New York: A. S. Barnes and Company, 1947.

"Mentors Help Us to Reach Higher SPORTS MAD JANE BORREN." *The Daily Post,* September 24, 2007. http://search.proquest.com/docview/432131482?accountid=2193.

Mill, John Stuart. *Utilitarianism*. New York: Macmillan Publishing Company, 1957.

Morris, Desmond. *The Soccer Tribe*. London: Jonathan Cape, Ltd., 1981.

Moss, Irv. "Colorado Sports Hall of Fame Mentors Fill Class of '08 April 8 Inductees – DeBerry, Lacroix, Shorter, Noxon, Finsterwald and Yelland – Were Men Who Excelled, and Then Helped Others Do the Same." *Denver Post*, October 10, 2007. http://search.proquest.com/docview/410858316?accountid=2193.

Murphy, Shane M., ed. *The Oxford Handbook of Sport and Performance Psychology*. Oxford: Oxford University Press, 2012.

Murray, Thomas H. "Making Sense of Fairness in Sports." *Hastings Center Report* 40, no. 2 (2010): 13–15.

"Nadia Comaneci: The World's First Perfect 10." http://www.olympic.org/nadia-comaneci . Accessed March 22, 2013.

Neihardt, John G. *Black Elk Speaks: Being the Life Story of a Holy Man of the Oglala Sioux*. Lincoln, NE: University of Nebraska Press, 1972.

Newman, Mark. "Baseball's 200,000th Game Played in Houston." http://mlb.mlb.com/news/article.jsp?ymd=20110921&content_id=25015352&c_id=mlb. Original post on September 25, 2011. Viewed March 22, 2013.

Niebuhr, Reinhold. *Moral Man and Immoral Society*. New York: Charles Scriber's Sons, 1960.

Novak, Michael. *The Joy of Sports: Endzones, Bases, Baskets, Balls, and the Consecration of the American Spirit*, Revised Edition. Lanham, MD: Madison Books, 1994.

Otto, Rudolf. *The Idea of the Holy: An Inquiry into the Non-Rational Factor in the Idea of the Divine and Its Relation to the Rational*, Second Edition. John W. Harvey, trans. London: Oxford University Press, 1952.

Overman, Steven. *The Protestant Ethic and the Spirit of Sport*. Macon, GA: Mercer University Press, 2011.

Owens, Jeff. "Knaus Not Fretting Reputation, but He Should Be." *Sporting News* http://www.sportingnews.com/nascar/story/2012-03-02/chad-knaus-cheater-not-worried -about-reputation-jimmie-johnson-hendrick-motorspo. Accessed March 2, 2012.

Pecora, Vincent P. *Secularization and Cultural Criticism: Religion, Nation, & Modernity*. Chicago: The University of Chicago Press, 2006.

Pinker, Steven. *The Better Angels of Our Nature: Why Violence Has Declined*. New York: Penguin Books, 2012.

Pro-Football-Reference.com. "2007 New England Patriots." http://www.pro-football -reference.com/teams/nwe/2007.htm. Accessed March 23, 2013.

Price, Joseph L., ed. *From Season to Season: Sports as American Religion*. Macon, GA: Mercer University Press, 2001.

Price, Joseph L. "The Super Bowl as Religious Festival." In *From Season to Season: Sports as American Religion*. Edited by Joseph L. Price. Macon, GA: Mercer University Press, 2001: 137–140.

Price, Joseph L. *Rounding the Bases: Baseball and Religion in America*. Macon, GA: Mercer University Press, 2006.

Price, Joseph. "Conjuring Curses and Supplicating Spirits: Baseball's Culture of Superstitions." *Martin Marty's Religion and Culture Web Forum*. Accessed January 26, 2015. http://divinity.uchicago.edu/sites/default/files/imce/pdfs/webforum/ 092004/ commentary.shtml.

Raglan, Lord. "The Hero: A Study in Tradition, Myth, and Drama." In *In Quest of the Hero*, edited by Robert A. Segal (Princeton, NJ: Princeton University Press, 1990).

Raissman, Bob. "When NBC Began to Crown the Seahawks as Super Bowl Champs, Cris Collinsworth Pumped the Brakes." *New York Daily News*. http://www.nydailynews.com/ sports/football/raissman-review-fresh-air-jackson-article-1.2100169. Accessed February 5, 2015.

Rank, Otto. "The Myth of the Birth of the Hero." In *In Quest of the Hero*. Edited by Robert A. Segal. Princeton, NJ: Princeton University Press, 1990.

Rendell, Matt Rendell. "The Perfect Ten: Great Athletes Relish Their Achievements; Nadia Comaneci Wants to Forget Hers." The Observer (London, UK). July 4, 2004.

Robb, Sharon. "A Resurrection, Bela Style: Romanian Gymnastics Coach Rushes Back in to Save the Day for the U.S., Reports Sharon Robb." *The Ottawa Citizen,* September 13, 2000. http://search.proquest.com/docview/240400998?accountid=2193.

Rosenthal, Gary. *Everybody's Soccer Book*. New York: Charles Scribner's Sons, 1981.

"Rugby Is a Sport Ruled by Emotion and, After Winning … [Derived Headline]." *The Argus,* September 09, 2011. http://search.proquest.com/docview /888271102?accountid=2193.

Ruth, Babe. *The Babe Ruth Story: As Told to Bob Considine*. New York: E. P. Dutton and Co., 1948.

Sands, Robert R., and Linda R. Sands. "Running Deep: Speculations on the Evolution of Running and Spirituality in the Genus Homo." *Journal for the Study of Religion, Nature And Culture* 3, no. 4 (December 1, 2009): 552–577. *ATLA Religion Database with ATLASerials*, EBSCOhost. Accessed February 6, 2015.

Sanneh, Lamin. "Saints and Exemplars." In *The Blackwell Companion to Religious Ethics*. Edited by William Schweiker. Malden, MA: Blackwell Publishing, 2008.

Schleiermacher, Friedrich. *The Christian Faith*. Edited by H. R. MacIntosh and J. S. Stewart (Edinburgh: T&T Clark, 1989).

Schwartz, Regina. *The Curse of Cain: The Violent Legacy of Monotheism*. Chicago: The University of Chicago Press, 1997.

Shapiro, Leonard. "1972 Dolphins Want to Remain The Big Fish: Team That Finished 17–0 Roots against 13–0 Broncos of 1998." *The Washington Post*. December 10, 1998.

Simon, Robert L. *Fair Play: The Ethics of Sport*, 3rd Edition. Boulder, CO: Westview Press, 2010.

Singer, Robert N., Milledge Murphey, and L. Keith Tennant, eds. *Handbook of Research on Sport Psychology*. New York: Macmillan Publishing Company, 1993.

Smart, Ninian. *Dimensions of the Sacred: An Anatomy of the World's Beliefs*. Berkeley, CA: University of California Press, 1996.

Smith, Huston. *The World's Religions*. New York: HarperCollins Publishers, 1991.

Sperber, Murray. *Shake Down the Thunder: The Creation of Notre Dame Football*. New York: Henry Holt and Company, 1993.

St. John, Warren. *Rammer Jammer Yellow Hammer: A Road Trip into the Heart of Fan Mania*. New York: Three Rivers Press, 2004.

Stuttard, David. *Power Games: Ritual and Rivalry at the Ancient Greek Olympics*. London, The British Museum Press, 2012.

Summers, Jeffery J., et al. "Middle-Aged, Non-Elite Marathon Runners: A Profile." *Perceptual and Motor Skills* 54, no. 3, Pt 1 (June, 1982): 963–969. *PsycINFO*, EBSCO*host*. Accessed February 5, 2015.

"Super Bowl Ticket Prices: Average Cost for Each Year's Game." SI.com (www.si.com), January 29, 2015.

Swaddling, Judith. *The Ancient Olympic Games*. London: The British Museum Press, 2011.

Taves, Ann. *Religious Experience Reconsidered: A Building-Block Approach to the Study of Religion and Other Special Things*. Princeton, NJ: Princeton University Press, 2009.

Taylor, Charles. *A Secular Age*. Cambridge, MA: Harvard University Press, 2007.

"Team USA." *TeamUSA.org*. http://www.teamusa.org/News/2009/August/05/Amazing-Moments-in-Olympic-History-Mary-Lou-Retton. Accessed February 11, 2015.

Tillich, Paul. *The Courage to Be*. New Haven, CT: Yale University Press, 1980.

Tinker, George E. "Native Americans and the Land: 'The End of Living, and the Beginning of Survival.'" *Word and World*, 6, no. 1 (Winter, 1986): 66–75.

Trothen, Tracy. "Better Than Normal?: Constructing Modified Athletes and a Relational Theological Ethic." In *Theology, Ethics, and Transcendence in Sports*. Edited by Jim Parry, Mark Nesti, and Nick Watson. New York: Routledge, 2011: 64–81.

Turner, Victor. *Dramas, Fields, and Metaphors: Symbolic Action in Human Society*. Ithaca, NY: Cornell University Press, 1974.

Turner, Victor. *The Ritual Process: Structure and Anti-Structure*. New York: Aldine de Gruyter, 1995

United Nations Office on Sport for Development and Peace (UNOSDP). *Annual Report 2013*. Geneva: UNOSDP, 2014.

UN News Centre. "UN, Olympic Committee Sign Formal Agreement on Role of Sport in Development, Peace." *UN.org*, April 28, 2014.

Venugopal, K. V. "World Cup Football—Will Brazil Regain Its Glory?" *Alive* 380 (June, 2014): 70–73.

Virgil. *The Aeneid*. Translated by Robert Fitzgerald. New York: Alfred Knopf, 1992.

Wagenheim, Kal. *Babe Ruth: His Life and Legend*. New York: Praeger Publishers, 1974.

Wahl, Grant. "American Nick Pugliese breaking barriers by playing in Afghanistan." *Sports Illustrated* (si.com), June 27, 2013.

Wallace, William. "Miami Wins in Bowl for Perfect Season." *The New York Times*. January 15, 1973.

Weber, Max. *The Protestant Ethic and the "Spirit" of Capitalism and Other Writings*. Translated and edited by Peter Baehr and Gordon C. Wells (New York: Penguin Books, 2002).

Yaeger, Don. With Sam Cunningham and John Papadakis. *Turning of the Tide: How One Game Changed the South*. New York: Center Street, 2006.

Zirin, Dave. *Bad Sports: How Owners Are Ruining the Games We Love*. New York: The New Press, 2010.

Zirin, Dave. *Welcome to the Terrordome: The Pain, Politics, and Promise of Sports*. Chicago: Haymarket Books, 2007.

Index

9 781472 514059